Radically Listening to Transgender Children

Radically Listening to Transgender Children

Creating Epistemic Justice through Critical Reflection and Resistant Imaginations

Katie Steele and Julie Nicholson

LEXINGTON BOOKS
Lanham • Boulder • New York • London

Published by Lexington Books
An imprint of The Rowman & Littlefield Publishing Group, Inc.
4501 Forbes Boulevard, Suite 200, Lanham, Maryland 20706
www.rowman.com

6 Tinworth Street, London SE11 5AL, United Kingdom

Copyright © 2020 The Rowman & Littlefield Publishing Group, Inc.

"Trans & Nonbinary BBI PoC New Pride Flag (Nebula version)" by Laurie Raye and Julia Feliz is licensed under CC-BY-SA-3.0. Special thanks to Mt Lemmon Skycenter.

All rights reserved. No part of this book may be reproduced in any form or by any electronic or mechanical means, including information storage and retrieval systems, without written permission from the publisher, except by a reviewer who may quote passages in a review.

British Library Cataloguing in Publication Information Available

Library of Congress Cataloging-in-Publication Data Available

ISBN 978-1-4985-9037-2 (cloth)
ISBN 978-1-4985-9039-6 (pbk)
ISBN 978-1-4985-9038-9 (electronic)

For Leelah Alcorn, who asked that her death mean something, and for all the beautifully gendered young people who leave this world much too soon.

Contents

List of Figures	ix
Acknowledgments	xi
Introduction	1
1 To be Twice Invisible: Professional Ethics in Early Childhood and the Epistemic Cliff Faced by Young Gender Expansive Children	15
2 Theorizing from the Edge: Dismantling Boy/Girl Boxes and Looking to the Starry Sky to Construct Gender Constellations	63
3 Testimonial (In)justice: Establishing Credibility in an Early Childhood Context of Identity Prejudice	101
4 Hermeneutical (In)justice: Rendering Lived Experience as Visible Truth for Young Children	125
5 Resistant Social Imaginations: Striating Paths for Gender Liberation in Early Childhood Classrooms	147
Conclusion	161
References	165
Index	175
About the Authors	179

List of Figures

Figure 2.1	Gender Boxes	68
Figure 2.2	Gender as a Spectrum	70
Figure 2.3	Genderbread Person	71
Figure 2.4	Gender Web	73
Figure 2.5	Intersectional Gender Constellation	77
Figure 2.6	Anthias's Multilevel Model of Intersectionality Adapted by Núñez	79
Figure 2.7	Joey's Gender Constellation	89
Figure 2.8	Asha's Gender Constellation	89
Figure 2.9	Intersecting Axes of Gender-Based Oppression	96

Acknowledgments

This book would not have been possible without the collective efforts of the rest of the Gender Justice in Early Childhood team (genderjusticeinearlychildhood.com) in our work together over the past four years as well as in individual support (often on short notice) during the writing process. Every member of our team has contributed meaningfully to the content and power of this work. I want to thank Encian Pastel for his thought leadership in resistantly imagining gender in early childhood and beyond, his time and effort in gathering stories and perspectives, and for his critical reflection and feedback on the book; Cyndi Maurer for her diligent and crucial research and writing support; Jonathan Julian and Julia Hennock for their artistic skills and their perspectives as mental health professionals; and Tess Urger and Nathanael Flynn for sharing their lived experiences supporting young trans and gender expansive children in the classroom. Our team is comprised of incredible trans, nonbinary, gender expansive, and allied thinkers, doers, and dreamers and this project was built on the foundation created by our work together.

We also would not have been able to bring so many trans and gender expansive experiences to life in these pages without the generosity and courage of the children, parents, teachers, and trans and gender expansive adults we interviewed. All of your stories are incredibly important. It was our honor and pleasure to listen to and learn from each person who has shared their experiences with us and to be able to amplify those stories here. I thank you for trusting us with your truths.

I also want to recognize and uplift the two artists who collaborated to create the image on the cover of the book. Illustrator and Founder of sanctuarypublishers.com, Julia Feliz—a gendervague, pansexual, Afro-Boricua (Puerto Rican)—created the flag design used in this image. In Julia's words, "The Trans & Nonbinary BBI PoC (Black/Brown/Indigenous/People of

Color) flag recognizes the history of the modern LGBTQIA+ movement, which was started by Trans People of Color of Marginalized Genders (Marginalized Genders, or MaGe, is a term coined by Black activist Crystal Michelle to mean everyone except men, particularly white cis men.)" The design acknowledges the need to center their voices and experiences and to fight for justice for those who are the most marginalized and who face systemic violence at disproportionate rates compared to the rest of the LGBTQIA+ community. More information can be found at newprideflag.com. This new flag design was then set in the Gender Galaxy by genderfluid artist Laurie Raye. This and many other pride flags from the LGBTQIA+ community can be found recreated by Laurie with images from space (including some taken by the Mt. Lemmon Skycenter) at https://www.artstation.com/artwork/Bm6dV6.

I also have to convey my sincere gratitude to my coauthor, Julie Nicholson. Without her guidance and encouragement, I would not have undertaken a project such as this. Julie has been the most thoughtful and empowering mentor I could have asked for in this endeavor. And to her family, whose generosity and graciousness is unparalleled and allowed me to continue in this work.

Finally, I want to thank my family. My parents, Marilyn and Alec Steele, and my brother, Ethan, who have always supported me without hesitation—including, and perhaps especially, when they didn't know how to relate to my experiences as a queer and transgender child. In a world that can be so hostile to children like me, I am incredibly fortunate to have such a loving family that has always been willing to learn something new. And my partner, Julie Walsh, who has been a patient, loving, and inspiring presence for me throughout this process as well as in the latest chapter of my gender journey. I love you all, and I wouldn't have had the strength of voice to put these words down if you hadn't been in my corner.

Introduction

A week before I was born, I was head down and ready to go, but by game day I had flipped myself back over. The doctor announced, "That doesn't feel like a head, that feels like a girl!" That was the first time someone decided for me which half of the human race I belonged to—the girls. And now you have a generic idea of what my genitals looked like the day I was born . . . it's what everyone wants to know when anyone has a baby. Are you having a penis baby or a vagina baby? After they have that question settled, they might ask if the baby is healthy, but probably not before. And while most of the time people don't ask quite so directly about the generic shape of someone's genitals after they are a few months old, people have been asking me my whole life. Both in the "Are you a boy or a girl?" way AND in the "So, do you have a penis or a vagina?" way. Yes, I have been asked that as an adult.

Most people throughout my life have taken one look and assumed I was a boy. Even when I had pigtails halfway down my back. Even though I had my ears pierced when I was 12, specifically so people would know I was a girl. Looking back, I can't say I blame them. It did not take me long at all to realize I didn't love being on team girl. I wasn't into the clothes. I didn't care for the toys. I got along a lot better with the boys. I remember having a small red journal, not long after I first learned to write. I wrote "I wish I was a boy" and then hid it in the basement. I just never felt like I knew how to do the whole "being a girl" thing. It seemed like all the other girls had gotten some manual that someone had forgotten to give me. Being a boy just seemed to make so much more sense. I think I told my parents that I was a boy when I was very young . . . maybe 3 or 4 . . . but they don't remember me saying that, at least not in so many words. They say I was always just me. Mom says that I was tearing off anything frilly or ruffled or pink by age 3. I threw a tantrum one day when my dad put me in a little denim skirt. He thought I looked cute. He had no idea what he had done that, given my response, amounted to some kind of torture.

I had an older brother, so I got away with lots of hand-me-downs, but I always had to get dressed up for school picture day. Dad says I would leave the house in a cute little dress and come home in a T-shirt and shorts that I had apparently packed for myself when I was in elementary school. Mom thinks she stopped trying to buy me skirts and dresses when I was about 9 or 10, and just let me pick my own clothes, but she had no idea that we should have been shopping on the other side of the store. My parents were supportive and loving. They always just wanted me to be me. But their vocabulary was limited to "tomboy" or "lesbian." They didn't know the word "transgender,"[1] so they never taught it to me.

It was confusing, honestly. Everyone—parents, teachers, friends—told me I was a girl, but I didn't feel like a girl. Not at all. Then everywhere I went I was called a boy, and not in a nice way. I was teased for being boyish, pushed out of the girls' bathroom in elementary school, pushed out of line to go in from recess when we lined up as girls and boys. It seemed like I just couldn't win. I was told that girls had vaginas and boys had penises, and that was that. So, in theory, I shouldn't have had to do anything in particular to succeed at being a girl. Just exist with genitals like mine, and I should qualify, right? But I was being teased for not being enough of a girl, for not looking like one. I was told "wow, you would make one ugly girl!", told I was a boy . . . but also not enough of a boy that the other boys would let me play with them.

I fought tooth and nail to be seen as a girl, starting almost immediately after that doctor declared it to be so, but the truth is I was a shy and soft little boy. I was sensitive, emotional, introspective, observant, and fairly delicate, but definitely a boy. So when I decided to do my best at being a girl because that was the only path open to me, that girl grew up fierce and strong and outspoken both because she was fighting for her right to qualify as a girl and because she was charged with protecting a shy and soft little boy who hadn't been given a chance to grow up himself.

I came out as trans in my late twenties, but not as just a man. Being only a man doesn't feel like it's enough for me at this point. That fierce girl worked so hard just to be seen as what she was told she had to be that she's a part of me now forever. To me, my journey is at least as important as wherever I end up, and she carried that boy on her back for so many of my early years. But I do still wonder what my journey might have been like if that shy little boy had been able to tell his story from the start.

—Katie, nonbinary/
transmasculine, he/him/she/her

Every young child has the right to feel seen and heard as their authentic self by the adults responsible for their care. Children need responsive and attuned caregivers who will show a genuine interest in continually learning about who the children are as individuals, the range of emotions they experience, what they desire, and the specific forms of support they need to feel safe, visible, and a genuine sense of belonging. When children experience relationships with adults in which they feel seen and heard, they build trust—trust in the adult, trust and confidence in themselves and their internal wisdom, and trust in the benefits of building relationships with others. A relationship between an adult and a child can be loving and caring without being *attuned* if the child is experiencing something the adult can't see, doesn't understand, or interprets significantly differently than the child does. Katie's experience of gender as a young child was not fully seen or understood by his parents, teachers, or home caregivers, and so they were unable to be truly responsive to her needs.

Children are constantly surveying their environment to understand the world and their place within it, asking themselves, "What, given the contemporary order of being, can I be?" (Butler, 2004, p. 58). Adrienne Rich (1994/1986) explains what happens to a child's understanding of who they are and who they can become when someone with the authority of a teacher describes the world, and they are not in it:

> There is a moment of psychic disequilibrium, as if you looked into a mirror and saw nothing. Yet you know you exist and others like you, that this is a game done with mirrors. It takes some strength of soul—and not just individual strength, but collective understanding—to resist this void, this non-being, into which you are thrust, and to stand up, demanding to be seen and heard.

No child should have to "demand to be seen and heard." The forms of injustice examined in this book are epistemic in nature, in which transgender and gender expansive (TGE) children are "wronged in their capacity as knowers" (Fricker, 2007) and in which TGE narratives are systemically excluded from contributing to general knowledge and the social imagination. These injustices have the capacity to cause deep and lasting harm to children. As much of the Western world is just barely awakening to the oppression experienced by the TGE community more broadly, it is imperative that some of this energy be directed at creating epistemic justice for the youngest members of this community, before they lose the chance to grow up knowing confidently who they are and are forced, instead, to rediscover their truths later in life, if ever.

Early childhood educators are ethically obligated to create environments where all children are visible and responsively cared for. Although child agency and child self-determination are tenets of high-quality early childhood pedagogy, they are rarely extended beyond activities and behaviors to enter the realm of identity. Dominant practices in the field of early childhood reinforce beliefs that young children like Katie are not in a position to know about their identity—in this case their own gender identity—nor to explore gender options beyond the gender assigned to them at birth. Most children are given no agency at all regarding their gender, having been assigned one at birth on the basis of their genitals. If offered any kind of choice, a predetermined binary (are you a boy or a girl?) is typically the only menu they have available. Instead of young children being given agency to define themselves, adults view themselves as having privileged knowledge and maintain unitary power to guide children to discover what they, as adults, already "know" to be true.

For decades, early childhood textbooks and experts have encouraged teachers to "help preschoolers understand that being a girl or boy depends on how their bodies are made" (Derman-Sparks & Olsen Edwards, 2010, p. 94).[2] However, the voices of many children belie this assumption as untrue. It is children who are keepers of this wisdom, yet our society has yet to acknowledge this truth. As Ehrensaft (2016a) states about gender identity, "it is not for us [adults] to say, but for the children to tell." Although parents, families, and teachers have no control over children's gender identities, she explains that they have extensive influence over children's feelings of affirmation (Ehrensaft, 2016b). We can choose to listen to our children and trust what they say, or we can lead them to experience moments of psychic disequilibrium by handing them mirrors that won't produce their reflection.

In her 2007 book, *Epistemic Injustice: The Power and Ethics of Knowing*, Miranda Fricker introduced the idea that certain categories of people suffer an injustice that is rooted in their unequal power to participate in the creation and sharing of knowledge. She described the phenomena of both *testimonial injustice*, in which a person is afforded less credibility in their sharing of knowledge simply for being a member of a given social group (e.g., women, people of color, transgender individuals), and *hermeneutical injustice*, in which a person is wronged by the simple fact that a given society does not have the linguistic, interpretive, or communication tools they need to fully understand and communicate a significant part of their experience (e.g., there are no words and no shared stories for a given experiential phenomenon in a person's native language). Without language to describe a specific experience, shared cultural narratives cannot be written, collective understandings cannot be formed, empathy for the experience cannot be culturally built, and the experiences cannot be fully interpreted and understood even by those who have them.

TGE young children like Katie exist at the intersection of several layers of epistemic injustice. One of these is both evidenced by and formed by the dearth of information about gender identity in early childhood that reflects expansive and nonbinary understandings of gender. Most resources for supporting TGE students start in middle school or high school (Payne & Smith, 2014) and very little attention has been paid to the experiences of TGE children in their earliest years (zero to five), when their gender identity is just beginning to develop (Mallon & DeCrescenzo, 2006; Petty, 2010). This is because young children are often thought of and imagined as being innocent and not yet mature enough to learn about transgender identities and lives, let alone communicate about their own (Payne & Smith, 2014). At the same time, transgender people of all ages are frequently not believed about their own identities, experiences, and needs (Serano, 2016; Stryker, 2008). These are two examples of testimonial injustice. The first time a young TGE child attempts to communicate about their gender is very likely to be their first experience of being silenced and discredited on a subject of great significance to them. The lack of credibility afforded to young children and to TGE individuals can have a lasting impact on their lives and even on their sense of self. When Katie's internal experiences of feeling like a boy were not validated by the external messaging he received, he began to doubt his own sense of himself and to try to be a girl instead.

Fricker's (2007) concept of hermeneutical injustice specifically refers to instances when the tools to understand and communicate about an experience simply do not exist. We argue that the same injustice occurs when the tools *do* exist but are kept from those who need them most. For TGE children growing up in many parts of the world today, there are already words and narratives in the cultural lexicon that can help them name and understand their experiences (e.g., picture books, images, role models, and videos). However, adults often restrict children's access to these because they do not think resources on gender that include transgender and gender expansive narratives are "appropriate" for young children (Payne & Smith, 2014). Or they do not have access to accurate information about gender diversity, as traditional child development theories that pathologize children like Katie still dominate coursework and professional development materials in the field of early childhood.

The absence of resources that acknowledge gender diversity prevents many young children from truly knowing themselves and being equitably and authentically included in early childhood classrooms. This can leave young TGE children feeling lost, unseen, and unknown. The majority of research studies and publications emphasizing transgender and gender diverse identities offer little mention of the experiences of children in early childhood (birth to age five). This is problematic on numerous accounts, especially as many transgender adults like Katie share testimonies that they were aware of their feelings about their gender as young as two to three years of age (Pyne, 2014). Sophie's story reflects the injustice TGE children experience when they don't have access to hermeneutical tools to help them name and understand their own experiences.

Sophie is a transgender woman in her late sixties. When she was born, she was labeled male by the doctor who delivered her. She was given a male name and raised as a boy by her family. Sophie attended an all-boys high school. She graduated college and entered a male-dominated field. She was perceived by the world around her as a kind and gentle man. She met a woman, got married, and had children, as boys are expected to do when they become men.

She recalls playing dress up one day with her older sister at their grandfather's house when she was young. Her sister was adorning her with makeup, a wig, a stuffed bra, shoes, and a skirt, and she recalls loving it until her sister wanted to show her off to their grandfather. Sophie remembers the look on her grandfather's face seeing her dressed as a girl and says "I knew immediately that it was a mistake. I flew back up the stairs and out of those clothes, hot with shame." She can't remember much else about her gender in her earliest years and believes she must have repressed some of it, but she still has a visceral recollection of that moment with her grandfather. Then, in adolescence, she started fantasizing about being a woman. She carried deep shame about these feelings, and learned to compartmentalize and repress them, only allowing herself an occasional indulgence in the fantasy and always feeling guilty and shameful about it afterwards.

In her fifties, when her children were grown and had moved out of the house, Sophie's fantasies had become consuming. "By this time," she recalled, "I was so good at denial and repression, that the only way that my mind was able to release some of this pent-up desire to be a woman was through the fantasies, which I wasn't able to control. They were so powerful. And then I would feel horrible and shameful. Then very slowly, as I got quite a bit older, it started just kind of leaking out as I was slowly becoming more and more aware of it." Sophie lived for nearly six decades working tirelessly to repress and deny her thoughts and desires about being a woman, trying to contain those feelings in brief fantasies with discreet start and end points—a character in a private play, then back to life as a man when the curtain closed—but she was finding it harder and harder to keep that character confined. The woman she was in her fantasies wanted to take up more space.

Sophie and her wife struggled in their relationship, as Sophie was feeling more and more overwhelmed by her feelings. They went to marriage counseling together, where the therapist asked Sophie if she had ever thought that she might be transgender. Sophie's wife encouraged her to explore the idea. "That was the first time in my life I had actually received permission to look at myself, and once I got that permission all hell broke loose. I've always looked at it like I'd been building this dam, trying to hold all this stuff away. And somebody said 'Well, just take out a brick and see what's behind there' and when I did, it just flooded over me. After that, there was no turning back."

After 58 years of living as a man—as a father, a brother, a son—Sophie informed her family and friends that the label she was given when she was born was wrong. She was a woman.[3]

Sophie's sense of being given "permission" to think of herself as transgender, a word she'd never heard until she was an adult, unlocked feelings she had held back for decades. Once she was given access to think of her life in the context of a transgender narrative, she experienced a freedom she had never realized she was missing. Many people have experienced this kind of relief or freedom upon accessing the terminology or the shared stories and experiences that help them understand an aspect of their life that was previously shrouded in confusion and frustration.

Through persistent and pervasive testimonial injustice, marginalized identity groups are denied equal participation in the development of shared hermeneutical resources (Fricker, 2007). As such, their experiences go comparatively unexamined, uninterpreted, unnamed, and misunderstood. In the case of transgender individuals, this has been true at many points in time in many communities. Simply having no visible transgender community members and no access to words or narratives for transgender experiences create a scenario in which a transgender individual might live their whole life simply searching for the right words to help wrap their mind around what they feel and know to be true about themselves inside.

> *I was born in rural Northumberland [England], and I met so very few people. I didn't meet a girl until I was five. I knew as soon as I met her. I thought [sigh] that's me. It wasn't like I could consider transitioning or thinking I was a girl. It just wasn't on the agenda. We had no Internet, we had no television, we had no radio. So, I was left in a village full of coal miners, quarry workers. It just steadily got worse inside of me, and by the time I was nine I knew that this body was wrong. There wasn't any words that you could use to tell people. (Josie, 70, trans woman, she/her)*[4]

Even worse, in some cases, members of a socially dominant group provide their own language and interpretation of oppressed experiences, and these exist as the only hermeneutical tools available to interpret and understand those experiences, even for those whose experiences they are. The few resources about gender there are for those who work with very young children are largely outdated and founded on theories of gender and identity development which do not reflect the lived experiences of the TGE community.

Additionally, the language and narratives produced by the TGE community are often resisted by the dominant group who fight to maintain the hermeneutical gaps that sustain their social power. Perhaps the most devastating example of this was the destruction of the Institute for Sexual Science in Berlin—"a combination of library, archive, lecture hall, and medical clinic, where [Magnus Hirschfeld, doctor and pioneering advocate for transgender individuals, among others] amassed an unprecedented collection of historical documents, ethnographies, case studies, and literary works detailing the diversity of sexuality and gender around the world"—by Nazis in 1933 (Stryker, 2008, p. 39). The most famous image of Nazi book burning actually captured the moment that decades of transgender knowledge and history went up in flames. While not so violent, censorship of TGE stories is widely seen in early childhood where vital access to language, stories, role models, and a connection to the gender expansive community is explicitly denied to TGE children who are searching the world around them for the hermeneutical tools they need to make sense of their own experiences (Payne & Smith, 2014).

Every young child deserves to feel seen and heard as their authentic self and to be in the care of responsive adults who are committed to helping them feel a strong sense of safety, visibility, and belonging in the classroom. This requires that children enter early childhood environments from birth that communicate and reinforce to TGE children—through words and actions and the planning and arranging of the environment—positive and affirming messages of who they are and an overall value for gender diversity.

This book was written for both direct service providers in early childhood programs as well as for early childhood graduate and undergraduate students, teacher educators, and researchers committed to learning about gender [in] justice as a foundation for creating gender affirming classrooms where all children, including TGE children, are listened to *and* heard. Where no child has to muster the strength of their soul to resist falling into an epistemic void. There must be urgency in the possibility of this vision across the early childhood field. As Judith Butler (2004) notes, "Possibility is not a luxury; it is as crucial as bread" (p. 29).

KNOWLEDGE CLAIMS: CENTERING LIVED EXPERIENCE AND COUNTERSTORYTELLING

Because this is a scholarly book, it is expected we will include traditional empirical research—studies published in peer-reviewed journals and reputable books from "experts" who have earned the credentials and skills to determine what "counts" as validated knowledge projects and truth claims. As researchers who participate in the construction of knowledge shaped by institutional review approvals and rigorous peer-reviewed protocols, we acknowledge the value of this format of knowledge construction. Therefore, officially sanctioned "expertized" knowledge is cited throughout the text. Yet, as scholars and individuals deeply committed to equity and social justice, we are also keenly aware of the limitations of the knowledge projects reified by the norms of the academy. As the quotes above reflect, empirical studies framed by a "researcher-centric way of defining knowledge" often privilege patriarchal and Eurocentric perspectives and as a result, can be complicit with further oppressing minoritized individuals and groups. This is evidenced in the types of research questions asked, the methods that are privileged and marginalized by the approving bodies in the institution and the theories that guide what researchers "see" and acknowledge as data in the course of their investigations. Empirical research on TGE individuals suffers from all of these limitations, especially research considering the experiences of very young TGE children.

There is a dearth of research examining TGE children that draws upon expansive conceptions of gender. Instead, the research examining gender—and especially gender identity development—is problematic for several reasons. (a) *Outdated measures*: Several of the most highly cited and recent studies rely on measures that are firmly based on patriarchal, heteronormative belief systems that strictly view gender as a binary. For example, Fast and Olsen's (2017) study comparing socially supported transgender children to "gender-typical" peers and siblings of socially supported transgender children concluded that transgender children do not differ from siblings and "gender-typical" peers on a number of measures. However, this study, like others, use measures that continue to unproblematically define gender as a binary (e.g., one measure asked participants if they wanted to be a mommy or daddy when they grew up). (b) *Small samples*: Most TGE research uses small populations, and many studies rely on self-identified TGE families who may not reflect the larger population of TGE children who do not utilize or have access to resources. (c) *Lack of consistency in terms used and their definitions*: As research expands regarding TGE children, definitions for concepts related to gender continue to develop and evolve. However, many researchers do not use consistent terms and, even if they do, the definitions can vary widely from one study to the next, making it difficult and/or problematic to compare results across studies. And (d) *Lack of research examining children between birth and five years old*: Most research on TGE individuals does not include children in the early childhood years, likely reflecting societal assumptions that young children are incapable of understanding their gender identity before they enter primary school. These factors highlight the need for understanding the *limitations* of the current empirical research on young children and gender. Using research based in binary conceptions of gender that pathologize TGE children in a book intending to accurately represent contemporary understandings of young children's gender where diversity is normalized, presents an important tension. With this in mind, we sparingly cite empirical research that represents theories, statistics, and narratives that position TGE children through deficit (or don't acknowledge their existence), as we do not want this book to contribute to the reproduction of oppressive knowledge projects and work against our goals of normalizing gender diversity for children, youth, and adults.

Understanding the limitations of empirical research, including what Patel (2016) describes as the colonial project of discovery in Western methods, we value and introduce other sources of knowledge—especially the narratives and stories of lived experiences of TGE children, youth, and adults—reflecting rich and important knowledge that is not yet well documented in empirical research. Such stories help us, as Gloria Anzaldúa (1990) explains, to make the "Borderland worlds" visible so we can push our theories and research to include those who have been traditionally "left out or pushed out":

> Necesitamos teorías [we need theories] that will rewrite history using race, class, gender, and ethnicity as categories of analysis, theories that cross borders, that blur boundaries—new kinds of theories with new theorizing methods. . . . We are articulating new positions in the "inbetween," Borderland worlds of ethnic communities and academies . . . social issues such as race, class, and sexual difference are intertwined with the narrative and poetic elements of a text, elements in which theory is embedded. In our mestizaje theories we create new categories for those of us left out or pushed out of existing ones. (Anzaldúa, 1990, pp. xxv–xxvi)

These stories challenge the dominant ideology—rejecting assumptions of neutral research, "objective" researchers, and damage-centered research (Tuck, 2009) that either silence or distort the epistemologies of gender-expansive people. The experiential knowledge of TGE people is positioned as legitimate and critical to understanding, analyzing, and teaching about subordination and resilience (Solórzano & Yosso, 2002). Research that denies the epistemological existence of TGE individuals is disrupted through the liberatory resistance such *counterstories* (Solórzano & Yosso, 2002) represent. Solórzano and Yosso (2002) describe four functions of counterstories that apply to how we use them throughout this text. Counterstories can

- build community among those at the margins of society by putting a human and familiar face to educational theory and practice;
- challenge the perceived wisdom of those at society's center by providing a context to understand and transform established belief systems
- open new windows into the reality of those at the margins of society by showing possibilities beyond the ones they live and demonstrating that they are not alone in their position; and
- teach others that by combining elements from both the story and the current reality, one can construct another world that is richer than either the story or the reality alone (p. 36).

Anzaldúa (1990) notes, "If we have been gagged and disempowered by theories, we can also be loosened and empowered by theories" (p. xxvi). The theorizing in this book attempts to do just that. We weave in the lived experiences of individuals who bend and break the social rules and norms of gender to examine the ways that TGE children are denied equal access to self-knowledge and, as a result, equal participation in the social and cultural production of and sharing of knowledge as it relates to gender. The intentional privileging of knowledge throughout the book that represents the lived experiences and counterstories of TGE children, youth, and adults aims to disrupt the hegemony of majoritarian narratives—theories that gag and disempower TGE individuals—and counter them with others that "loosen, empower and liberate . . . and open new windows into the reality of those at the margins of society" (p. 37). Their voices are woven throughout every chapter as a political act to continually acknowledge their presence and intentionally make their perspectives and narratives visible and valued. Quotes and anecdotes uplifting the voices of TGE individuals and their families and teachers will be differentiated from other block quotes by the use of italics. Some of these will tie to the topic at hand and will be discussed directly, while others are included for the sole purpose of keeping these voices and counterstories centered at all times. Some of the individuals we interviewed asked to have their real names used, while others are presented with pseudonyms. It is important to note that, though the voices included here are rich and varied, no small sample of TGE voices can be fully representative of the incredible diversity of gendered experiences.

CHAPTER OUTLINE

Chapter 1, "To be Twice Invisible: Professional Ethics in Early Childhood and the Epistemic Cliff Faced by Young Gender Expansive Children," begins with a review of the values and principles that are core to the early childhood field. Next, we summarize research describing milestones in children's gender awareness. We also discuss language and gender (specifically focusing on the English language), analyzing how words have been used to limit conceptions of gender. We provide alternatives that liberate and normalize gender diversity. This chapter ends with a discussion of the use of critical reflection to inspire transformative learning and the introduction of an equity focused reflection tool for teachers.

Chapter 2, "Theorizing from the Edge: Dismantling Boy/Girl Boxes and Looking to the Starry Sky to Construct Gender Constellations," describes the need to problematize the dominant child development theories and their assumptions about gender. Next, we describe a range of models that scholars, clinicians, and transgender activists use to conceptualize gender and advocate for the progression toward more complexity, intersectionality, and acknowledgment of gender diversity. This is followed by a description of identity power and several forms of gender-related oppression. The chapter ends by emphasizing the commitment to the nonideal as essential for teachers on a path to gender justice.

Chapter 3, "Testimonial (In)justice: Establishing Credibility in an Early Childhood Context of Identity Prejudice," introduces Miranda Fricker's (2007) concept of testimonial injustice and the two main components of this phenomenon: credibility judgments and identity prejudice. We connect these constructs to young TGE children and their experiences in early childhood classrooms. Negative cultural images of both young children and transgender people of all ages are reviewed. We end with strategies teachers can use to improve TGE children's opportunities to experience testimonial justice in their care.

Chapter 4, "Hermeneutical (In)justice: Rendering Lived Experience as Visible Truth for Young Children," explores Fricker's concept of hermeneutical injustice, wherein children are unable to understand their gendered experiences or even attempt to talk about them because there are no linguistic or interpretive tools available to them to help them fully understand and communicate about their gender. We conclude with several strategies teachers can implement to work for hermeneutical justice by expanding opportunities for children to learn about and see examples of gender diversity and to express their authentic gender selves.

Chapter 5, "Resistant Social Imaginations: Striating Paths for Gender Liberation in Early Childhood Classrooms," introduces Medina's (2013) concept of resistant social imaginations. The social imagination represents the collective reaches of a society's ability and willingness to consider how things are or could be. We discuss the gender injustices TGE children experience that result from a limited social imagination. Next, we share stories and strategies from early childhood classrooms where teachers committed to anti-bias education are using resistant social imaginations to work for gender justice for our youngest children.

Throughout the book, we use the word "teacher" to represent the diverse range of early childhood professionals who work with young children and their families. We understand that many adults who serve our youngest children use a range of other formal titles—for example, provider, caregiver, care teacher, care provider, childcare provider, teacher aide, instructional aide, home-care provider, substitute, volunteer, parent, and others. Our decision to refer to "teachers" throughout the book is only to provide a consistent term for readers. The content of the book applies to all adults who work directly with, or on behalf of, infants, toddlers, preschoolers, and early elementary-aged children as well as to academics, scholars, teacher trainers, professors, and others, who work in the field of early childhood education.

NOTES

1. The term "transgender" will be defined at length later in this book, but briefly, it refers to all individuals who identify with a gender other than the one they were assigned at birth.

2. The first edition of *Anti-Bias Education for Young Children and Ourselves* by Louise Derman-Sparks and Julie Olsen Edwards was groundbreaking in the field of early childhood education for bringing equity and anti-oppression work to the center of working with young children. The book, in its first and second editions, has been one of the most impactful works on equity in the field. A third edition of the book is in production at the time of the writing of this text. The chapter on gender in this upcoming edition will reflect the importance of child agency in gender identity and gender exploration.

3. Note the use of "she" and "her" as well as Sophie's chosen name, even when referring to her childhood. Unless a transgender individual specifies otherwise, it is currently considered the most respectful practice to use a person's current name and gender pronouns even when discussing events that occurred before they began using that name or those pronouns.

4. Source: *Young Trans Girl Speaks with an Older Trans Woman* by My Generation. See: https://www.youtube.com/watch?v=sxMcGRZCz24.

Chapter 1

To be Twice Invisible

Professional Ethics in Early Childhood and the Epistemic Cliff Faced by Young Gender Expansive Children

THE ETHICS OF PRACTICE: REVISITING EARLY CHILDHOOD EDUCATORS' PROFESSIONAL RESPONSIBILITY TO CHILDREN AND FAMILIES

Early childhood education is a profession concerned with promoting and ensuring children's healthy development and learning. This is accomplished through the intentional creation of meaningful, safe, and dynamic learning environments that are culturally, linguistically, developmentally, and contextually responsive to diverse children, families, and communities. As with other professions, the field of early childhood has developed codes of ethical conduct and guidelines that represent the shared responsibilities adults agree to engage in and strive toward in their direct work with or on behalf of young children and families. Following are excerpts of the values and principles that are core to the early childhood field across the United States and internationally. These principles should inspire and inform a collective desire to work for gender justice for children of all genders.

The Code of Ethical Conduct and Statement of Commitment for The National Association for the Education of Young Children (2005, 2011) describes the following core values, ideals, and principles:

- Respect the dignity, worth, and uniqueness of each individual child
- Respect the diversity of children
- Recognize that children achieve their full potential in the context of relationships that are based on trust and respect
- Base program practices upon current knowledge and research . . . as well as on particular knowledge of each child

- Recognize the vulnerability of children and their dependence on adults
- Create and maintain safe and healthy settings that foster children's social, emotional, cognitive, and physical development and that respect their dignity and their contributions.
- Above all, we shall not harm children. We shall not participate in practices that are emotionally damaging, physically harmful, disrespectful, degrading, dangerous, exploitative, or intimidating to children.

My family loves and supports me. I used to think they didn't because they would say things that were ignorant. And I don't think they necessarily prepared the world for me as much as they were trying to prepare me for the world. (Jen, twenty-four, nonbinary, she/he/they)[1]

The *International Code of Ethics for Educators* (ICoEE), a code aligned to internationally recognized human rights documents (e.g., United Nations Universal Declaration of Human Rights, and others) for educators worldwide, states the following as ethical responsibilities of all teachers who work with children:

- Value and nurture *the voice and unique contribution* of each child as an agent in the construction of the learning environment and learning process
- *Foster child agency* as a human right and the foundation for social justice by creating learning environments where learners can be actors and leaders in creating positive social change

When I was younger and people told me I was a girl and told me I needed to be certain things, that made me reject femininity. So I didn't like skirts, I didn't like accessories, I didn't like pink. But at the same time, there was just this inner struggle about, "why don't I feel comfortable with myself?" (Paulina, seventeen, nonbinary, prefers no pronouns)[2]

Additionally, *Anti-Bias Education* (ABE) (Derman-Sparks & Olsen Edwards, 2010), the most widely circulated resource for early childhood teachers in the United States addressing anti-oppression pedagogy, emphasizes the following as key tenets of all professional practice with young children: All children will experience a sense of belonging, affirmation of their identities and cultural ways of being, comfort and joy with human diversity; accurate language for human differences, and deep, caring human connections.

None of my family was listening. . . . To this day, my grandmother passed away and I never told her I was trans, but she saw me with a full beard. We just didn't talk about it. My grandfather switched his lexicon to grandson, and my mother eventually came around as did my father. But for the most part they didn't listen. (Ikaika, trans and māhūkāne, he/him)

These documents collectively emphasize supporting children's voice and agency, affirmation of children's diverse identities, a value for building trusting relationships and most importantly, ensuring that our education and caring practices *do no harm*. These values and principles of practice are critical foundations that are emphasized in various ways throughout this text.

Early educators' responsibility to listen to what children have to say about their gender identities begins from birth. Many TGE youth and adults report they began to *hide their authentic gender self* from their families, teachers, peers, and communities as young as the age of two (Brill & Pepper, 2008; Ehrensaft, 2016b; Steele, 2016). Although current research on young children's gender has significant limitations, as discussed above, there is strong evidence that children are aware of gender at very early ages. Many TGE adults report that they were aware that their gender was different than the one they were assigned at birth as young as two to three years of age (Pyne, 2014; Miller, 2016). In the largest survey of TGE adults ever conducted, with a sample size of nearly 28,000 respondents, the National Center for Transgender Equality (NCTE) found that 32 percent of respondents began to feel their gender was different from the one on their birth certificate by the age of five, and another 28 percent by the age of ten (James, Herman, Rankin, Keisling, Mottet, & Anafi, 2016). Further, outpatient clinics specializing in working with TGE children have seen referrals and client bases triple over the past thirty years (de Vries & Cohen-Kettenis, 2012; Keo-Meier & Ehrensaft, 2018; Zucker, Bradley, Owen-Anderson, Kibblewhite, & Cantor, 2008).

Empirical studies document the following milestones in gender awareness among young children:

- By twelve months, *children begin to categorize individuals by gender* (Quinn, Yahr, Kuhn, Slater, & Pascalis, 2002). There is no biological or intellectual reason why children categorize gender as a binary. Instead, this is a reflection of children's active reading of the social norms that privilege a gender binary. If they grow up in environments that are inclusive of gender diversity, they will learn from the earliest ages that gender is not restricted to a binary.
- By eighteen months, *children begin to understand their gender identity* (Halim, Bryant, & Zucker, 2016), or a person's deeply held "sense of fit with a particular gender category," multiple gender categories, or no gender category at all (adapted from Stryker, 2008, p. 13).
- By two years, *children can communicate awareness that their gender identities are incompatible with their legal designations* (Steensma, Biemond, de Boer, & Cohen-Kettenis, 2011; Steensma, McGuire, Kreukels, Beekman, & Cohen-Kettenis, 2013). At this age, children also begin to recognize gender stereotyping, which may be displayed through toy preference

or an expectation for other children to present gender a particular way. For example, children may invalidate or reject a boy wearing a dress (Zosuls, Ruble, Tamis-LeMonda, Shrout, Bornstein, & Greulich, 2009).
- By two and half years, most children have awareness of their gender identity and can communicate about it using language (e.g., I am a boy, I am a girl, I am an in-betweener, I am a boy and a girl, etc.). *Children understand how they are feeling inside about their gender* (e.g., I am happy to be a girl) (Halim, Bryant, & Zucker, 2016).
- By four years, children *construct a personal belief system of gender stereotypes that is reinforced by cultural and social norms* (Halim & Ruble, 2010). For example, children may have strong feelings about what are male or female tasks, such as cleaning or fixing something. This may be seen in their play or descriptions of experiences (Halim, Bryant, & Zucker, 2016).

The same NCTE survey of nearly 28,000 TGE individuals mentioned above also found that 40 percent of respondents had attempted suicide at some point in their life, which is nearly nine times the rate in the U.S. population generally (James, Herman, Rankin, Keisling, Mottet, & Anafi, 2016). Additionally, the survey found that suicide rates were higher among respondents who experienced intersecting forms of oppression (e.g., people of color or individuals experiencing homelessness) and among respondents who did not find support in their families and educational spaces in their childhoods. Over one-third of those who had attempted suicide at least once in their life reported that their first attempt was at the age of thirteen or earlier. Another 39 percent reported that their first attempt occurred by the age of eighteen. However, rates of suicidality were significantly lower for those with supportive families and accepting school environments when they were growing up (James, Herman, Rankin, Keisling, Mottet, & Anafi, 2016). These statistics are staggering, but they should be seen as a call to action and to support TGE children before they internalize the oppression they will face in their lives. Reducing these rates means recognizing that harm is already being done to very young TGE children, and it is the responsibility of all early childhood professionals to learn how they can contribute to ending this cycle.

Such evidence reinforces that young children are not only old enough to start talking about gender, but they will have already formed foundational understandings of themselves and the world of gender by the time they enter elementary school. This is why it is so critical for early childhood educators to disrupt the restrictive and oppressive norms of the gender binary system and create environments that align with the values and principles at the core of our commitments to children: honoring their voices, agency, and identities and striving to do no harm. Yet, many early childhood educators are hardly prepared to work with TGE children in ways that actively support their gender health, including offering them narratives and role models with which they can connect or granting them agency over their gender identities and expressions.

Supporting early childhood teachers to create more inclusive environments that normalize and value children of all genders and support children to have agency in determining their gender identity begins with a critical deconstruction of their *image of the child*. The "image of the child," a phrase coined by Loris Malaguzzi (1994), refers to the cultural understandings and assumptions about the role of children in education and society, and specifically, varying beliefs about what children are capable of, what motivates them, how much agency or autonomy in decision-making and actions children should have, and goals for their learning and development. Social connections, cultural and family beliefs, and the historical context of communities influence different "images of the child" (Martalock, 2012; Rogoff, 2003), and significantly shape the types of practices and settings adults create to support children (Rogoff, 2003). As Malaguzzi (1994) states, "There are hundreds of different images of the child. Each one of you has inside yourself an image of the child that directs you as you begin to relate to a child. This theory within you pushes you to behave in certain ways; it orients you as you talk to the child, listen to the child, observe the child. It is very difficult for you to act contrary to this internal image" (p. 52).

INTERROGATING THE "IMAGE OF THE CHILD" IN EARLY CHILDHOOD EDUCATION

To honor children's voices and agency requires an interrogation and deconstruction of the "image of the child" in Western Eurocentric early childhood education—which is rooted in knowledge claims from developmental science (Dahlberg, Moss, & Pence, 2013; File, Basler Wisneski, & Mueller, 2012). Western developmental science scholarship has historically constructed beliefs about children as egocentric, naive, concrete, and immature thinkers who need age-appropriate interventions in order to mature into independent fully-human beings because, as Murris (2018) describes, to be a child is to be "vulnerable, fragile and in need of adult surveillance and controlled opportunities and experiences" (p. 7). Childhood is assumed to be a time of "immaturity" where children are assumed to be "lacking" across several domains including cognition, morality, rationality, and agentic ability. Murris (2018) describes six configurations that inform the dominant images of the child embedded in Western early childhood theories and practices:

> the "developing child" who lacks maturity by nature and needs culture's guidance; the "ignorant child" who lacks rationality and experience from birth and needs instruction and training; the "evil child" who lacks natural goodness and

requires cultural intervention of control and discipline; the "innocent child" who lacks responsibility, therefore needs culture to provide protection and to facilitate learning; the "egocentric child" who lacks social norms and cultural values and requires socialization by elders; the "fragile child" who is assumed to lack resilience by nature and needs culture to diagnose, protect and possibly medicate. All these deficit figurations of child assume childhood as an inferior stage in human development with the mature, developed, rational, autonomous adult self as the normative ideal. (2018, p. 8)

The Western perspective of "child/childhood" in the field of early childhood also has deep roots in heteronormativity, cisnormativity, and patriarchy, where a "mature, white, able-bodied, heterosexual man (Braidotti, 2013) is the yardstick by which 'normal' and 'natural' child development is measured" (Murris, 2017, p. 2). This worldview situates the TGE child as abnormal and unnatural by comparison, and therefore TGE children are marginalized in the hierarchy of patriarchal power (Cannella & Viruru, 2004). Young-Bruehl (2012) discusses at length what she calls *childism*, a systematic prejudice that is "built into the very way children are imagined" in our society where social, political, legal and cultural structures fail to meet children's needs and fully respect their human rights (p. 5). Given the Western propensity for *childism*, listening to children's voices and respecting their agency requires deep disruption, a commitment to reform our attitudes toward children (Young-Bruehl, 2012). Murris (2018) describes this as a project of dismantling identity prejudice that systematically privileges adults and the imperialist assumptions of their superiority:

Children are not listened to because of their very being a child and are therefore unable to make claims to knowledge, because it is assumed that they are (still) developing, (still) innocent, (still) fragile, (still) immature, (still) irrational, and so forth. As a result, the child is denied ethically, epistemically and ontologically. . . . Knowledge is offered by the child, but not heard by the adult, because of identity prejudice. (pp. 15–16)

The binarized conceptions of immaturity/maturity that shape current images of the child ordain a reciprocal reasoning. Imagining children as deficient in reason, emotion control, responsibility, and maturity have consequences for how we imagine ourselves (Murris, 2013, p. 9). Re-imagining children through a lens of capacity and equality would, in this hierarchical worldview, diminish adults' sense of being and purpose. The act of listening to children is a radical redistribution of power. When children are understood to be knowledge coconstructors, they are given opportunities to influence the decisions that impact their lives, including their experiences in early childhood programs (e.g., curriculum, instructional methods, arrangement of the environment, and policies and family engagement practices). Dislike of such a loss of control is likely a powerful motivation fueling adults' insensitivity in hearing the voices and supporting the agency of young children.

> *We had a creek that was in the back of the house and I remember we were playing the equivalent of "king of the hill" but it was "king of the creek," so we were pushing each other off these stepping stones and trying to get the other person wet, and I remember winning, and one of the neighbor boys who was a year older than me saying that I couldn't be the king of the creek because I was a girl. And of course, I was just absolutely enraged, and punched him, and he ran home crying, and then I hear my grandmother yelling my full name out of the window and I knew I was in trouble because his screams could be heard for miles around. She asked me what happened because she heard him wailing. And she goes, "Well, you have to be nice to boys," and I said, "Why?" And she goes, "Well, you're gonna have to marry one of them eventually." And I was like four and a half, you know, on the cusp of five and I was just like why? Why? I felt like I wasn't heard. (Ikaika, trans and māhūkāne, he/him)*

Despite the stability of the Western Eurocentric child development canon, theoretical shifts in the ontological and epistemological anchors referenced in early childhood scholarship have emerged to critique the intellectual impoverishment reinforced in the Cartesian dualisms and traditional western views. These knowledge projects aim to reconfigure the nature of the child to be competent epistemic agents. Studies in the sociology of childhood (Christensen & Prout, 2012; Corsaro, 1997; Greene & Hill, 2012; Greene & Hogan, 2012) are an example of this disassembling as they resist positioning children as "adults in the making," preferring to emphasize children as "beings" versus "becomings" (Hogan, 2012, p. 27). Sociology of childhood studies neither emphasize the "biological incompleteness of children" nor do they position children as passive and dependent on adults for an expression of personal agency (Liebel, 2012, p. 18). By contrast, these studies reframe children as active stakeholders who are self-determined, regularly act in their own interest and have a right to be taken seriously, not only at a future point in time but also in their present experiences (Liebel, 2012). Shifting away from historical signification of children as needy, vulnerable, and irrational, the sociology of childhood studies recast children through a strengths-based discourse signifying children as competent social agents whose ideas and contributions can fundamentally inform the social institutions created to support them (Graham & Fitzgerald, 2010; Loveridge, 2010). Each child is understood to be "a unique and valued experiencer of his or her own world" (Christensen & Prout, 2012, p. 50) and a reliable and capable informant able to provide accurate information about their lives.

Similarly, queer theory applied to early childhood disrupts the traditional image of the child. Ruffolo (2009) explains:

> Queer theory . . . offers tools to disturb normative practices and binary ideologies by exposing how there are no fixed and stable bodies that are essentially normal . . . [it] exposes how bodies become *normatively essentialized*: what is considered "normal" and "essential" is in fact a complex networking of social, cultural, political, and economic desires that seek to produce what it means to be normal. . . . Queer theory is concerned with challenging such constructions in order to move away from essentialized understandings of experience (e.g. all children in kindergarten can "use, read, and represent whole numbers to 10 in a variety of meaningful contexts"). It specifically focuses on the ways in which children become intelligible through the reiteration of identity norms that are often upheld in fixed and stable binary categories: able/disabled, male/female, masculine/feminine, gay/straight, etc. . . . This binary framework is problematic for queer theory because it places and restricts subjects in fixed identity categories that unavoidably majoritize and minoritize subjects. In other words, the privileged category relies on an unprivileged other for its intelligibility: to be masculine is to not be feminine. (p. 295)

More recent research drawing on the perspective of critical posthumanism disrupts the anthropocentric nature of binary thinking in a manner that supports a new way of imagining the child (Barad, 2007). Murris (2017) explains, "a postdevelopmental move away from the exclusive anthropocentric focus on language and the discursive in education is particularly urgent to enable more just educational encounters with people who are not only young, but who might also live in poverty and not have English as their 'home' language. Critical posthumanism does so by removing language as the main hub of knowledge production and with it the 'fully-human' sophisticated language speaker of age as the sole producer of knowledge" (p. 3). In Barad's (2007) words, posthumanism invites "females, slaves, children, animals and other dispossessed Others (exiled from the land of knowers by Aristotle more than two millennia ago) into the fold of knowers" (p. 378).

INTERSECTIONS OF KNOWLEDGE, TRUTH, AND DISCOURSE

In addition to an interrogation of the image of the child teachers hold, the road to gender justice and creating gender inclusive early childhood classrooms also requires a comprehensive evaluation of the discourse available to children to talk about gender. Using the most currently accepted and inclusive language will require both learning new ideas and terms *and* unlearning previously taken-for-granted lexicon considered problematic when examined under the magnifying glass of more accurate understandings about gender and its diversity. As discourses are "bodies of language, text and communication patterns that 'systematize and frame' our thinking, feelings, understanding and practice in relation to particular ideas" (Foucault, 1980; MacNaughton, 2005, p. 20), each discourse "naturalizes" particular relationships of power in society by privileging certain ideas as "truths" (Foucault, 1980) while marginalizing or leaving invisible other equally valid but unknown perspectives. Foucault (1980) and poststructural scholars (Chapman, 2003; English, 2005) emphasize how the production of knowledge is intimately related to politics, as certain voices and stories are heard, privileged and counted as knowledge or "truths" in discourse while others are systematically hidden from view, marginalized and excluded from circulation.

> *At the snack table, kids were talking about invisible "Mr. Nobody" sitting in one of the chairs. Kerry comes over and says, "Mr. Nobody's sitting here, and Mrs. Nobody's sitting here, and in-betweener Nobody's sitting here!" My co-worker, Crane, identifies with the term "in-betweener" and uses it with the kids as an umbrella word for everyone outside the cisgender binary. (Luke, transgender preschool teacher, he/him)*

Poststructuralism destroys claims of *objective truth* by spotlighting the political foundations and subjectivity pervasive within the discourses circulated, privileged, and used to construct majoritarian narratives that set the metrics for what is considered normative in society (Foucault, 1980). Made visible is the asymmetry of the narratives we have access to, how the "storying" of our lives is always impacted by the limitations of language that simultaneously sorts, contains, entitles, censors, dominates, and eclipses the expression of experiences and constructions of meaning (Nicholson, 2017). Poststructuralists suggest that the politics shaping a particular context influence which stories are privileged and circulated as "truth" and knowledge in that environment and which mental models, stories, and perspectives are cast to the margins, rendering them silent from public imagination and discourse. Poststructuralism brings attention to the process of "signification," that is, how individuals are named and politically positioned through linguistic signifiers, for example, "male," "female," "transgender," and the highly political process in which social norms and ideology influence the meaning and power associated with different signifiers.

Language, and the act of representing experience or signifying it, becomes an expression of power as dominant groups signify the world according to their ideological worldview, as the privileging of cisnormativity and the gender binary illustrates. Bringing the personal stories and voices of those who have gone unheard or whose experiences have not been counted as knowledge into the discourse where it can be heard offers alternative, often contradictory, versions of reality (Ewick & Silbey, 1995; MacNaughton, 2005). This process becomes an inherently political act as bringing visibility to silenced stories provides opportunities to challenge the normalized "truths" circulating and privileged in society (Ailwood, 2011; Foucault, 1980; MacNaughton, 2005). Further, for minoritized individuals, learning how one has been signified while also learning to give voice to one's personal experience can be a catalyst for critiquing, resisting, and reauthoring how one is signified in society.

In the words of Foucault (1981), "power is not something that is acquired, seized, or shared, something that one holds onto or allows to slip away, power is exercised from innumerable points, in the interplay of non-egalitarian and mobile relations" (p. 94). Thus, although individuals do not have unrestricted agency, they do have degrees of freedom and ability to be powerful in working for positive change in making intentional choices with the discourse and signifiers they use. Language, and the act of representing experience or signifying it, is a "powerful means of constructing an ideological worldview that furthers the interests of particular dominant groups" and sustains particular hegemonic power relationships in society (Fletcher, 1999, p. 23).

It is with the intersections between discourse, knowledge, and power firmly in mind, that we turn to the importance of language in discussions of gender. To date, the act of representing experience and signifying it has privileged the ideological worldview of patriarchy and cisnormativity, and maintained power for individuals who most benefit from the status quo (e.g., white "men") in a world forced into a rigid gender binary. Thus, disrupting the use of language that reproduces this dominant social order is an essential transformative and liberating process for teachers committed to gender justice. The next section provides a comprehensive examination of the intersections of power and knowledge with a wide range of terms used to talk about gender.

I often explain to other service providers that while the constantly evolving language and concepts of gender and sexual identity in youth populations can be overwhelming at times, if we don't keep up we lose the ability to connect and therefore to do effective work. When we sign up as health care providers, educators, parents, we sign up to sometimes make ourselves uncomfortable in order to make our young people comfortable. (Kyle Taylor-Shaughnessy, Trans author, he/him for present/future and she/her for childhood [Taylor-Shaughnessy, 2016, p. 28])

THE EXPANDING LEXICON OF GENDER: LEARNING THROUGH UNLEARNING

Contemporary Western understandings of gender are evolving rapidly and moving strongly in the direction of diversity and expansiveness. For forms of injustice and oppression experienced by young TGE children to be explored in depth, a working understanding of the complex and dynamic concept of gender itself must be established. There is an inherent challenge associated with this task. Introducing a progression of terms with their own working definitions is necessary for documenting the evolving boundaries of gender as a dynamic construct. However, the danger is a list that appears more glossarial and authoritative than shifting and evolving. The order and length of our presentation of terms in this section is intentional as we believe it is necessary for situating readers' understanding of the arc of change in Western Eurocentric scholars' conceptions of gender and both the learning and the unlearning required for teachers who are committed to adopting language that signifies a value for gender diversity.

It is important to note that there is no universal consensus within the gender diverse community on language to use to discuss gender. The terms used below and throughout this text represent the authors' best effort to use the most empowering, current, progressive, and justice-based language for discussing gender diversity at this moment in time. However, our lexicon is not a definitive set of universally accepted terms, nor should it be assumed that these definitions will stand the test of time. We will continue to learn and adapt our use of language to respect and align with the words that individuals find most empowering and accurate for themselves. To that end, quotations are included at times with terms that are considered outdated or offensive to some (e.g., transsexual, transgendered), as we respect the language that others choose for themselves. When someone identifies personally with an outdated label, it is very possible that they fought hard for that label when they first donned it. The history of gender liberation can often be seen in its evolving lexicon and in the labels associated with its generations.

As we introduce the terms below, we discuss how different words have been used to limit conceptions of gender and provide alternatives that liberate and normalize gender diversity. While the word *gender* itself will be used throughout this section, we will be going through a process of unlearning and learning to build a working definition of *gender* that will be used throughout the rest of the book.

The Gender Binary: An Unjust Hegemony

Much of Western language, laws, social norms, customs, and ways of understanding gender are rooted deeply in the *gender binary* (Bornstein, 2013a; Fausto-Sterling, 2000). The gender binary is defined in this book to mean the belief system which dictates that there are two mutually exclusive and collectively exhaustive gender categories—male and female—and that the category a person belongs to is determined conclusively by their anatomy and physiology. Because so many aspects of life are commonly associated with gender—behaviors, interests, expressions, mannerisms, temperaments, sexuality, aptitudes, and so forth—such a binary system resting on anatomy and physiology for its means of categorization inherently implies that those aspects of life are significantly determined or influenced by biology (Bornstein, 2013a; Fausto-Sterling, 2000).

> *Gender is also, like, sometimes there's gender themed bathrooms, like there's girls' bathrooms and boys' bathrooms. (Oak, eight years)*
>
> *I don't think I really had a good sense of what gender even was, just that women and girls were told they couldn't do stuff and I was like, "That's silly, why not?" There was kind of this continual petulance and defiance. (Ikaika, trans and māhūkāne, he/him)*

Anatomy and Physiology

As subsets of biology, *anatomy* in humans is the science of the structures and parts of the body, and *physiology* is the science of the functions, processes, and relationships of those body parts. Most children are assigned a gender in the gender binary, on the day they are born or even before, based on a visual inspection of external genitalia (one aspect of anatomy) (Fausto-Sterling, 2000).

Since, according to the gender binary, anatomy determines gender and gender is associated with so many aspects of life, the assumptions and expectations for a particular child's lifelong gender journey begin at the first moment they are categorized into a binary gender. For example, a growing trend in the United States over the last several years is for those who are expecting a child to throw a "gender reveal party"—using frosted cakes with hidden pink (for girl) or blue (for boy) centers or other suspenseful methods of revealing the gender of their unborn baby. A Google image search of "gender reveal cake" displays an array of pink and blue frosting designs posing playful questions like "baseballs or bows?" "touchdowns or tutus?" and "guns or glitter?" Before a child is out of the womb, adults begin making plans for the types of activities and clothing styles they assume the child will prefer someday, based entirely on the fetus's anatomical assignment of *boy* or *girl*. Embedded in these questions are the assumptions that a blue cake will mean a child who one day will like sports, rugged activities, and possibly even violence while a pink cake foretells a child who will be interested in pretty clothes and accessories, dancing, and aesthetics.

The period of feminist activism in the United States known as Second Wave Feminism, beginning in the 1960s and lasting roughly twenty to thirty years, centered around many issues related to the gender binary as a system that limits the paths available to a person based on their gender—sending men to colleges and to work while women stayed home to raise children, placing men in positions of power and authority while women were expected to be subservient and deferential (Budge, Orovecz, Owen, & Sherry, 2018). After World War II, when many of the men in the United States were sent to war, and the number of women in the workplace increased dramatically, it was clear that women were not simply incapable of pursuing those paths. Rather, they were being held back by societal norms and expectations about their roles in society. It was against this social backdrop that a conceptual split proposed in the fields of medicine and psychology was popularized—that is, that there is a difference between bodies and behaviors, and that the former does not always predict or determine the latter (Fausto-Sterling, 2000; Haig, 2004).

Sex and Gender: A Double-Edged Sword

In 1955, John Money introduced the concept of "gender roles" as all those behaviors that individuals engage in to signify their status as a boy, girl, man, or woman (Haig, 2004). Prior to that point, the term "gender" was almost exclusively used in academic publications in the context of grammatical gender (the linguistic classification of nouns in certain languages as grammatically masculine, feminine, or neuter), while "sex" was the term used to describe how people were categorized based on anatomy (Haig, 2004). Money and Ehrhardt (1972) shifted this conceptual distinction from *gender* being related to grammar to both *sex* and *gender* being ways to categorize and describe people. They argued that *sex* pertained to one's anatomy and physiology (their physical body), while *gender* pertained to one's internal conviction of being a man, woman, boy, or girl and the external behaviors used to signify this conviction.

This sex-gender distinction began to take hold in much of second wave feminist theory and messaging, through the 1970s and 1980s (Haig, 2004). Since then, arguments about sex and gender have flowed largely along nature-nurture lines, respectively. They have pushed on restrictive gender roles and behavioral expectations by claiming that, aside from reproductive functions, most of the behavior that falls under *gender* is culturally and socially learned (nurture) rather than biologically determined (nature) (Fausto-Sterling, 2000). Perhaps the largest push of this period of feminist activism was to liberate women from restrictive, oppressive, and socially constructed gender roles and expectations by showing that they are not inevitabilities of anatomical difference (Fausto-Sterling, 2000).

In discussions that differentiate between sex and gender, *sex* is often framed as being distinctly binary and relatively immutable. According to Dr. Anne Fausto-Sterling (2000), a leading expert in the biology of gender, *sex* is presented as being based soundly in biology, a hard science, which is therefore understood to be clear-cut, straightforward, and objective. *Gender*, on the other hand, is presented as a social construct that captures much more nebulous and subjective concepts than physical bodies, such as personalities, social roles, and presentations as they relate to masculinity and femininity. Fausto-Sterling (2000) notes, "sex and nature are thought to be real, while gender and culture are seen as constructed. But these are false dichotomies" (p. 27).

Fausto-Sterling (2000) documents the sex-gender distinction being used by second-wave feminism in the support of those who bend and break the social rules of gender, allowing them to behave and enact their genders differently than their bodies might otherwise dictate if sex and gender were one and the same. She describes this sex-gender distinction then being extended to the cultural dialogue around transgender lives and experiences. Indeed, the idea that a person might be a "woman [gender] born in a man's body [sex]," or vice versa, is becoming a more well-known narrative (Vade, 2005). This distinction, however, has allowed the concept of *sex* to remain relatively unquestioned as a binary classification, while *gender* has seen a great deal of conceptual expansion in recent decades. But a binary view of *sex* is inadequate to accurately capture human anatomical diversity. In fact, John Money, a sexologist and psychologist, first introduced the concepts of gender roles and a sex-gender distinction based on his work with people whose anatomy and physiology resisted simplistic binary categorization (Fausto-Sterling, 2000; Haig, 2004).

Sex classification of humans has evolved as the scientific fields of biology, medicine, anatomy, physiology, and others have made inroads to understanding the complexities of the human body—from external genitalia to gonads and internal reproductive organs to compounds categorized as "sex hormones" to chromosomes and more. However, in her book, *Sexing the Body*, Fausto-Sterling (2000) argues that legal, political, and cultural decisions have had as much, if not more, to do with drawing the line between male and female than doctors and scientists. Also, some of those doctors and scientists who *did* have significant influence on modern classifications were shown to be socially and culturally motivated to maintain a *sex binary*—a binary system of belief, much like the gender binary, but specifically related to the categorization of bodies into two distinct and separate groups (Fausto-Sterling, 2000).

In reality, bodies are not so simple to categorize. Some of the anatomical and physiological attributes that are most commonly used to try to define binary sex categories—genitals, XX or XY chromosomes, the presence of either ovaries or testes (both are referred to as gonads), and reproductive capacity—have significant degrees of variation in normal human diversity (Fausto-Sterling, 2000; Vade, 2005; Intersex Society of North America, ISNA; InterAct Advocates). Other aspects of anatomy and physiology often associated with sex—especially certain growth hormones (estrogens, androgens, and others), and many of the physiological changes that occur during puberty (facial and body hair, breast development, voice changes, fat distribution, etc.)—come in even more varied and diverse combinations (Fausto-Sterling, 2000). The umbrella term *intersex* is used to describe all those who are born with bodies that do not fit conventional ideas of male or female anatomy and physiology (ISNA; InterAct).

According to Fausto-Sterling (2000), documentation of infants born with ambiguous genitalia date back at least to Aristotle in the fourth century BCE. Accounts of individuals who embodied both male and female physical traits exist in many of the world's religions and mythologies. Early interpretations of the Bible describe Adam as being both male and female before splitting into two separate bodies. The term "hermaphrodite"—largely considered outdated and offensive now[3]—comes from the Greek Hermes and Aphrodite and myths of their child who blends maleness and femaleness so much as to be uncategorizable as either one or the other (Fausto-Sterling, 2000).

Some children are born with XY chromosomes but are completely insensitive to androgens (the growth hormones associated with masculinization), and so develop physically such that they are categorized as female and may never know about their chromosomal makeup. Some children may develop one ovary and one teste or have a single gonad with both ovarian and testicular tissues, called ovotestes, or have other various combinations of gonads. While XX and XY are the most common chromosomal variations, children are born with XO, XXY, XXX, XYY, and several other combinations (Blackless, Charuvastra, Derryck, Fausto-Sterling, Lauzanne, & Lee, 2000; Greenberg, 1999; Fausto-Sterling, 2000).

There simply is no aspect of anatomy or physiology that can be used to cleanly divide people into two groups—male and female (Fausto-Sterling, 2000). Further, "choosing which criteria to use in determining sex, and choosing to make the determination at all, are social decisions for which scientists can offer no absolute guidelines" (Fausto-Sterling, 2000, p. 5). Intersex and trans sociology professor, Cary Gabriel Costello (2014), likens the slicing of bodies into two groups to the slicing of the color spectrum into discrete and distinctly named colors.

In cases of ambiguous genitalia, many individuals have historically been, and are often still today, subjected to invasive and unnecessary "normalizing" surgeries as infants in order to more neatly place them in binary sex boxes, sometimes without even the parents of the child being informed of the real reason their infant is taken into surgery (Fausto-Sterling, 2000). These surgical sexual assignments of intersex infants "focus primarily on reproductive abilities (in the case of a potential girl) or penis size (in the case of a prospective boy)" (Fausto-Sterling, 2000, p. 5), and in the case of a possible male assignment, "what counts especially is how the penis functions in social interactions" (p. 58) meaning in heterosexual intercourse. These surgeries have been defended as necessary for the child to grow up well adjusted to society—the hidden assumption being that society is and must always be founded on a binary interpretation of sex. Despite the scientific evidence of a wide spectrum of bodies, the sex binary mandates that all babies be placed in one of two boxes as neatly and as quickly as possible.

The very existence of intersex bodies is antithetical to the sex binary and places the gender binary on unstable ground as well. That intersex bodies could destabilize the gender binary is the real reason behind medically unnecessary surgeries performed on infants to make them "fit in" better. As will be examined in chapter 2, multiple axes of gender-based oppression and privilege rest on maintaining the false binaries and related hierarchies of bodies and genders. As Fausto-Sterling (2000) notes, "since intersexuals[4] embody both sexes, they weaken claims about sexual differences" which is why doctors have historically employed a "surgical shoehorn" to force intersex bodies into binary classifications (p. 8).

In his discussions of *sex* and *gender roles*, John Money largely advocated for the idea that intersex children could be surgically assigned a sex, and then, with "proper" rearing, they could be molded to fit the corresponding societal gender role (Haig, 2004; Fausto-Sterling, 2000). This stance aligns somewhat with second-wave feminism in the claims that one is not unilaterally defined by their body and that gender roles are socially conditioned, which is why it was picked up in feminist discourse. It also rings true for many transgender individuals, who do not wish to be defined by their bodies or their birth assignment. However, Money applied those beliefs in an attempt to use social conditioning to force intersex individuals to accept an assigned gender role, which is distinctly at odds with feminist, intersex, and transgender goals of behavioral autonomy (Fausto-Sterling, 2000; Haig, 2004).

The adult intersex community today advocates strongly for the cessation of all medically unnecessary "normalizing" surgeries and for child agency in both gender development and bodily autonomy (ISNA; InterAct; Costello, 2014). Costello (2014) notes, "Intersex advocates believe that no intervention should be forced—but also that once an intersex person is old enough to give full informed consent, that hormonal, surgical, or other interventions should be performed if that's what the individual truly wants." While some feminist discourse today is in favor of both bodily and behavioral autonomy, other factions are only in favor of the latter, and argue that all individuals should accept their bodies as they are (Costello, 2014). Individuals who advocate against *any* medical interventions (e.g., hormones therapies, surgeries, etc.) are further split between those who accept that someone may identify differently than their birth assignment and those who believe that birth assignment based on anatomy should also dictate gender and gender role assignments. But both groups argue that one's *sex* assignment is immutable because *sex* (as a categorical notion) is considered innate and must be accepted along with one's anatomy and physiology (Costello, 2014). This stance has been used against both intersex and transgender individuals who seek bodily autonomy (Costello, 2014; Vade, 2005).

When looking at the whole of this brief history, distinct contradictions of ideologies become clear, but the motivations appear to be the same. An argument that one's rearing, not their body, defines their societal role is used to bind intersex individuals to their surgically sculpted and then socially enforced sex and gender assignments. Then, an argument that *sex* dictates one's societal role and is unchangeable is used to deny agency over self-identification and *wanted* medical interventions for both intersex and transgender individuals. In both cases, some kind of externally controlled, binary classification is enforced and individual autonomy to self-define and self-determine is removed. In both cases, power is removed from individuals who challenge the gender binary and given to institutions and structures that uphold it.

Eliminating the Sex-Gender Distinction

While the distinction provides some glimmer of hope for autonomy of individuals not to be defined by their bodies, the pitfalls of this conceptual divide are too many and the damage it has done to the intersex and transgender communities is too great. In examining the sex-gender distinction, transgender activist and lawyer Dylan Vade (2005) reflects, "Sex is natural and biological and medically objective and fixed. Gender is cultural and changeable and subjective and in the head. Transgender people are those whose sex and gender do not match. I strongly disagree with this conceptualization" (p. 278). Vade (2005) puts forth four arguments in favor of eliminating this false dichotomy, which can be summarized as follows:

1. Despite the ways sex and gender are discussed, both concepts are socially constructed, and both concepts are real.
2. The sex-gender distinction removes power and agency to self-identify from transgender and intersex individuals and gives it to cisgender authorities in the medical and legal fields, which results in transgender self-identifications being viewed as delusional, deceptive, or less credible.
3. The delegitimization of self-identities creates a physically dangerous environment for transgender and intersex individuals, whose *deceptiveness* is used as a justification for violence perpetrated against them.
4. The conceptual divide unnecessarily cuts transgender and intersex individuals' bodies off from their minds—for example, being described as "female bodied" but "male-identified"—and is "self-alienating."

The first and second arguments are demonstrated in the analysis of intersex bodies and the history of classifications above. The second argument's assertion of a cultural image of transgender individuals as not credible, as delusional, and as deceptive, along with the third argument that that image creates a physically dangerous environment for transgender individuals will be explored in much greater depth throughout this book. The fourth argument rings true for many transgender individuals, who do not ascribe to the common "born in the wrong body" transgender narrative. For example, many transgender women prefer to think of themselves as a "woman with a large clit" rather than as being "male-boded." However, this argument may not feel compelling to other transgender individuals who do feel alienated by their bodies. Our proposed use of language respects all of these narratives and does not impede individuals from expressing discord between their genders and their bodies.

Furthermore, Haig (2004) notes that, despite the significant discourse about the sex-gender distinction, the two terms are often used interchangeably both colloquially and academically, and *sex* is also linguistically inextricable from reproduction and erotic activity or behavior. It is clear that distinct and empowering definitions of both terms are needed.

In this book, we will not endorse the idea that sex and gender are two separate concepts that can be used to categorize individuals. Gender will be used to encompass all that can be used to categorize (including bodies, social roles, and identities) as well as one's gendered social experiences (how others view and treat one as a gendered being). We will adopt transgender activist and writer, Kate Bornstein's (2013b) handling of the word "sex," by consigning it to mean only "erotic energy at rest or in motion" (p. 49). By limiting this term in this way, the reduction of people to their reproductive or sexual capacities, or to a checklist of body parts and functions, is avoided. With this treatment of *sex* and *gender*, the components of anatomy and physiology that are used to categorize bodies as male, female, or intersex become aspects, but not determinants, of one's gender. Many more aspects of gender are discussed below.

The intentional use of the terms *anatomy* and *physiology* (or simply bodies), rather than sex, is a political act that intends to honor and make visible the true diversity of human bodies. Anatomy and physiology are more affirming and inclusive terms than *sex*. They are more open-ended and can be used with children to discuss bodies in descriptive, rather than deterministic and prescriptive, ways. These terms allow for bodies to change throughout one's life, both through physiological processes of aging and through medical interventions, whereas *sex* as a categorical concept is considered innate and unchanging. For example, an intersex child born with 5-α-reductase deficiency has XY chromosomes but is typically born with an unfused scrotum and very small penis, which are often thought to be labia and a clitoris, respectively, and so that child is likely to be assigned female at birth (Fausto-Sterling, 2000). Then during puberty, their scrotum fuses, testicles descend, and penis grows significantly. By discussing this child's anatomy and physiological processes, rather than trying to classify them into a sex category, much confusion can be avoided, especially for the child. As another example, a child who is born with a penis, but who identifies as a girl, may eventually choose to surgically alter her body so as to have a vagina instead. By discussing anatomy and physiology, rather than sex, she can be empowered to change her body in ways that affirm her gender without being tied to some immutable classification. While (consensual) medical intervention is not as relevant for children in early childhood (e.g., Tanner stage II of puberty, when a child's incipient body changes are in evidence, is the time that many clinicians currently believe a child is ready to consider medical intervention; Ehrensaft, 2016b), it is important to use language that encourages children to think of their bodies as diverse and dynamic and under their own control, rather than binary and static and deterministic of their futures. Further, we want children to begin to learn from their earliest years that bodies are only one of many aspects of the complex concept of gender.

> *I ask. I used to ask the kid, like, "What do you call this?" if they're more verbal. I used to ask, "Can I call this your penis?" or "Are you okay if I call this a vagina?" But since our last conversation, I've tried avoiding labeling kids' genitals in those binary ways, unless that's the language they're using for themselves. So I'll just say, "aim your body part into the toilet." And it's part of consent, right? If we're teaching them the word consent, if we're teaching them the word inclusion, how am I modeling that and practicing that as an educator? (Mitali, trans* genderqueer nonbinary community educator, they/them)*

Legal Designation: A More Honest Accounting than "Sex"

Another aspect of gender, which is derived directly from the cultural importance placed on anatomy, is *legal designation*. In most countries, the (typically) binary category assigned to individuals at birth is then codified by law. Indeed, it is the requirement that binary legal designation be made at birth that has fueled some of the immediacy of intersex "normalizing" surgeries (Fausto-Sterling, 2000; Gabriel Costello, 2014). One's legal designation at birth as either male or female has far-reaching ramifications, depending on when and where a person is born in this world. Throughout history, up through the present-day, being assigned female at birth has typically meant incurring significantly more restrictions on one's legal rights and opportunities in life. In many countries, women are not given basic rights of citizenship such as voting, holding property, and speaking for oneself in legal matters. Even in countries where women do have such rights, they have been primarily granted in the last century. One's legal gender designation is a key card to much of their life as a member of an organized society (Fausto-Sterling, 2000).

For transgender individuals, legal designation can become mired with complexity due to the constraints imposed by various sociocultural, historical, and political systems (Stryker, 2008). The process of changing one's legal designation varies widely state by state and country by country. In many places, it is simply not allowed (e.g., Tennessee[5], Puerto Rico, and sixty-seven countries[6] as of 2016). In others, it is so onerous or expensive that it is effectively impossible for a community that also has to contend with rampant oppression and economic disadvantage. Many transgender individuals find themselves with different designations across legal, medical, and other records, which can cause difficulty navigating society (e.g., a state driver's license that says "F" and federal passport that says "M" or a trans man who is denied insurance coverage for a hysterectomy because he has legally changed his gender marker with his insurance). Not having access or the ability to change one's legal designation is an example of structural and institutional oppression faced by transgender individuals—where inequality is built directly into the laws and structures of a society.

> *[After checking in to an ER for suicidal thoughts] . . . this is my first visit to the hospital after having the gender marker on my health card corrected, so I'm very optimistic that it will go better than others in the past. There were little Fs (for "female") all over the place: in the hospital documents, on my wristband, and on my chart. This made me pretty happy. That happiness was crushed when I left the waiting room and entered the emergency room. It only takes minutes for me to realize that whatever is on my chart will be trumped by my appearance—the very same appearance that causes my dysphoria, the very same appearance that is a major contributing factor to me being in the ER to begin with. Unbeknownst to the staff in that ER, by calling me "he" and "him," they have all become a grim reminder of exactly why I'm here. (Xeph Kalma, she/her [Kalma, 2016, p. 204])*

As with anatomy and physiology, "legal designation" is a term we intentionally choose to disambiguate the many connotations of *sex*. Since *sex*, as a categorical concept, is assigned at birth based on anatomy and then codified by law on documents like birth certificates, its false binary assumptions are then given legal weight and power. Additionally, the conceptualization of *sex* as being immutable and unchanging (unlike anatomy and physiology) is reinforced by the legal hoops one must go through to change their legal designation, if doing so is even possible where they live. "Sex: M/F" is often used on government forms, identification cards, medical paperwork, and in other administrative contexts, when the information that is truly being conveyed is one's legal designation (or even more narrowly, their *institutional* designation as a person is documented in a specific institution's records such as at an insurance company or a school). Having a driver's license that states, unambiguously "Sex: M" can be a painful reminder to a transgender woman that her self-identification is seen as less valid than her legal designation or it can be an empowering moment of victory in a transgender man's life when he is able to change his legal designation to match his self-identification. Using the term "legal designation" rather than *sex* allows for nuanced discussions of both the agency to change one's designation to affirm their identity and the complexity of legal and logistical barriers to doing so. It also names the power structures—the medical and legal establishments—that are maintaining the gender binary, rather than falsely conceptualizing the binary as existing within bodies themselves.

Using the term legal designation instead of sex acknowledges the discrimination faced by transgender individuals. Many states in the United States have proposed laws that would require people to use public restrooms based on some version of the concept of "biological sex."[7] However, the lack of a universally accepted medical definition of such a binary category as "biological sex" means that they typically have to use one's legal designation as a stand-in. In 2017 in Arkansas, SB774 was introduced, which defined sex as "a person's immutable biological sex as objectively determined by anatomy and genetics existing at the time of birth." However, because that definition is unenforceable, the law then stated that "a person's original birth certificate can be relied upon to establish his or her sex." In this case, it is not any *immutable* characteristic of the individual that is used to enforce the law, but one's legal gender designation specifically on their original birth certificate. Again, by eliminating *sex* as a way of categorizing, we resist the kind of reductionist thinking based on false representations of anatomy that is used to discriminate against transgender individuals, and which routinely ignores the existence of intersex individuals.

Only one of these bathroom bills has been passed in the United States at the time of this writing, and it has since been repealed. However, if these kinds of laws get more of a legal foothold, someone who has medically altered their anatomy and physiology to affirm their gender would be legally required to use a restroom where they would not just look very out of place, but where they may be in very real danger of experiencing violence. The NCTE's 2015 survey of transgender adults devoted a whole chapter to the violence and harassment experienced by transgender people in public restrooms, with 12 percent reporting experiences of verbal harassment, physical assault, and/or sexual assault in a public restroom in the preceding year. As Vade (2005) noted in his arguments against the sex-gender distinction, recognizing a conceptual category of *sex* over gender puts transgender individuals at physical risk. As with anatomy and physiology, one's legal designation(s) and institutional designations are aspects of their gender. They play an important role in how an individual is allowed to participate in a given society, but they do not dictate who the person is or should be. The only person who can do that is the person themself.

Gender Identity: Only the Person Themself Can Tell

In this book, *gender identity* is defined as a person's deeply held "sense of fit with a particular gender category," multiple gender categories, or no gender category at all (adapted from Stryker, 2008, p.13). It is not within the purview of this book to claim to know what precise balance of internal and external influences bring about one's gender identity, nor is it the responsibility of early childhood educators to speculate the same. Gender identity is ultimately a personal understanding and awareness of self that is determined individually and internally (Stryker, 2008; Bornstein, 2013b; Ehrensaft, 2016b).

> *Gender is . . . all different kinds of people. (Ivy, five years, she/her)*

As reported previously, most children start becoming aware of their gender identities between eighteen and thirty months of age (Halim, Bryant, & Zucker, 2016). Some children will develop gender identities that align with their original legal designation as assigned based on anatomy (cisgender), and some children will develop an identity that is different from that designation in some way (transgender/trans). An individual's gender identity may stay constant throughout their life (fixed), or it may change over time and/or across contexts (fluid). A person might identify with a single gender, or they may identify with multiple genders (e.g., bigender, ambigender), or with no gender at all (agender).

Most importantly, gender identity cannot be determined just by looking at someone. Because gender identity is a deeply personal sense of self, the only way to know someone's gender identity is for that individual to tell us who they are. This is also true for young children who are actively learning about the world and working out their place within it. As Diane Ehrensaft (2016a), the director of mental health at the University of California San Francisco's Child and Adolescent Gender Clinic, says, "If you truly listen, the children will tell you who they are. It is not for us to dictate, but instead it is for us, parents and professionals, to give them the space to establish their authentic gender." As Carlina Rinaldi notes, "It is impossible to observe without interpreting because observation is subjective" (Edwards, Gandini, & Forman,

2011, p. 241). But it is the responsibility of early childhood educators to help foster an environment in which children can self-determine and self-identify, and we won't truly know a child's identity until they tell us who they are.

Cisgender and Dyadic: Decentering "Naturalized Truths"

The majority of young children will develop gender identities that align with the male/female assignment given to them at birth—an identity known as *cisgender* or *cis* (Center for Disease Control and Prevention, 2018). Although many cisgender individuals have never heard the term "cisgender," designating a distinct term to describe the majority of the population who fall into this category is essential. Cisgender derives from the Latin preposition "cis-" which means "on this side" (as opposed to "trans-" which means "on or to the other side: across : beyond" or "so or such as to change or transfer"). Without the term *cisgender*, gender identities are seen through a binary cisnormative lens casting all cis individuals as *normal*, while marginalizing anyone else as *other*. Although cisgender identities may be the most common, they are no more or less "normal" than transgender identities. It would be *abnormal* for human experiences to be entirely uniform.

Using the term *cis* allows individuals to see the oppression that exists when less-common gender identities are signified through deficit language and considered *other* or outside of the norm. For example, without a name for cisgender identities, cis women enjoy the privilege of being simply *women*, while trans women are rarely afforded this label without the qualification of "trans." Stryker (2008) notes, "it's the same logic that would lead somebody to prefer saying 'white woman' and 'black woman' rather than simply using 'woman' to describe a white woman (thus presenting white as the norm)" (p. 22). Naming cisgender experiences decenters cis "truths," making room for a more honest accounting of the diverse gender identities individuals claim.

It is not uncommon for cisgender individuals to resist or reject their signification with the term "cisgender." Comments the first author has observed in online forums include "I hate being called cis. Because I'm not cis. I'm a woman. I always have been a woman and always will be," "*Cisgender* is an insult," "You are not 'cisgender.' You are normal." "I detest the word 'cis.' The word woman is a stand-alone for adult female human. We are not 'cis women.' We are women." Until recently, cisgender individuals have been in positions of privilege in having their experiences labeled "male" and "female" or "man" and "woman," without qualification. Resistance against the more specific term of *cisgender* is an example of the intersection of discourse, knowledge, and power, and the resistance those who benefit from the privileged discourse—and the worldviews it represents—often display when marginalized thruths challenge majoritzed ones. Individuals' identities are influenced by the language used to signify themselves and others, both internally and interpersonally. Having control over the choice of words and their definitions is both a marker of and an exercise of social power.

Similar to the importance of naming of the majoritarian experience of cisgender identities, a term has come into use by the intersex community to label the majoritarian experience of those who are not intersex: *dyadic*[8]—referencing the duality of bodies which are labeled unquestioningly as male or female. As with the term *cisgender* and identities, without the term *dyadic*, bodies are seen through a binary lens that *normalizes* some while *othering* those that resist binary classification. Although dyadic bodies may be more common, they are no more or less "normal" than intersex bodies. Again, it would be *abnormal* for bodies to be uniform rather than wonderfully varied.

Transgender or Trans: Making Visible a Truth That Has Always Been

In this book, we use the umbrella terms *transgender* or *trans* to describe all those who develop gender identities that are somehow different from their original gender assignment—including those who identify outside the gender binary, with multiple genders, or with no gender at all. It is important to note that this is not a universally agreed-upon definition of either term within the population that they describe. Some individuals consider identities that are nonbinary (e.g., genderqueer, bigender, ambigender) or identities that resist gender altogether (agender) to be outside of the trans/transgender umbrella. This includes binary transgender people who wish to more narrowly define *transgender* and nonbinary or agender people who do not identify as *transgender*. Many people do not see *trans* and *transgender* as interchangeable terms. Some people see trans as being a wider umbrella term with transgender subsumed within it, while others see them as the inverse. For example, some people believe *transgender* only includes binary identities, but *trans* includes binary, nonbinary, and agender identities. Many of these differences are geographical or generational.[9]

Many intersex adults do not agree with the cis-trans dualism, as these terms have grown out of the sex binary, which excludes intersex bodies. Costello (2014) asks the hypothetical question, "if a person is born genitally indeterminate, is surgically assigned female in infancy, and grows up to identify as a woman, is she 'transgender' because she was surgically altered to become female, or 'cis gender' because she identifies with the sex she was assigned at birth?" Costello (2014) suggests a third term, *ipso gender*, referring to intersex individuals who grow up to identify with their assigned gender, to distinguish them from cisgender individuals who are not intersex. This third category of gender identity is valuable in avoiding the creation of a new false dualism, giving agency to a marginalized group who has had little power to self-identify historically, and preventing intersex experiences from being hegemonized by cisgender narratives.

Oak's mom is gay or queer—I'm not sure precisely which word she identifies with—and a single parent. She has been supportive of Oak's gender exploration and preferences. However, her parents have not. In Oak's first year with us, he would wear dresses often and was growing out his wispy toddler hair, and often expressed a preference for "she," or more often, indicated that he didn't care which pronoun people used. Halfway through his second year, he spent 12 days with his grandparents, and when he got back, he stopped wearing dresses and only wore pajamas for the remainder of the year. He also got his hair cut around the same time, but I can't remember if that was directly after or not.

My way of responding to Oak in the classroom is to try and figure out his wishes in terms of name and pronouns, and then use them and model using them for others (kids and adults). Also, fielding many questions from other kids where it feels appropriate, and directing them to ask Oak himself when that feels more appropriate. Oak's out-ness with gender seems to be an enabling factor for others to explore gender. Jorin started wearing dresses every day and it didn't strike anyone as out of the ordinary, and another teacher overheard a private conversation between Oak and Martin, one of his besties, where Martin said, "Right now I'm a boy, but when I grow up I'm going to be a woman." Since it was private, we decided not to respond to that from Martin unless we heard more.

As a staff, people were at different places in their ability to handle a gender fluid child. David is in his mid-fifties, cisgender, and had the hardest time with it. I remember one statement he made about how it was hard to call Oak "she" when he was always playing with his penis! But the second year for staff development day we had Gender Spectrum come do a workshop, and it was super helpful in shifting his thinking. At that point we had three staff members including myself who identified as some kind of gender-variant, and for us three, the workshop felt very 101 but afterwards, it was apparent how helpful it was for other staff members because although many of them had worked together for 10+ years, they had never had this explicit conversation where gender identity vs. expression vs. sexual orientation was all broken down. And after that is was easier for us all to discuss together as a staff.

I want to let children know that they get to tell me who they are. I strive to share the idea that activities, dress up, colors, objects, and ideas are here for everyone. When I see children talking directly about gender or clearly self-censoring their behavior because of their sense of their own gender versus others' expectations of gender, I reinforce the idea that they're able to question those expectations.—Luke, transgender preschool teacher, he/they [Oak currently uses he/him pronouns, which is why they are used in this anecdote.]

Gender Expression: Creative Playground or Protective Shield

The myriad ways in which people externally communicate their gender to the world through behaviors, style, names and nicknames, mannerisms, activities, interests, vocal pitch and intonation, and other manifestations of masculinity, femininity, and androgyny (a mixture of or ambiguity between the masculine and feminine) are collectively called *gender expression*. What is meant by masculine or feminine varies across cultures and throughout history (Fausto-Sterling, 2000; Brown & Mar, 2018). Each individual develops their own ways of expressing their gender(s) within the context of their place and time in this world. However, Christian colonization[10] and conversion campaigns have had a significant impact on TGE people and their gender expression globally (Brown & Mar, 2018).

Most people explore various gender expressions throughout the course of their lives. One's expressions are likely to shift across the different contexts in which they exist (e.g., dressing differently at sporting events than at weddings, embodying gender differently with friends than with family or sexual/romantic partners, etc.). In many cases, gender expressions are bound by restrictive gender roles and rules through laws, dress codes, and unwritten social pressures and stigmas (Fausto-Sterling, 2000). Laws have existed in the United States from 1848 to the last one enacted in 1974, making it a crime to wear clothing in public that was not considered appropriate based on one's legal designation (Stryker, 2008).

> *If I wore a sari without having grown my hair, I would be seen as a man wearing a sari, and that meant dishonor for the entire household. I learnt too that while we felt like women, it was equally important to look like them, and that long hair was an important marker of being feminine. (A. Revathi, she/her, The Truth about Me: A Hijra Life Story, 2010, p. 28)*

The extent to which an individual expresses their gender authentically or adopts a gender expression that is designed to hide their true gender from others is impacted by all manner of external forces and messages. Ehrensaft (2011) discusses the idea of a *false gender self*—"the face a child puts on for the world, based on what the world expects from that child and what the child then takes in as either 'appropriate' or adaptive gender behavior" (p. 86). In other words, this false self is a manifestation of gender expression which the child develops in response to what they believe they are *supposed* to do because of their assigned gender and/or as a protective shield to prevent others from knowing who they really are inside. The adults in a young child's life have significant control over a child's options and decisions for their gender expression (e.g., purchasing clothing and toys for a child; encouraging, discouraging, forcing, or forbidding certain kinds of gender expression).

> *My grandfather, he had referred to me at a younger age as "māhū," but I didn't know exactly what that meant . . . it was always brought up in the family context, when I would go back to the Islands to visit our extended family, as a pejorative. I knew it had to do with gender . . . my grandfather [was very] matter of fact. It's like, "Of course you're playing football, you're māhū." And I'm just like, "Well, what does that mean?" And my grandfather's like, "Well it's just*

a Hawaiian term for the third kind." . . . I didn't quite understand the context because I was so removed from anybody who was Native Hawaiian. And when I would go back to visit my Hawaiian family on that side, like every now and then for the summers, for the reunions, it would be, like, jokes about māhūs, or, "Who's a māhū?" . . . they were all Mormon and making jokes about māhūs . . . when I went to Hawaii I think is when I started to really identify as trans . . . I started to come out as trans and as māhū sort of simultaneously, more specifically māhūkāne. And trans, I think, continued to get redefined in different ways. (Ikaika, trans and māhūkāne, he/him)

Throughout a person's life, one will have varying degrees of agency over their gender expression in different contexts. In early childhood, this aspect of gender has the potential to be narrow, limiting, and repressive, but it can also be a rich and creative source of positive gender exploration for all children given the right support from adults.

Gender Attribution: Evidence of Assumptions and Identity Biases

According to Bornstein (2013b). "Gender attribution is what we all do when we first meet someone: we decide whether they're a man or a woman, or something indeterminable. We attribute a gender to someone based on an intricate system of cues, varying from culture to culture. The cues can range from physical appearance and mannerisms to context and the use of power" (p. 51). These cues may include gender expression, observable aspects of anatomy and physiology such as facial hair or breasts, clothing and mannerisms, name, occupation, and more. They are impacted by one's culture, personal beliefs, upbringing, and the situational context of meeting someone. This process of attributing a gender to someone generally happens in most cases without conscious awareness.

I have a lot of my friends who are like, "but I thought you were a trans man," and I say, "I never said that, you know?" I identify as trans, and identity is always twofold: it's both how we self-identify and how people perceive us, and if they confer that identity or not, at some point someone's going to be like, "yes, I see you and recognize you," and/or we're going to be shaped by the voices around us. So like being butch, I somehow became "less" butch by dating another butch person and I'm like, "I don't feel less butch." Ironically, my butch girlfriend brought me closer to other identities that resonated more. So I think as new words come up, like non-binary, I'm like, "does this feel like it fits?" I mean I wake up some mornings, feeling—I don't know if this is a new word, but very "binaried" by others. And I don't think that the reflection of what people see is always still in alignment with how I see myself. (Ikaika, trans and māhūkāne, he/him)

Even as a very young child I identified as non-binary. My mom talks about us fighting when I was around 3 or 4 and I'd get mad and insist I wasn't a girl and to not call me a girl. My mom said, "well, you're not a boy." To which I replied, "no, I'm a kid." I insisted I was a kid and my mom and I would often fight over my gender with hair and clothing being the major battles. But, my grandfather somehow "got" me. He let me ride the riding lawn mower and hang around while he worked on cars. He gave me a pocket-knife, even though mama said no, and called me "kiddo." He let me tag along, go fishing, and just be a kid. It's like he saw the me that I felt I was even though I certainly didn't have the vocabulary to express that except to say, "I'm a kid." He treated me like a person and my time with my grandfather was a safe space to just be. (Raven, "I identify as non-binary, genderqueer, handsome butch, m-o-c, Mx, I guess. Actually, when it gets down to brass tacks, I still identify as kid/person/human.")

While someone may influence the ways others attribute gender to them through gender expression and medical interventions, gender attribution is an aspect of one's gender over which they have very little control. People have no agency over the internal associations, assumptions, and beliefs of everyone with whom they interact. While a white Christian from Chicago might immediately attribute an amount of femininity to someone wearing a skirt-like garment, someone from Scotland who is used to men in kilts, or a Muslim who is familiar with men in Ihram attire would have a different set of gender attribution heuristics and might perceive that person differently. One's own gender expression is informed by their own life experiences, but gender attribution is informed by another's.

Gender Pronouns: Discovering the Ubiquity of Gender in Many Languages

In many languages, personal pronouns (pronouns replacing names or nouns describing people) denote a person's gender. These are called *gender pronouns* to distinguish them from those in languages that do not denote gender with personal pronouns. In keeping with the idea that the best terms to use to describe a person are the words that person chooses, we define an individual's *gender pronouns* as the pronouns (he, she, they, ze, per, and more) with which that person identifies. While the term "preferred pronouns" is often used to mean the same thing, many TGE individuals have felt that the qualification of "preferred" delegitimizes the concept. The effect tends to be that cisgender people have pronouns, but transgender people have *preferred* pronouns. In reality, *all* people whose native language uses such pronouns have *gender pronouns* with which they identify and, subsequently, pronouns with which they do not identify. It is disrespectful to use any *gender pronoun* to refer to a person if they don't identify with that pronoun.

In many languages, including English, personal pronouns reinforce the gender binary (e.g., he/him/his and she/her/hers). It is difficult to communicate about a person in these languages without ascribing a gender to them through the use of gender pronouns, even when gender is not being discussed at all (e.g., "Where is Henry? I haven't seen *him* all day"). As such, actively learning which pronouns a person identifies with and using them consistently is an extremely important aspect of honoring and respecting that person. Gender pronouns, like gender expression and gender identity, may be fixed or fluid throughout one's life.

> *Gender is what pronouns you wanna be. So, an example of pronouns is he, she, they, or just you could be nothing, without one, and you could just be called by your name. (Oak, eight years)*

> *It was international pronoun day a week ago, and so we decided to celebrate at school by making pronoun necklaces for everyone. Teachers asked the kids what their pronouns were, and then made them a necklace, and then the kids decorated them. Then they went around Lake Merritt and they handed out little slips explaining what a pronoun is and why it's important for you to ask people what their pronoun is, and they would first say, "What is your pronoun?" to the stranger, and then they would give them the slip. And it was really cute. It was a great little action we did with them because we're like "Oh, if people don't know what a pronoun is do you think we need to educate them?" They're like, "Yeah! How can people not know what a pronoun is? We know what a pronoun is." That was a really special day. (Mitali, intersex teacher and trainer, they/them)*

As children acquire language skills and begin to learn the association between pronouns and gender, and as they develop their own gender identity, they may find that they do or do not identify with the pronouns assigned to them. Young children may use pronouns indiscriminately before understanding the connection between pronouns and gender. They may also try on different pronouns to see what fits or switch pronouns quite determinedly, if given the agency and respect to do so.

Individuals typically make assumptions about a person's gender pronouns based on that person's appearance, name, or other cues (one aspect of gender attribution is the assumption of pronouns). Using incorrect pronouns for any person may feel hurtful or disrespectful to that person. Incorrect pronoun usage, by a slip of the tongue or by way of inaccurate gender attribution, is bound to happen occasionally, and can happen to anyone—both as speaker and as subject. The harm done in those instances can often be minimized by correcting oneself and moving on. However, using incorrect pronouns deliberately or consistently after learning a person's self-identified pronouns is disrespectful and can be confusing, degrading, belittling, and traumatic over time (Russell, Pollitt, Li, & Grossman, 2018; also see National Center for Lesbian Rights: Katharine Prescott versus Rady Children's Hospital San Diego[11]). The intentional use of incorrect pronouns, often coupled with the use of a transgender person's birth name when they no longer go by that name, is a common form of harassment and verbal aggression experienced by transgender individuals (James Herman, Rankin, Keisling, Mottet, & Anafi, 2016; Sharman, 2016). The use of a child's self-identified pronouns, even if they may change in the future, is an important act of support for, and trust in, the child and the child's agency to self-identify.

Every time we—teachers, parents, and students—use a pronoun, we're making a statement about gender. Usually a "this is what gender I think that person is" type of statement. Usually without verbal confirmation that this pronoun is preferred. (Luke, transgender preschool teacher, he/they)

Since gender pronouns are almost impossible to avoid when talking about someone, many trans and gender-expansive adults and allies are working to normalize the practice of including gender pronouns in regular introductions. For example, an introduction might sound like, "Hi, I'm Amber, and I use she/her/hers." This eliminates the need for others to guess or assume Amber's gender pronouns and allows them to talk about *her* without accidentally disrespecting *her* by making wrong assumptions. By normalizing this practice for everyone, the spotlight is taken off TGE individuals—whose pronouns may not be obvious based on conventional gender attributions, and who often have to announce their pronouns when gender is not the topic of conversation to interrupt or avoid being called the wrong pronoun. In languages that use gendered personal pronouns and other gendered identifiers (e.g., English, French, Russian), people must be committed to everyday practices by which they can learn each other's correct gender pronouns without making prescriptive guesses.[12] It is important to note that not all cultures divide themselves linguistically by gender. Nigerian anthropologist Oyeronke Oyêwùmí (2011) notes that in the language of the Yorùbá people of western Africa, personal pronouns do not indicate gender, but rather the age of the subject relative to the speaker. In such a culture, knowing accurately who is older or younger than oneself is critical, as this helps a speaker determine how to speak respectfully to and about others.

We refer to individuals in this book using the last pronouns we are aware of them using for themselves. We use the singular "they" and "themself" if we do not know someone's correct pronouns. We may also just use a child's name and no pronouns. It is worth reflecting throughout this book whether these conventions feel awkward or uncomfortable, as it is indicative of how much we feel compelled to assign gender to an individual. Many transgender individuals prefer to be referred to by their current pronouns even in stories about their past, while others want their stories to reflect their journey and ask others to refer to them using the pronouns they were using at the time a given story took place. For example, Baz is a transgender man who does not like to be referred to as his birth name or as "she" or "her" even when his mother is talking about when he was a baby. Kyle Taylor-Shaughnessy (2016), another transgender man, prefers his friends and family to talk about "little Katie" and use she/her pronouns when they discuss his childhood. Without this kind of preferential information about a person, it is best to default to using their most recent pronouns for discussing all stages of their life. Pronouns, and other gendered language used to describe a person, are another aspect of one's gender.

Gender: Deconstructed and Reconstructed Anew by Centering Complexity and Diversity

In this book, *gender* is defined as a person's unique constellation of anatomy and physiology, legal designation(s), gender identit(ies), gender expression(s), experiences with gender attribution, the gender pronouns and labels they use and related gendered experiences. This definition is used to build a working theoretical model of gender in the next chapter. As seen, a theoretical model of gender which only recognizes two types of people (e.g., the gender binary) is inadequate and insufficient to truly capture the diversity and complexity of human gender.

> *Only you get to decide what gender you are. You can't tell other people's genders just by looking, the only way to know is to ask. There are more than two genders. People's genders can change but yours won't change unless you really want it to. Your gender doesn't limit your play choices, style choices and what you can do. (Luke, transgender preschool teacher, he/they, describing the foundational messages about gender they strive to impart to children in their classroom)*

Gender Expansive(ness): Breaking Down Boxes

While transgender individuals may make up a relatively small percentage of the population, a much larger percentage bends or breaks the social rules and expectations of gender in ways besides, or in addition to, identity. Any person who pushes or breaks the boundaries of dominant cultural understandings and expectations of gender with their identities, expressions, or other explorations of gender falls under the umbrella of the term *gender expansive*. Wider than the umbrella terms *transgender* or *trans*, gender expansiveness also includes cisgender or ipso gender individuals whose gender expression and/or use of pronouns and gendered language are not limited by binary expectations based on their gender identity. If everyone truly reflected on their own gender journey, most would realize they have pushed the boundaries of binary gender in at least small ways throughout their lives. The concept of gender expansiveness makes space for all those who are breaking down gendered barriers, regardless of their gender identities. It also evokes an image of gender as something that can be stretched and pushed and built upon, an ever-*expanding* field of possibilities if only one has the courage to venture outward from what they think they know.

Further Terms for Discussing Gender and Understanding Gender

The terms introduced above provide a solid foundation for building a theory of gender in early childhood. Below, we discuss a few additional words and concepts that are important to know for critical discussions of gender justice and gender-based oppression.

Misgender. To refer to someone as a gender other than their gender identity is to *misgender* that person. Misgendering might look like using the wrong pronouns, using a name that the person does not want used (e.g., using the birthname of a transgender person who has chosen a different name and no longer wishes to be called by their birthname[13]), or using other incorrect gendered language or behavior in referencing someone (e.g., asking a child to sit with "the other girls" if that child does not identify with being a girl). As noted under pronouns, occasional and accidental misgendering is often relatively harmless. When someone we have known for a while changes their pronouns and/or name, it is easy and common to slip up while adjusting to using new language for them. It is also very common to make mistakes if someone is learning to use pronouns with which they are grammatically unfamiliar, such as the use of "they" as a singular personal pronoun. For example, "Tyler forgot their backpack again. I hope they come back to get it." Correcting the mistake, apologizing briefly, and moving on is usually enough to minimize any harm done. However, when misgendering is intentional, malicious, and/or persistent it can be very upsetting and harmful. As will be discussed later, persistent misgendering with or without malice or even awareness can cause lasting damage for a young child.

Sexual Orientation. While related to gender, *sexual orientation* is an entirely different concept that refers to one's interpersonal sexual attractions. One can be transgender and heterosexual or homosexual or pansexual or asexual, and so on, just as one can be cisgender and any sexual orientation. The only reason this term is included here is that gender and sexual orientation are often conflated and frequently considered to be interdependent. As noted in the discussion of the sex-gender distinction, the concept of categorical *sex* and *sex* as an interpersonal act have historically been linguistically conflated (Haig, 2004). Additionally, reproductive capacity, which is associated with sexual activity, has been used as a significant consideration in the implementation of categorical concept of *sex*, especially for intersex infants (Fausto-Sterling, 2000). Since "sex" and "gender" are so often used interchangeably, it is no wonder that gender and sexual orientation are frequently conflated as well. They are related but *not* interdependent aspects of identity. One's deeply held sense of their gender identity is not the product of their sexual attractions, nor the other way around.

> *In Black families we have these sayings about being soft or about "having sugar in your bowl . . ." and it all just means you're gay. And so from a young age, I had some sugar in my bowl, and I was soft. . . . At age four, I had a doll and I would take the doll to church, and it was my grandpa's church and it was like, "People are gonna think you're this way if you carry a doll with you," and I was like, "I don't care. I'm gonna carry my doll." (Jen, twenty-four, nonbinary, she/he/they)*

Carrying a doll as a young child is entirely unrelated to one's sexual attractions later in life, but it is possibly a gendered behavior. Jen's family interpreted their gendered behavior as an indicator of their sexual orientation. Often, when someone expresses gender-expansive behavior as a child, the first assumption by adults is not that they might be transgender, but that they might be gay. Because the two most well-known sexual orientation labels (homosexual and heterosexual) indicate one's sexual attraction to a particular gender relationally to one's own gender (e.g., a homosexual person who is attracted to men would necessarily be a man himself, while a heterosexual person who is attracted to men would be a woman), the two concepts are inextricable. Understanding the difference between them is important in order to avoid inaccurate interpretations of young children's gendered behaviors and expressions.

Heteronormativity & Cisnormativity. The cultural assumptions that lead to the conflation of gender and sexual orientation are rooted in *heteronormativity* and *cisnormativity*. Heteronormativity is both the cultural belief that heterosexuality is the privileged, desired, and only "normal" and "natural" sexual orientation and the system of social structures and pressures that encourage compulsory heterosexuality. Cisnormativity is the correlating system of beliefs that insists that only cisgender men and women are valid and the system of social structures and pressures that push everyone to stay neatly in the binary gender they are assigned at birth.

> *When I went to kindergarten, I went to Catholic school, I had to wear a dress and that was again reinforcing certain things. And the ways that young girls in that school were disciplined around what they wore, or how they looked, or how*

they acted was really difficult. And what I saw the boys be able to do, and what I saw their permissions were, that mine weren't, I think that was hard. (Kelly, transgender preschool teacher, he/him)

THE INJUSTICE OF TEACHERS WHO DON'T "SEE" THE CHILDREN THEY TEACH AND THE RADICAL REQUEST TO TRUST CHILDREN

When I started menstruating at 10, I don't feel like I was entirely heard by my mother. I was scared shitless I think. And all I could think about in my head was it was the day that I got my cast off on my leg so I was so excited I could go to softball practice. And I remember trying to communicate this is a nuisance, like, as best as a ten-year-old could. "Make it go away." My mother was like, "Now you're a woman." And I'm like, "no". And saying "No." But her being like, "Yes, and this is wonderful." And so there was a kind of fantasy that she was playing out in her head, and my reality was a horror flick and it was making me late to practice. (Ikaika, trans and māhūkāne, he/him)

I wore nail polish to school and some people thought I was a girl. One kid said I was a girl and I said "I'm not" and he said I was a girl again which made me feel kinda bad. (Tobble, seven years, he/him)

Gender-expansive children experience harms just by existing in a world that does not fully see them. While many educators are working diligently to reduce overt examples of gender-based bullying (Derman-Sparks & Olsen Edwards, 2010), transgender and gender-expansive young children experience a source of injustice which has largely gone unnamed and unaddressed. These experiences of injustice can leave TGE young children without a sense of confidence or agency over their gendered lives. They can experience a loss of their sense of self that is very deep and can be at least as damaging as overt bullying, if not more so. When a young child says, "I'm a girl!" and twirls around in a dress made out of a bedsheet, and is told "No, son. You have a penis, and that makes you a boy," it might just be a creative bubble bursting, or it might be a deeper existential experience of epistemic injustice. It might be a moment when a child attempted to communicate something they knew to be true about their identity, yet they were not believed and were even "corrected." The insistence by someone a child trusts that the child is not who they feel themselves to be, can leave that child feeling as though they themselves are not trustworthy observers of the world. When experienced frequently and persistently, this cycle can lead the child to lose confidence in their own ability to interpret their experiences (Murris, 2013; Fricker, 2007).

Despite many cogent critiques, highlighting the problematic assumptions about what counts as knowledge and an essentialized image of the child (Burman, 2008; Dahlberg & Moss, 2005), discussions of child development and developmentally appropriate pedagogy in early childhood is still significantly influenced by the tenets of developmental psychology. This has led to "detached observation rather than engaging with children and listening to their ideas, position[ing] children as the objects of teaching and research, rather than as subjects with their own stories, interests and views . . . and as . . . 'persons in the making,' not 'persons'" (Haynes, 2009, p. 30; John, 2003, p. 42 cited in Murris, 2013, p. 10). Imagining children as "persons in the making" leads adults to diminish the credibility they afford to young children and to fail to hear important messages children communicate about what they are feeling, what they know and the trust and acknowledgement they desire from the adults around them. This credibility gap resulting from an adult hearer's prejudice and inability to "see" and "hear" a child has significant consequences. Carried to its most tragic end, children conclude that a life where adults don't see them, don't acknowledge them, and don't listen to their cries for validation, visibility, and support, is not a life worth living. Leelah Alcorn, a seventeen-year-old transgender girl who committed suicide in 2014, shared these feelings in a suicide note she posted on social media that included a description of her experience coming out, not being accepted by her family, being forced into conversion therapy, and finally choosing to leave this world (Alcorn, 2014). Her last request was that her death mean something. She knew who she was at the age of four but did not have the language or resources to understand her experiences, and she did not have the support she needed to live as her authentic self:

If you are reading this, it means that I have committed suicide and obviously failed to delete this post from my queue.

Please don't be sad, it's for the better. The life I would've lived isn't worth living in . . . because I'm transgender. I could go into detail explaining why I feel that way, but this note is probably going to be lengthy enough as it is. To put it simply, I feel like a girl trapped in a boy's body, and I've felt that way ever since I was 4. I never knew there was a word for that feeling, nor was it possible for a boy to become a girl, so I never told anyone and I just continued to do traditionally "boyish" things to try to fit in.

When I was 14, I learned what transgender meant and cried of happiness. After 10 years of confusion I finally understood who I was. I immediately told my mom, and she reacted extremely negatively, telling me that it was a phase, that I would never truly be a girl, that God doesn't make mistakes, that I am wrong. If you are reading this, parents, please don't tell this to your kids. . . .

That won't do anything but make them hate them self. That's exactly what it did to me.

The only way I will rest in peace is if one day transgender people aren't treated the way I was, they're treated like humans, with valid feelings and human rights. Gender needs to be taught about in schools, the earlier the better. My death needs to mean something. My death needs to be counted in the number of transgender people who commit suicide this year. I want someone to look at that number and say "that's f***ed up" and fix it. Fix society.

Please.

Goodbye,

(Leelah) Josh Alcorn (2014)

There is an inherent injustice in any context where adults do not see and hear the children they teach and/or care for. Leelah Alcorn is asking that no other young children have to experience the injustice she did—not being trusted as a credible knower of her own gender. As outlined in the opening of this chapter, early childhood educators have codes of ethical conduct and practice commitments that reflect a set of values and principles to guide their teaching and caring practices. Primary among these professional responsibilities is a commitment to *do no harm* to children. On its surface, this statement may appear perfunctory, but more deeply it asks teachers to be in a continuous state of inquiry—observing, listening, and responding to children as each individual child reveals what they are asking of adults and peers to help them feel a sense of belonging, inclusion, and visibility. It is impossible to know whether we are harming children if we are not in a dynamic dance of relationship, attunement, and what Carlina Rinaldi (2001) names as "a pedagogy of listening":

Listening as sensitivity to the patterns that connect, to that which connects us to others; abandoning ourselves to the conviction that our understanding and our own being are but small parts of a broader, integrated knowledge that holds the universe together.

Listening, then, as a metaphor for having the openness and sensitivity to listen and be listened to—listening not just with our ears, but with all our senses (sight, touch, smell, taste, orientation).

Listening to the hundred, the thousand languages, symbols, and codes we use to express ourselves and communicate, and with which life expresses itself and communicates to those who know how to listen.

Listening as welcoming and being open to differences, recognizing the value of the other's point of view and interpretation.

Listening that does not produce answers but formulates questions; listening that is generated by doubt, by uncertainty, which is not insecurity but, on the contrary, the security that every truth is only such if we are aware of its limits and its possible "falsification."

Listening is not easy. It requires a deep awareness and at the same time a suspension of our judgments and above all our prejudices; it requires openness to change. It demands that we have clearly in mind the value of the unknown and that we are able to overcome the sense of emptiness and precariousness that we experience whenever our certainties are questioned.

Listening that takes the individual out of anonymity, that legitimates us, gives us visibility, enriching both those who listen and those who produce the message (and children cannot bear to be anonymous).

Listening as the premise for any learning relationship—learning that is determined by the "learning subject" and takes shape through his or her mind through action and reflection, that becomes knowledge and skill through representation and exchange.

Listening, therefore, as "a listening context," where one learns to listen and narrate, where individuals feel legitimated to represent their theories and offer their own interpretations of a particular question. In representing our theories, we "re-know" or "re-cognize" them, making it possible for our images and intuitions to take shape and evolve through action, emotion, expressiveness, and iconic and symbolic representations (the "hundred languages").

Understanding and awareness are generated by sharing and dialogue. We represent the world in our minds, and this representation is the fruit of our sensitivity to the way in which the world is interpreted in the minds and in the representations of others. It is here that our sensitivity to listening is highlighted; starting from this sensitivity, we form and communicate our representations of the world based not only on our response to events (self-construction), but also on that which we learn about the world through our communicative exchange with others. (Rinaldi, 2001, pp. 80–81)

It is through such a pedagogy of listening that teachers will be in a position to support children of diverse genders like Leelah and so many others who need adults who are willing to cede power to children and acknowledge them as full epistemic individuals. When we engage in a pedagogy of listening to children, we listen to connect, listen to give children visibility, listen as a premise for building and sustaining a learning relationship, and listen with humility and awareness that our "truths" have limits and we may need to re-cognize and allow our understandings to evolve.

> We were at a Native American cultural center and this woman was showing people how they make something. She thought I was a girl and then when my sister told her I'm not a girl they're just like, "I'm so sorry if I made you feel bad." And she was really nice about it. When we were talking about it, I remember she said, "I'm so glad that you forgive me." She said, "I realized I made a mistake and I just jumped to conclusions." It was a lot better because she was realizing her mistake. She wasn't saying, "well, you have long hair" She was like, "oh wow, I made a mistake and it means so much to me that you would forgive me." (Tobble, seven years, he/him)

DETACHING FROM DOMINANT KNOWLEDGE PROJECTS THROUGH CRITICAL REFLECTION AND TRANSFORMATIVE LEARNING

Journeying toward gender justice where early childhood teachers develop Rinaldi's conception of a pedagogy of listening to be responsive to children of all genders requires a level of "epistemic disobedience" and delinking from the privileged knowledge they take for granted. Transformative learning (Brown, 2004)—where adults are guided to change the "specific knowledge, beliefs, value judgments, and feelings that constitute their interpretations of experience" (Mezirow, 1991, pp. 5–6, e.g., their "image of the child" and/or beliefs about gender)—is supported when adults have opportunities to experience what Medina (2013) describes as *beneficial epistemic frictions*. He explains:

> [Through] encounters and engagements with differences, we experience epistemic frictions that can lead us to feel the contours of our social gaze and the blind spots of our cognitive-affective sensibilities ... what is required in order to be exposed to the appropriate epistemic friction that can expand one's sensitivity is an interactive process in which the subject can learn to empathize with others and to become sensitive to those aspects of their experience that have been marginalized, suppressed, or rendered unintelligible. The process of expanding one's sensitivity to insensitivity—of overcoming one's cognitive-affective numbness, of attaining greater degrees of lucidity with respect to injustices—is always a social interactive process. Although one should always tap into one's own experiences of difference, these are always limited. For that reason, the process of expanding our sensitivity requires that we connect the differences and excesses that we feel in ourselves with those felt by others that we may be ill-equipped to understand and to which we may remain insufficiently or improperly sensitive. This requires seeking others with significantly different experiences and engaging with their heterogeneous perspectives. Openness to differences—both to one's own internal differences as well as to those of others—is the key to sufficient degrees of lucidity, sensitivity, and epistemic responsibility. (pp. 204–205)

Learning to detach from the dominant knowledge projects that perpetuate harm and oppression (e.g., unnecessarily reinforcing gender binaries through classroom routines) is enhanced when teachers have opportunities to engage in critical reflection and collaborative dialogue that embody the principles of epistemic friction:

1. Actively searching for more alternatives than one's own perspective
2. Acknowledging these alternatives (or their possibility)

3. Attempting to engage with them whenever possible
4. And seeking a new equilibrium (Medina, 2013).

Critical reflection is a combination of reflection and an explicit examination of the role of power, privilege, and oppression in relation to one's teaching practice (Sensoy & DiAngelo, 2017). *Critical* in this context does not mean criticism. Instead, the goal of critical reflection is to support adults to become cognizant of oppressive structures and practices that marginalize individuals and groups and to develop their knowledge of various strategies and tactics they can use to work for positive change (Brown, 2004). Critical reflection involves teachers in a process of *asking questions that focus their attention on power, privilege, and oppression* and helps them evaluate how their communication, interactions, and teaching practices benefit some children while simultaneously disadvantaging or even harming others:

- Whose stories am I listening to and why? Who do I automatically attribute with credibility? Who don't I trust and why? How are my beliefs and/or actions limiting the range of stories that children can share in the classroom?
- Which linguistic signifiers am I using to represent children? What meanings are associated with these signifiers? What are the consequences of being signified in this way? How can I reframe, redirect, or disrupt signification that may be marginalizing, misrepresenting or harming a child/children?
- How am I supporting children to give voice to their personal experiences in my class? Whose voices am I hearing? Whose voices are silent or unacknowledged? Why is that so?

Critical reflection is strengthened when teachers pair their own personal time for thinking with opportunities for *collaborative dialogue and interaction with others where they have opportunities to experience beneficial epistemic friction*. As Medina (2013) explains, the expansion of our sensibilities is not a task we can take on ourselves. Instead, transformative learning requires sustained interactions with significantly different individuals and groups because "although one should always tap into one's own experiences of difference, these are always limited. . . . This requires seeking others with significantly different experiences and engaging with their heterogeneous perspectives" (p. 204). A third element of critical reflection is a process of planning and taking *transformative social actions* that are inspired by what is surfaced and destabilized during the process of asking questions and engaging in dialogue with others. This additional process engages teachers in activism as they use their new understandings to inform a commitment to plan and implement new practices aimed at improving equity (Brown, 2004).

Barbara Dray and Debora Wisneski (2011) developed a process that supports teachers to experience beneficial epistemic friction through the use of critical reflection, collaborative dialogue, and transformative social actions. Their intention in developing the process was to support teachers to strengthen their sensitivity in working with a diverse student population, especially with children and families whose backgrounds are unfamiliar to the teacher (Harry & Klingner, 2006). The process—which includes the principles of epistemic friction—guides teachers to examine their deeply held beliefs and to learn how to "be willing to listen and change to respond to the student who may be different in some way" (Dray & Wisneski, 2011, p. 29). The process creates a critical pause for teachers and helps them to shift away from "automatic-pilot or mindless responses that are based on a person's own cultural frames of reference" (p. 30).

They outline a series of steps that involve both reflection and collaborative dialogue to help teachers become aware of their assumptions, beliefs, biases, and behaviors and then use this information to take transformative social actions that interrupt any inequitable teaching practices they discover (seeking a "new equilibrium"). Originally designed to support teachers to become more culturally responsive in their practice, we adapt the process to focus on teachers' journey in learning to support children of all genders. The process helps individuals uncover and detach from their "privileged knowledge projects"—including their underlying gender assumptions, attributions, and value judgments that influence how they interact with and respond to children in their care, especially children who break gender norms in ways that make them uncomfortable.

DRAY AND WISNESKI'S MINDFUL REFLECTION PROCESS

(Adapted from Dray & Wisneski, 2011 and cited in Pastel, Steele, Nicholson, Maurer, Hennock, Julian, Unger & Flynn, 2019)

1. *Reflect on your gender attributions.* Think about a child whose gender (identity, expression, pronouns, etc.) is challenging for you in some way. Ask yourself the following questions:
   - Am I making assumptions about this child and their gender?
   - Have I already judged this child's gender as being acceptable or unacceptable? Stop and describe what the child said or did that led you to the conclusions you have made.
   - What leads me to believe that the child's gender is concerning or wrong? What about the child is leading to my interpretation?

2. *Write out and reflect on your feelings and thoughts when you work with this child.* Think about a specific interaction you have had with this child that involved your awareness of the child's gender identity/expression in some way. Write freely and describe what you can recall about the interaction. What happened? What was the child doing/saying? How did you respond? Then read through your written reflection and ask yourself:
   - What attributes am I assigning to the child? Have I made assumptions about this child's motivations, emotions, and intents relating to their gendered behavior?
   - How does this child make me feel? What thoughts went through my mind during this interaction?
   - What are my worries or fears for this child? What are my worries or fears for other children in the class related to this child's gender? Can I identify specifically what it is I am afraid of or concerned could happen?
     - Not knowing the best way to support the child?
     - Not knowing the best way to support the rest of the children?
     - Not knowing how to balance the two?
     - Saying the wrong thing(s)?
     - Having to facilitate challenging conversations with the children and families or with my colleagues?
     - Accidentally "outing" a child who has not shared their gender identity with others?
     - Not "outing" a transgender child, and then facing community members who find out from someone else and are upset?
     - Backlash either for acting or failing to act in a certain way?
   - What might the impact of my fears be on this child in my care? Are there ways my own discomfort is limiting my ability to truly support and affirm the gender health of children?
   - What are my assumptions—why do I find the child's behavior problematic or concerning? Have I evaluated, interpreted, or judged their behavior?
   - Answering these questions can help teachers acknowledge their beliefs and assumptions about gender and support a process of making visible if they are using deficit thinking in the attributions they are associating with a child and the actions they are taking as a result. Being honest and the discomfort associated with an honest auditing of oneself is a difficult and essential part of any transformative learning experience.
3. *Consider alternative explanations by reviewing your documentation and reflections.* This next part of the process supports us to more deeply examine the ways in which we are perceiving children and communicating with them, and then to rethink our initial interpretations. In order to do this, review your answers to the questions in Step 2 describing your

interaction with the child. Reflect on the reasons this child may be doing what you observe them doing in your classroom (e.g., using a certain pronoun, wearing specific clothing, identifying with a gender different than their legal designation, engaging in aggressive masculinity, refusing to expand their gendered play choices, excluding others on the basis of gender). Consider how this child's behavior and choices are similar to or different from other children's behavior and choices in the classroom. Ask yourself:
- What are my expectations for the situation?
- How is this child meeting/not meeting my expectations?
- In what ways is this child's behavior supporting their learning and/or interfering with their learning? In what ways is this child's behavior supporting or interfering with other children's learning? Is there a type of learning happening that I previously have not seen or valued, but that is valuable to the child?
- Consider how the child's family responds to and interacts with this child and the messages they are communicating to the child about gender. What do I know about how they interact with the child at home?

4. *Check your assumptions.* After you have reflected on the child's behavior and developed alternative explanations to expand or challenge your assumptions and surface your biases, it is helpful to identify individuals to act as critical friends who can help you further check your assumptions. For example, you might identify a colleague or friend you can share your reflections with and invite them to ask you probing questions and then provide you with their honest reactions to your ideas and to share their own perspectives. You might also consider identifying someone with expertise in gender diversity to share your reflections with, with their consent. Perhaps a professional who provides training or coaching on diversity, ideally gender diversity would be willing to meet with you. It is also important to learn from the child's parents and family members about how they perceive their child's gender identity and expression and the gender expectations and norms they hold and value in their family. After listening and learning from these conversations, teachers can ask themselves:
   - Can I spend time sitting with, reflecting upon and trying to understand why I have discomfort about children who embody gender in this way? What can I learn and unlearn from my discomfort?
   - What are some alternative explanations or interpretations of the child's behavior that I had not considered previously?

5. *Make a plan.* Now it is time to ask yourself the following questions:
   - How can I change or respond differently to this child?
   - What can I do to reduce my own fears and anxieties prior to engaging with a child who makes me feel this way? If I am not able to prepare in

advance, what can I do now to be attuned and responsive to the child so they feel safe, acknowledged, and supported in my care?
- What additional resources do I need to implement this change?
- What is one thing I can do daily to affirm this child's gender and support their gender health while I process through these feelings on my own?
- What is one thing I can commit to *not* doing anymore because it was a reaction that served to make me more comfortable, rather than to support the child?
- After you have considered alternative explanations and developed a different interpretation of a situation, you will be able to change your behavior. You should develop a plan for making a change (e.g., a change in the way you communicate with this child, or a change in your classroom environment) and commit to trying it out. Make a change and observe what happens as a result, reflect on your reactions and feelings, as well as the child's/children's response.

6. *Continuously revisit this process to reassess your attributions and your progress in being responsive to children.* Learning to identify the attributions you associate with others, especially young children who are different than you, is challenging and long-term work. You will need to continuously reflect upon your relationships with children and honestly assess whether you are creating attuned, supportive, and caring relationships with every child. All teachers need to think about mindful reflection as a process that is ongoing. Remain committed to revisiting each step as needed as this will allow you to continue strengthening your ability to support all children to be successful in your classroom.

Below we provide an example of how this tool could be used by an early childhood teacher striving to develop a pedagogy of listening, to detach herself from beliefs about gender that reinforce cisnormativity and the gender binary, and to shift toward new interpretations of experience that normalize and value gender diversity. This process of transformative learning occurs because of the epistemic frictions and counterpoints she experiences that support her to actively search for alternatives to her own perspective, acknowledge them and their possibility, attempt to engage with them and try them out and establish a new equilibrium. Through critical reflection, thought partnership and dialogue with diverse others, and trying out new practices, Grace learns about the "contours of [her] social gaze and the blind spots of [her] cognitive-affective sensibilities . . . attain[s] greater degrees of lucidity with respect to injustices . . . and openness to differences—both to [her] own internal differences as well as to those of others . . . and to [strengthen her] epistemic responsibility" (Medina, 2013, p. 204).

Mindful Reflection in action to Strengthen Gender Inclusive Practices

(Adapted from Dray & Wisneski, 2011 and cited in Pastel, Steele, Nicholson, Maurer, Hennock, Julian, Unger & Flynn, 2019)

In this scenario, a preschool teacher, Grace, is reflecting on an interaction she observed between two children in her classroom, Marcel and Sasha. Grace is using mindful reflection to pause and observe her own responses to Marcel, the impact of her words, and how she could react differently in the future.

1) *Reflect on your gender attributions.*
   - *What did you observe? What happened?* Marcel and Sasha playing together in the dramatic play area. Marcel was pretending that he was pregnant, and he said to Sasha, "I'm going to have three babies. I'm the mama!" Sasha looked confused and insisted that Marcel was a boy and could not have babies or be a mother. Marcel protested, "yes I can!" and he looked at me and said, "Sasha said I can't be a mother!" I looked over and said, "Marcel, Sasha is right. You can't be a mother. You are a boy and only girls can be mothers. Why don't you pretend to be a father in the family?"
   - *How did the child react to your actions or comments?* Sasha smiled and nodded her head up and down feeling acknowledged. Marcel started to cry and ran away. I found him in the corner of the room in a little ball, sobbing and saying to himself, "Yes, I can be a mother. I don't want to be a father. No fair!"
2) *Write out and reflect on your feelings and thoughts when you work with this child. Consider the potential for misinterpretations resulting from deficit thinking, prejudice, or overgeneralizations.*
   - *How does this child make you feel? What are your worries or fears?* I feel uncomfortable when Marcel talks about wanting to be a mother. I worry because I don't know what to say in response. I also have fears that the other children might make fun of him or that my supervisor will get upset if she overheard Marcel and I don't interrupt this play.
   - *What are your assumptions? Why do you find the child's behavior problematic?* My assumptions are that there must be something wrong with Marcel if he wants to be a mother because he is a boy. I find this behavior problematic because boys are supposed to think about becoming fathers when they grow up and I want to protect Marcel because I care about him.

- *What might the impact of my fears be on this child in my care? Are there ways my own discomfort is limiting my ability to truly support and affirm the gender health of children?* By correcting Marcel, I shut down his play and it caused him to withdraw and cry. He seemed really distressed, and I feel guilty about hurting him and not knowing how to support him in that moment.

3) *Consider alternative explanations by reviewing your documentation and reflections.*
    - *Review the explanations and reflect on why the child may be doing what they are doing. Look for patterns in your behavior and the child's behavior.* Marcel might be using play to explore gender identity, or it might just be about exploring being pregnant and playing out the "mama" role. Or maybe Marcel knows that his gender identity does not match his legal designation at birth and he is trying to communicate this to a safe adult. I see in my observational notes that Marcel often takes on the role of females (e.g., mothers, sisters, princesses, etc.) in his play. I consistently discourage him from continuing with these roles.
    - *What are your expectations for the situation? How is the student not meeting your expectations? In what way is the behavior interfering with learning?* I have been expecting that Marcel's gender identity and expression would be determined by his anatomy, physiology, and legal designation at birth. Pretending to be a mother, sister, or princess in his play is not interfering with his learning.
    - *What external factors and/or personal factors could be influencing the child's behavior?* Marcel may not have opportunities to play at home. His family is often food-and-housing insecure, and they often move from one relative's house to another and sometimes have short stays in a local homeless shelter. Being at the childcare center may be the only place where he has time to engage in pretend play.

4) *Check your assumptions. Share your reflections with a colleague, parents, and/or community members. Meet with parents to learn more about expected and observed behaviors in the home.*
    - *Share your list of alternative explanations or interpretations of the child's behavior with a colleague, parents, and/or community members.* I described my observations with a colleague who serves as a mentor for other early childhood teachers who want to learn about ABE. I asked for her opinion about my reactions to Marcel. Should I be responding in a different way? She appreciated that I asked her opinion. She encouraged me to allow Marcel to have freedom in his play to explore and make discoveries about himself. She also loaned me a few books I could read and have available in the classroom (e.g., *They She He Me: Free to Be!*

by Maya Gonzales or *One of a Kind, Like Me / Único Como Yo* by Laurin Mayeno and Robert Liu-Trujillo). Finally, she gave me the name of a local organization that had some information I could read about TGE children and youth.
- *Meet with the family to learn more about their perspective in understanding the child. Do they notice the same behavior at home? Do they find it problematic?* It's a bit challenging to speak with Marcel's parents because of all of the pressures they face on a daily basis, but I did ask Marcel's mom if she could find time to talk with me briefly. I explained that I wanted to learn more about Marcel and their family so I could be a supportive and responsive teacher. We had fifteen minutes to check in together recently and Priya, Marcel's mom, shared that Marcel likes to draw and play with his younger cousins when he is with his family. Sometimes he asks if he can try on her makeup. She doesn't mind and sometimes allows him to do so and notices that it makes him happy. But this makes his father very upset so she has started telling him that he can't do so anymore.

5) *Make a plan.*
- *How will you change or respond differently?* I learned from my colleague that I should support Marcel to have the agency to choose the roles he wants to take in play so I am going to try hard to not discourage and redirect him any longer. I am going to change my approach and instead, work on listening to Marcel and taking seriously what he is communicating to me.
- *Brainstorm ideas on how to change the environment, your actions, and/or expectations for this child.* I need to learn more about gender because these ideas are so new to me. I will add some new books into my classroom. My colleague said that she would be willing to come into my classroom to introduce a new persona doll who is gender expansive.
- *Experiment with responding differently. Note what happens. Reflect on your feelings as well as the child's response.* Two weeks later, Marcel wanted to be the mother again while playing with Sasha. Sasha said he had to be the dad. This time, instead of agreeing with Sasha, I interrupted by saying: "Sasha, Marcel can be the mom if he wants. He gets to decide who he is, and you get to decide who you are." Then I remembered my colleague's advice to take an inquiry stance and asked, "Why did you say Marcel had to be the dad?" Sasha said, "Because you said boys can't be mothers!" I felt hot in the face at that! I took a deep breath and responded, "I did say that. But I was wrong. Now I'm learning about all the things that boys and girls and all kids can be in play and in real life too.

- *Consult with colleagues, parents, and/or community members while you experiment to check your assumptions and interpretations.* I will continue to share what I am observing with my colleague and maybe ask her to come in and observe in my classroom independently.
6) *Continuously revisit this process to reassess your attributions and your progress in being responsive to children.*
    - *Notice when you are overgeneralizing, attributing behavior from a deficit perspective, or behaving in prejudiced ways toward certain children.* I want to learn how often and in what ways I am discouraging children from exploring gender and/or attributing any behavior that diverges from traditional binary norms and expectations as problematic. I am going to start paying attention to my language more carefully and think about any fears I have about children and gender and whether my fears are based in deficit thinking.
    - *Remember that this process is a continuous one, so revisit the steps periodically to continue your growth and understanding of children.* Yes, there is a lot for me to learn about gender and creating a gender inclusive environment for young children. I look forward to using this process to keep learning and improving my teaching practice.

NOTES

1. In Their Own Words, Beyond the Binary. See: https://yr.media/interactive/in-their-own-words-beyond-the-binary/.

2. In Their Own Words, Beyond the Binary. See: https://yr.media/interactive/in-their-own-words-beyond-the-binary/.

3. Intersex Society of North America. See: http://www.isna.org/faq/hermaphrodite; InterACT Advocates for Intersex Youth. See: https://interactadvocates.org/faq/.

4. This term is considered outdated and offensive by many intersex individuals.

5. See: https://transequality.org/documents.

6. See: https://www.nationalgeographic.com/magazine/2017/01/gender-identity-map-where-you-can-change-your-gender-on-legal-documents/.

7. See: National Conference of State Legislatures for "Bathroom Bill" legislative tracking: http://www.ncsl.org/research/education/-bathroom-bill-legislative-tracking635951130.aspx.

8. See: http://aisdsd.org/intersex-faq-interact-mtvs-faking/.

9. It is everyone's responsibility to continuously learn as language evolves and to be respectful of each individual's agency over the words used to describe them.

10. Brown and Mar (2018) report: "African, Asian and Indigenous cultures of the Americas had a consistent pattern of gender diversity, pre-Christianity." Documentation of the *Bianxing* ("one who changes sex") in China, *Kathoey* (historically "ladyboy," although this definition is being replaced with "transgender woman") in

Thailand, *Hijras* ("third sex") in India, and *Fa' afafine* ("third gender") in Samoa shows TGE people held valued social roles, such as healers and spirit mediums (Chung & Singh, 2009). In 2011, Nepal was the first country in the world to allow people to register as third gender in their national census. India, Pakistan, and Bangladesh have also legally recognized people as third gender. History points to more than fifty African tribes with practices of gender diversity embedded in their social structures (Roscoe & Murray, 2001). The *yan daudu*, of the Hausa's in sub-Saharan and West Africa, are "men" who take on feminine gender expression and consider themselves lesbians when partnered together. The Bala of southern Africa identify *kitesh* as a third gender, and the Bantu in northern Africa have acknowledged the mixed- and cross-gendered as healers (Roscoe & Murray, 2001). Precolonization representation of nonbinary genders was observed in Indigenous communities of the Juchitán and in representation of Aztec and Mayan deities. The Muxes, a third gender, from the Zapotec people, were individuals assigned male at birth but who dressed in "female" clothing (Mirandé, 2014). The Muxes are still a recognized third gender category in Oaxaca, Mexico, and have an annual parade. The term "two-spirit" is applied in contemporary times to a person embodying both feminine and masculine spirits in American Indian, Alaskan Native, and Canadian First Nations communities (Balsam, Huang, Fieland, Simoni, & Walters, 2004). Each of these communities was impacted by the role of Christian colonization and conversion campaigns in their language, social practice, and acceptance of nonbinary genders. The Christian (Catholic and Protestant) colonization of the Americas decimated Indigenous populations and targeted nonbinary gender representation for the most horrific treatment. Explorers of Asia and Africa brought their Christian morals and aggressively challenged the presence of nonbinary genders on both continents. With 63 percent of the populations of Africa and 42 percent of Asia identifying as Christian, the remnants of forced conversion are reflected in the morality laws jeopardizing the safety of TGE people throughout both continents (Funk & Lugo, 2012; Hackett, Connor, Stonawski, & Skirbekk, 2015)" (pp. 55–56).

11. See: http://www.nclrights.org/wp-content/uploads/2016/09/Prescott-Complaint-USDC-Southern.pdf.

12. See: https://deepbaltic.com/2018/03/20/being-non-binary-in-a-language-without-gendered-pronouns-estonian/.

13. Transgender individuals who no longer use their birthname often refer to it as their *deadname* and the act of calling someone by that name as *deadnaming*. See: https://www.healthline.com/health/transgender/deadnaming.

Chapter 2

Theorizing from the Edge

Dismantling Boy/Girl Boxes and Looking to the Starry Sky to Construct Gender Constellations

Any truly meaningful retheorizing about gender in early childhood requires first that we interrogate, problematize, and dismantle those knowledge projects that do not fully reflect the lived experiences of TGE young children. As Patel (2016) encourages,

> We must all learn to regard all knowledge as incomplete, partial, contextually created, and perspectival . . . there is an implicit premise that research should be universal, generalizable, and immutable, key constructs of coloniality. Instead, knowledge should be seen as an entity, specific, mutable, and impermanent itself. Such a regard does not mean to resign ourselves to a less than desirable form of knowledge but a more realistic one that can ask better questions. Instead of asking how to pursue mythical objective truth (which is a façade for coloniality), we can ask what knowledge might be useful at this moment, in this place, and how does our pursuit of it stay attentive to its material effects? This will involve giving up some of the mantle of expert. (p. 79)

In this chapter, we will interrogate that which has been claimed as objective truth in both child development and gender theories, seeking instead knowledge that might be useful in our work with TGE children.

PROBLEMATIZING THE CHILD DEVELOPMENT CANON

To ask "what knowledge might be useful at this moment, in this place" emphasizes the need to give up some of the privileged canons—the mantel of expertise—that has been circulated as taken-for-granted majoritarian "truths" in child development and across the field of early childhood. Many of the most widely circulated theories of child development—which influence teachers' understandings of what is typical/atypical, appropriate/inappropriate, and normal/abnormal for children and their gender development—must be replaced by new knowledge projects formed in response to asking different—and better—questions seeking to understand how adults can authentically and responsively support children of *all* genders. Dominant views of gender development in early childhood share several inaccurate assumptions that contribute to epistemic harms. They

- reinforce the idea that anatomy and physiology determine a child's gender,
- associate pathology (mental illness) with anyone who rejects the gender that was legally designated for them at birth, and
- stigmatize children who do not identify as cisgender and express their gender according to the strict norms associated with the gender binary.

All of these assumptions have been disputed and are not supported by the evidence emerging from contemporary research studies on young children's gender development (Keo-Meier & Ehrensaft, 2018). Which traditional child development theories are most problematic and require critical examination and unlearning?

- Lawrence *Kohlberg's* (1966) *theory of gender constancy* claims that young children realize their gender identity—that they are *either* male or female, dictated strictly by genitalia—by the age of three. The next stage, he proposed, happens about four years of age when children begin to understand that gender is "fixed" or stable, and they will still be male/female when they are older. Finally, between the ages of five and seven, Kohlberg asserted that children begin to understand that changes to clothing, names, or behavior will not change a person's gender. Kohlberg believed that children first learn that gender is permanent or constant, and then they use this understanding to learn to behave in "gender-appropriate" ways. Kohlberg's theory of gender constancy is widely cited in child development courses as the most important developmental theory related to children's gender development. As a result of Kohlberg's theory of gender constancy, TGE children whose gender identities and gender expressions fall outside traditional male/female categories are perceived as atypical in their developmental progression. Further, it leads to a developmental view that children need to be at least seven years of age before they would be given any credibility in questioning the gender they were designated at birth. Strangely, many people subconsciously hold both beliefs that children must know and accept their genders in early childhood, as proposed by Kohlberg, *and* that early childhood is too soon for children to know their gender identities. The catch is that, they usually employ whichever logic works against TGE children in a given context. When working with young children, many people will subtly or not so subtly enforce Kohlberg's theory—directing children into their designated boxes and making sure those children "know" exactly what their gender is (by assignment). Then, when faced with a transgender child who is *very* confident about what their gender is, the same people will claim that this child is too young to know. This invalidation of TGE children comes so naturally that most people don't even notice the contradiction.

- *Erik Erikson* (1968), an American developmental psychologist and psychoanalyst long venerated across the field of early childhood, is most known for his *theory of stages and "identity crises" in psychosocial development* across the lifespan. In describing development in the earliest years, he asserted that preschool-aged children, ages three to five, experience the *Initiative vs. Guilt* stage of life, during which identity shifts from the self to the self in relation to and with others. He proposed that during this stage, children begin to articulate a sense of autonomy, an ability to self-reflect, and they improve their capacity to group concepts into categories, including gender, which he understood to be rigidly binary and stable over time. Erikson's ideas have been advantaged for decades in textbooks and college courses in child development. His theory perpetuates the oppressive belief that children whose gender identities and gender expressions fall outside traditional male/female categories, are "atypical" in their developmental progression, often in "identity crises," and assumed to be "at risk" for lifelong negative psychosocial consequences.
- *Piaget's* (1958) *stage theory of children's cognitive development* created images of children as naive, egocentric, and unable to see a situation from another person's point of view. These theories influenced decades of thinking about young children as too young and intellectually immature to have much awareness of their own participation in social categories (e.g., gender, race, etc.). A by-product of this theory was an assumption that young children are incapable of participating in intentionally harmful or oppressive interactions (racism, classism, sexism, etc.); an assumption that led to a professional practice of excluding such topics from early childhood curricula. There is now significant evidence that children at very young ages have an awareness of various social categories of identity (e.g., race, gender, class, etc.) and that they understand and read the cultural norms that associate some social categories as privileged (e.g., being white, English speaking), and others as marginalized (being a person of color, immigrant, etc.) (Terry, 2012). There are also many studies that document how children often reproduce oppressive dynamics in their play and other interactions with each other (Campbell, Smith, & Alexander,

2016; Derman-Sparks & the A.B.C. Taskforce, 1989; Derman-Sparks & Olsen Edwards, 2010; Grieshaber & McArdle, 2010; Kroeger, 2006; Rogers, 2011; Zosuls, Ruble, Tamis-LeMonda, Shrout, Bornstein, & Greulich, 2009).

As these theories influence the majoritarian narratives about child development and early childhood discourse in the United States, *unlearning* their impact on ideas of typicality, appropriateness, and normalcy in relation to gender is critical given their inaccuracies and the oppressions they reproduce. For example, teachers and administrators report that early childhood and early elementary school is an "innocent space" in childhood where the topics of sex, gender, and sexuality should not be discussed (Smith & Payne, 401). However, children's continual exposure to prince and princess stories and pretend play scenarios where they act out being "the mom" or "the dad" are rarely critiqued and acknowledged as deeply representative of these taboo topics. When children are regularly participating in the reproduction of heterosexuality and strict binary gender norms, but the designation of early childhood as an "innocent" space is used to continually silence and marginalize transgender and nonheterosexual stories and experiences, those stories and experiences are signified by comparison as deviant, taboo, and mature.

Even in progressive scholarly writing on gender in early childhood, there is a dearth of acknowledgment of transgender and TGE children. For example, Blaise (2005) introduces postdevelopmental descriptions of gender to expand beyond traditional conceptions that position gender as a binary concept determined from biology and/or socialization. She defines postdevelopmentalism as a new theoretical perspective that can "support pedagogies that aim to explore assumptions about identities, diversity, and learning" in order to emphasize equity and social justice over "individual child's developmental progress" (p. 3). Although her theorizing critiques conceptions of male/female gender identity boxes, her writing does little to encourage a paradigm shift where gender is reconceptualized as trans inclusive and represented by a complex multitude of gender identities and gender expressions.

Kroeger and Regula (2017) *do* talk about transgender and TGE children in early childhood classrooms and, importantly, recommend that teachers use antibias practices with young children to create inclusive classrooms. They explain, "Connecting our arguments for the provision of early childhood ABE practices to some of the larger problems faced by LGBT+ youth and families in North America and other parts of the world is an important conceptual step for argumentation. If teachers of young children understand the larger social problems faced by LGBT+ youth or families, we hope they will take responsibility for positive actions, rather than avoidance, in the classroom" (p. 107). Kroeger and Regula's discussion of gender diversity in early childhood stands out given their acknowledgment of TGE children and emphasis of ABE.

GENDER THEORIES AND MODELS

To understand why it is essential to retheorize gender in early childhood, it is also important to understand the range of models scholars and clinicians have used to conceptualize gender and how they have evolved over time. Below, we introduce how Western Eurocentric models of gender have progressed over the last few decades to become more complex, intersectional, and gender diverse as trans and gender-expansive narratives have demanded more voice and cultural credence. The final model presented, the intersectional gender constellation, is a new model we introduce and is the conception of gender used throughout subsequent chapters.

The models introduced in this chapter do not represent universal understandings of gender. As previously mentioned, many Indigenous and non-western cultures have long recognized genders outside of the gender binary (Brown & Mar, 2018). Conversely, some cultures are so invested in the gender binary that they have not made nearly as much progress as is represented in this section. Also, the progression presented here is still far from being accepted in systemic, institutional, or academic contexts, and within education, this is especially the case within the field of early childhood which is still primarily stuck in the grip of the gender boxes model. The more progressive models discussed below—the gender spectrum, GenderBread Person™, Gender Unicorn, Gender Web, Gender Galaxy, and Intersectional Gender Constellation—are not yet recognized in most places by law, nor have they yet displaced old binary theories of gender identity development taught in colleges or teacher credential programs. These models are largely the work of activists in the gender-expansive community and the medical professionals who work with gender-expansive people.

Gender Boxes

This model is based firmly in the gender binary and is the model that is embedded in law in most Western societies. Under this model, "male" and "female" exist as two discreet and nonoverlapping categories—or boxes (see figure 2.1). An individual's gender assignment at birth (the first and most far-reaching instance of *gender attribution* in one's life) places one in a metaphorical box, which comes complete with all the other aspects of

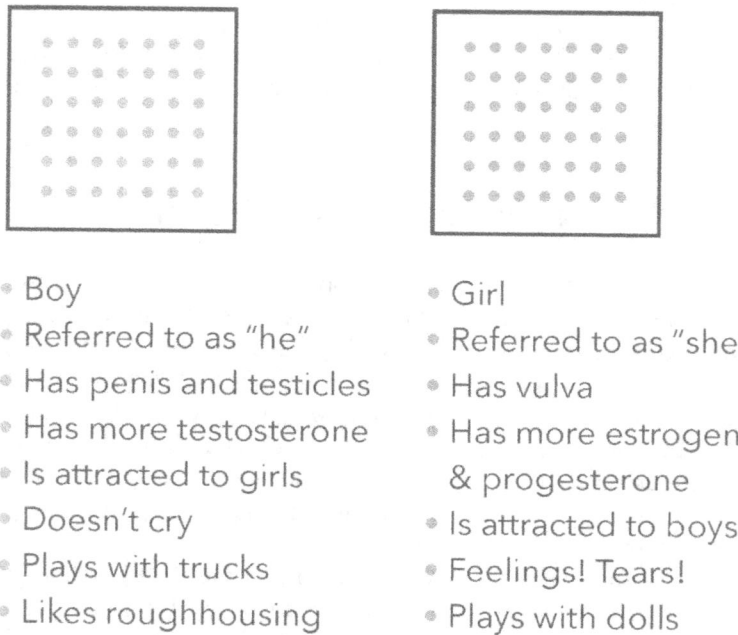

Figure 2.1 **Gender Boxes.** *Credit*: Julia Hennock.

gender included—legal designation, gender identity, pronouns, anatomical and physiological assumptions, expected and accepted gender expressions, etc. Additionally, wrapped up in this model is the conflation of gender and sexual orientation. When a doctor announces, "It's a girl!" heteronormative and cisnormative assumptions lead adults to imagine this child in a beautiful wedding dress in front of the man of her dreams before the child can even walk. Onesies that say "Ladies' Man" are a clear representation of these assumptions at work.

Many people, including cisgender individuals experience the constraining nature of the gender box model (Ehrensaft, 2011). They have felt the need to push the boundaries of their gender box to express themselves in ways that are frowned upon for someone of their gender and to have more diverse experiences than those that are allowed by this restrictive system.

> *[Reflecting on 58 years living as a man before transitioning] The thing about being a girl, what I love about it which was always a problem being a guy, is to really express yourself. Not to worry about, you know, showing weaknesses. Just all of those things that were just really important to me. I feel like I gained a lot from that. (Sophie, sixty-eight, trans woman, she/her)*

Boys and men who want to express a greater emotional range than just happy or angry, who want to be able to cry and to be tender, find themselves up against the walls of their gender box. They are socialized to hide emotions that might make them look "weak" or "feminine." Similarly, girls and women who exhibit strength and exert power can encounter push back, and often violence, for their efforts to escape or expand their gender boxes as illustrated in the story of Malala Yousafzai—a Pakistani activist for female education who was shot in retaliation for her activism. This model of gender is not nearly sufficient to accurately capture all possible combinations of bodies, identities, expressions, and more, but it is also creates limitations and negative impacts even for those who are relatively comfortable with their gender assignment at birth.

While most of the trans and gender-expansive community has left the boxes model behind, there are some transgender individuals whose belief in the gender binary is still strong. Many people, including some transgender people, hold the idea that transgender identities are valid, but only if someone leaves their assigned binary box altogether and transitions "completely" (meaning medical interventions, name change, pronoun change, etc.) to the other binary box (e.g., It is acceptable for a person to have been assigned female, but to identify as male, provided one adopts a new male name, uses he/him pronouns, takes testosterone to produce masculine features such as facial hair, undergoes surgery to remove breast tissue, and possibly also genital surgery. However, it is not acceptable for that person to identify as male without doing at least a few of those things.). In a society that is deeply invested in the gender binary, this mindset may be conscious or subconscious, and it results in a hierarchy of social acceptance for different trans individuals. If a person is able to enter their new gender box so fully as to *pass* as if they were placed in that box at birth, they are often more socially accepted and rewarded than others who (intentionally or incidentally) do not fit as neatly into binary boxes. Binary *passing* transgender people (those who are often interpreted by others as being their self-identified gender, but as cisgender) may not challenge the gender beliefs of someone who ascribes to the gender binary, especially if they believe in the sex-gender distinction. However, many TGE and intersex individuals destabilize the gender binary as a whole—resisting neat and orderly classification into one of two nonoverlapping boxes and raising questions of the legitimacy of any binary categorizations.

Gender as a Single Spectrum

The first major departure from the boxes model of gender is the idea of gender existing along a linear spectrum. In this model, male/masculine and female/

Male	Nonbinary/Agender	Female

Figure 2.2 Gender as a Spectrum. *Credit:* Julia Hennock.

feminine exist at opposite ends of a continuum (see figure 2.2). The middle point of the spectrum is typically understood to be either an equal blending of masculinity and femininity or an absence of both, often referred to in either case as androgyny or specifically as "agender" in the second case. The basic spectrum model is often coupled with the sex-gender distinction, whereby one's *sex* is seen as binary and immutable but one's *gender* can be anywhere on the spectrum.

In the gender spectrum model, people can position themselves at either (male or female) end or anywhere along the middle. One's gender may shift along the spectrum throughout their life—gender fluidity—or it may remain at roughly the same spot—fixed gender. Individual agency over one's gender is highlighted by the ability to place oneself on the spectrum regardless of their assignment at birth, but it is still based largely on the idea that male and female are oppositional and binary. To move toward one end of the spectrum inherently means moving away from the other. In other words, to express or embody an amount of femininity, one's masculinity is conceptually decreased in this model. Also, like the boxes model, placing gender on a single spectrum ties all aspects of one's gender together. As a result, if one's expression shifts along the spectrum, it is assumed that their identity has shifted too. If one's identity shifts, they are expected to alter their expression, pronouns, and body as well.

Gender as Multiple Spectrums

In an effort to highlight the many aspects of gender, models such as the Genderbread Person™ have now been used in the TGE community for several years (see figure 2.3). These models take the idea of gender as a spectrum and apply it to each of the various aspects of gender separately. Accordingly, there might be one spectrum for gender identity with woman at one end and man at the other. Another spectrum shows gender expression as masculine to feminine. A spectrum to represent *sex* (these models do often still reflect the sex-gender distinction) shows female at one end, male at the other, and intersex in the middle. Sexual orientation is also often included in these multiple spectrum models, from heterosexual to homosexual, in order to acknowledge that it is a separate but related aspect of a person.

Using models like these, it becomes much clearer that there are many possible combinations of the different aspects of gender. Diversity even among cisgender individuals, who all might position themselves near the ends of a

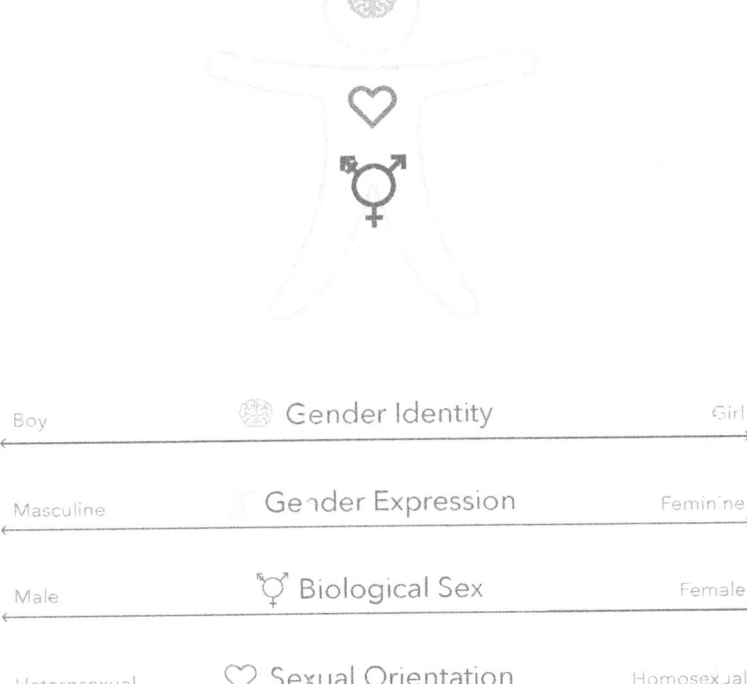

Figure 2.3 Genderbread Person. *Credit*: Julia Hennock.

single gender spectrum, can be revealed when gender expression and diverse anatomical and physiological elements are taken into account.

The first generation of these models were still limited by the binary and the assumptions of opposition embedded in the single spectrum model, that is, where moving toward one end of a spectrum means moving away from the other. Newer versions of these models use separate rays or rating scales for each end of a given spectrum. For example, on a scale from one to ten, how masculine is one's gender expression? And on a separate scale from one to ten, how feminine is it? By allowing these measures to operate independently, someone who loves gendered expression of all kinds might rate themself a ten on both, while someone who aims for neutral or agender expression might give themselves two 1's. On a single spectrum, both of those gender expressions would land in the middle of the line between masculine and feminine, with no way to differentiate The Gender Unicorn (Trans Student Educational Resources[1]) is one such example of a model that has worked to eliminate the oppositional nature of linear spectrums.

Multiple spectrum models have helped many people to grow their understanding of and appreciation for the complexity of gender beyond bodies and binaries. The Genderbread Person™ and the Gender Unicorn are currently two of the most widely circulated models in the world of TGE friendly and inclusive education. They are often quite well-received, especially by cisgender allies, as they give a fairly digestible visual explanation of many of the terms used to discuss gender and how those concepts might play out in an individual. While there are still some limitations to these models (e.g., the lack of an intersectional identity framework), which community members and activists largely acknowledge, they have been very useful in moving cultural understandings of gender forward.

Gender as an Active Process: Spinning a Gender Web

While the multiple spectrum models are helpful in visualizing some of the different aspects of gender and how they may operate independently, they lack social context and do not illustrate the process of one's gender construction. Ehrensaft (2016b) introduced a model for understanding gender in young children in her book, *The Gender Creative Child*. In Ehrensaft's model, gender is a unique and beautiful web woven actively by each child out of three major threads—nature, nurture, and culture (see figure 2.4). This is the most explicit illustration of agency in gender construction out of the models reviewed thus far, as the child is imagined actively and creatively building their *own* gender web using threads that are unique to them. It is easy to imagine how two individuals with similar nature, nurture, and culture threads may end up spinning very different webs.

Ehrensaft's (2016b) concept of *nature* includes chromosomes, hormones, hormone receptors, "primary sex characteristics" (e.g., genitals and gonads), "secondary sex characteristics" (e.g., breasts and facial hair) and what she describes as "brain and mind"—she explains, "for some time we have been talking about gender not being located between our legs, but between our ears—in our brain and mind" (p. 31). She defines *nurture* as including "socialization practices and intimate relationships . . . usually housed in the family, the school, peer relations, and religious and community institutions" and *culture* includes "a particular society's values, ethics, laws, theories, and practices" (p. 25).

The final element that Ehrensaft recognizes in her web model is *time*. As spinning a web is a process, her model communicates the important idea that we are not born with our genders fully developed for life, but that we create them over time. According to Ehrensaft (2016b), "we all, you and I and everyone around us, will always be tweaking our gender webs until the day

Figure 2.4 Gender Web. *Credit*: Julia Hennock.

we die" (p. 25). This reinforces that even those with gender identities that remain fairly stable throughout their lives are constantly responding to the changing contexts in which they exist and to the things they learn about gender. For example, in the fall of 2017, many heterosexual men began to reevaluate and "re-spin" their gender webs in response to the #MeToo movement in the United States, which shed light on the prevalence of sexual harassment and some of the harmful effects of hyper masculinity. Re-spinning of gender webs is also seen with the shifts in the social construction of norms related to what it means to be "male" and "female," "masculine" and "feminine" over time as with trends in fashion or hairstyles. For example, a woman whose femininity in the 1980s included big hair, stirrup pants, leg warmers, and oversized sweatshirts may have re-spun her gender web as those trends went out of style. As seen with the intersectionality framework for identity we discuss below, historical contexts inform people's understandings and beliefs about gender considerably.

Ehrensaft's model gives rise to an image of infinite possible gender webs, with active and creative agents spinning the threads of their lives. It also opens the door to discussing what Keo-Meier and Ehrensaft (2016b) call *gender health*. Gender health is "the opportunity for a child to live in the gender that feels most real and/or comfortable for the child and the ability for children to express gender without experiencing restriction, criticism or ostracism" (p. 13). If others "grab the thread of the web from us as we are spinning it, and tell us what our gender has to be, rather than listening to us as we spell out our gender, or rather than watching us do our own creative work, we are at risk of ending up with a tangled knot of threads, rather than a beautifully spun web that shimmers and glows" (Ehrensaft, 2016b, p. 25). Thus, if adults insist that a child is, and must be, the gender they were legally assigned at birth despite the child's communications otherwise, they risk putting that child's own sense of self at odds with the child's need to trust the adults who are supposed to nurture and care for them. This discord can be confusing, frustrating, isolating, and shameful for a child, and it is harmful for their gender health. This idea of gender health, and the ways it can be either impinged or supported for a young gender expansive child, is one that will be explored in depth in this book.

Gender as a Galaxy

Transgender activist and lawyer Dylan Vade (2005) offers another model of conceptualizing gender, the gender galaxy—"a three-dimensional non-linear space in which every gender has a location that may or may not be fixed" (p. 261). Vade strongly rejects both the sex-gender distinction and any attempt to examine male/female or masculine/feminine as linearly related and oppositional concepts. In the gender galaxy, every individual's gender is a location in space, rather than an assignment to a predetermined box or something that can be mapped onto a linear spectrum. As Vade (2005) notes, even within the cisgender population, there are infinitely different ways to enact maleness and femaleness, to express masculinity and femininity. In the transgender community, there is no homogenized way to be a trans man, trans woman, nonbinary person, or agender person. There are infinite ways to be and act within each identity category. In the gender galaxy model, each of those ways of being gendered is seen as a unique location in the galaxy.

> *I identify in the "male" region of the gender galaxy, but not really as female or male. Once, a law school exercise required that students divide into groups of women and men. I looked at the side of the room with the feminine women. I looked at the side of the room with the masculine men. At that point, I strongly identified as neither female nor male. That identification was both visceral and*

political. I needed more space . . . In contrast, at one transgender meeting in San Francisco, I was told I was welcome only if I did not identify as either female or male. Here as well, I had a visceral and political reaction. Again, I needed more space. In that space, the male parts of my identity felt erased, so I needed to assert them. In that space, I identified as male. My gender is situational. (Vade, 2005, p. 267, he/him)

In the gender galaxy, there is no imperative to lock a person into a particular gender or way of being that gender. There is space for individuals to move, to be unique, to identify, and re-identify themselves. We can imagine a child named Joey—assigned male at birth and comfortable with the term *penis* and with using the boys' bathroom, but who does not like to be called "he" or referred to as a boy specifically. Joey would rather just be called "Joey." Joey likes to twirl in the sparkly skirts from the dress-up bin at preschool. Joey's whole complex and unique gender stakes out a location in the galaxy, and Joey's location may move around in the wide-open space of the gender galaxy over the course of Joey's life. Another child, Asha, also likes twirling in the sparkly skirts at school. Asha was born with ambiguous genitalia, but she knows she is definitely a girl. She has tried out using both of the bathrooms at preschool, but she decided she likes the girls' room better. Asha occupies a separate and distinct location in the gender galaxy. Her location may be somewhat nearby Joey's because they both like twirling in sparkly skirts, but there are lots of things about their genders that they don't have in common.

In the previous models, excluding Ehrensaft's web, there is some need to draw lines around Joey and Asha to identify where they fall between male and female, masculine and feminine. In order to place Joey on a linear spectrum model, one might feel like they need to force Joey to either accept an assigned gender or pick a new one, but at least for now, Joey just wants to be Joey. On the single spectrum model, would Asha be placed in the middle by her body or at the female end because she knows she is a girl? A value judgment is required in order to answer that question. On the multiple spectrum model, her body and her identity are separated from each other, even if she thinks of her body as a girl's body because she knows she is a girl. In the gender galaxy, these two unique children are allowed to exist exactly where they are without pressure to be otherwise, pressure to "make up their minds," or judgment of their unique positions.

It is important to note that everyone—old, young, transgender, cisgender, ipso gender, intersex, and dyadic—has a location in the gender galaxy. A cisgender male who likes to watch sports, works on cars, wears baseball caps, and smokes cigars with other male friends is a location in the gender galaxy. A cisgender male who dances ballet, wears tuxedos to house parties, and goes to the theater with his male friends is another location in the galaxy. Both are in the cisgender and male regions, but they differ in their expressions and enactments of gender and maleness.

Vade (2005) is keen to point out that space in the gender galaxy is not to be thought of as a void. That is to say, there is no location in the galaxy that is completely without gender, and nobody can exist without being located somewhere in the galaxy. This model assumes that every person has a gender, whether they have spent much time reflecting on it or not. Even someone who identifies as agender (no gender) exists in a gendered society, and their experiences within that society are impacted both by how they view their own positionality outside of gendered systems of belief and by how others perceive and treat them through a gendered lens (gender attribution). Because gender-based systems of power and oppression continually work to establish and maintain gender hierarchies, nobody is exempt from gender in Vade's gender galaxy. This model also assumes that one's location in the gender galaxy impacts their perspective on, experiences with, and knowledge about, the rest of the galaxy. For example, a cisgender adult who has not reflected much on their positionality in the gender galaxy is not a neutral observer of a gender-expansive young child. Instead, they are observing that child from their own distinct location in the gender galaxy.

The gender galaxy departs notably from the other models presented, with its infinite nature, its rejection of linearly related gender categories, and its denouncement of the sex-gender distinction. However, the concept of gender "locations" does not present a very clear embodiment of agency in how a young child might construct their own complex gender, in the way Ehrensaft's (2016b) web does. The gender galaxy also does not account for one's intersectional identities.

Intersectional Gender Constellation

The intersectional gender constellation model of gender combines elements of the multiple spectrum models, Ehrensaft's (2016b) web, and Vade's (2005) gender galaxy (see figure 2.5). It also illustrates the *intersectionality* of individuals' multiple social identities and the systems of power and oppression that influence how these identities are developed, expressed, marginalized and privileged in different contexts and times across the lifespan.

We describe the intersectional gender constellation model below in two parts. First, we zoom out and consider how gender fits into a larger context of intersectional identities. Then, we zoom in on the metaphor of the "gender constellation" to identify for readers how it builds upon the important role of children's agency introduced in the gender web model while also expanding and extending it in important ways.

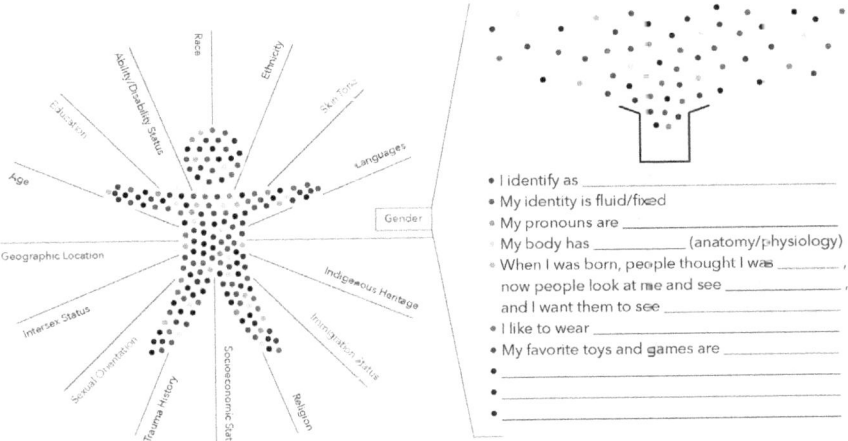

Figure 2.5 Intersectional Gender Constellation. *Credit*: Julia Hennock.

Zooming out: Gender and Intersectional Identities

Intersectionality represents "the critical insight that race, class, gender, sexuality, ethnicity, nation, ability, and age operate not as unitary, mutually exclusive entities, but as reciprocally constructing phenomena that in turn shape complex social inequalities" (Hill Collins, 2015, p. 2). Although the literature reflects great variance in definitions and applications for intersectional knowledge, Hill Collins (2015) suggests the following as representative of its shared tenets:

- Race, class, gender, sexuality, age, ability, nation, ethnicity, and similar categories of analysis are best understood in relational terms rather than in isolation from one another.
- These mutually constructing categories underlie and shape intersecting systems of power and power relations (e.g., racism and sexism are interrelated).
- Intersecting systems of power catalyze social formations of complex social inequalities that are organized via unequal material realities and distinctive social experiences for people who live within them.
- Because social formations of complex social inequalities are historically contingent and cross-culturally specific, unequal material realities and social experiences vary across time and space.
- Individuals and groups differentially placed within intersecting systems of power have different points of view on their own and others' experiences with complex social inequalities, typically advancing knowledge projects that reflect their own social locations within power relations.

- The complex social inequalities fostered by intersecting systems of power are fundamentally unjust, shaping knowledge projects and/or political engagements that uphold or contest the status quo. (p. 14)

Identity has been a focal area for scholars using an intersectionality approach, especially examination of the manner in which intersecting identities lead to diverse social experiences for individuals and social groups (Crenshaw, 1991). Intersectionality research examining identities often analyzes how individuals experience both privilege and marginalization in accordance with their various social identity categories (e.g., race/ethnicity, immigration status, citizenship, income, and language(s) spoken) and how oppression is perpetuated through power dynamics (Anthias, 1998, 2013; Bonilla-Silva, 2013; Cho, Crenshaw, & McCall, 2013).

It's hard to be black and be seen as feminine regardless of what you are doing—regardless of whether people think you're fruity, you're this, you're that, [or] you're born with certain parts. So I have to navigate a gender nonconforming body and a black body. (Jen, twenty-four, nonbinary, she/he/they)[2]

There are really strict gender roles in the Mexican community. Growing up I was told to "be a girl" and "be a lady." I had to learn how to cook. I was expected to want kids and want a family, and I didn't want any of that. (Paulina, seventeen, nonbinary, prefers no pronouns)[3]

I come from a place of pretty high privilege. I'm white, and I'm upper-middle class. Both my parents went to college. They both have graduate degrees. So I think for me, being non-binary and being under the trans umbrella has enabled me to access a lot more information and just learn a lot more than I would have if I were cis and stayed in my white, suburban neighborhood. (Peter, seventeen, he/they)[4]

The intersectional gender constellation model explicitly acknowledges that an individual's experiences with gender are significantly influenced by their other social identity categories (categories they claim or those they don't claim but are attributed to them) and the privileges and/or marginalization and social inequalities associated with each of these categories. This is seen, for example, with transgender people of color whose identities are not accurately represented by thinking about race and gender as "unitary, mutually exclusive entities" (Hill Collins, 2015, p. 2) influencing their daily experiences. Instead, the unparalleled level of oppression faced by Black trans women (Human Rights Campaign, 2018) is best understood by examining the mutually constructing categories of race and gender in relational terms rather than in isolation from one another as these reciprocally constructing phenomena and their intersecting systems of power and power relations shape the complex social inequalities they experience.

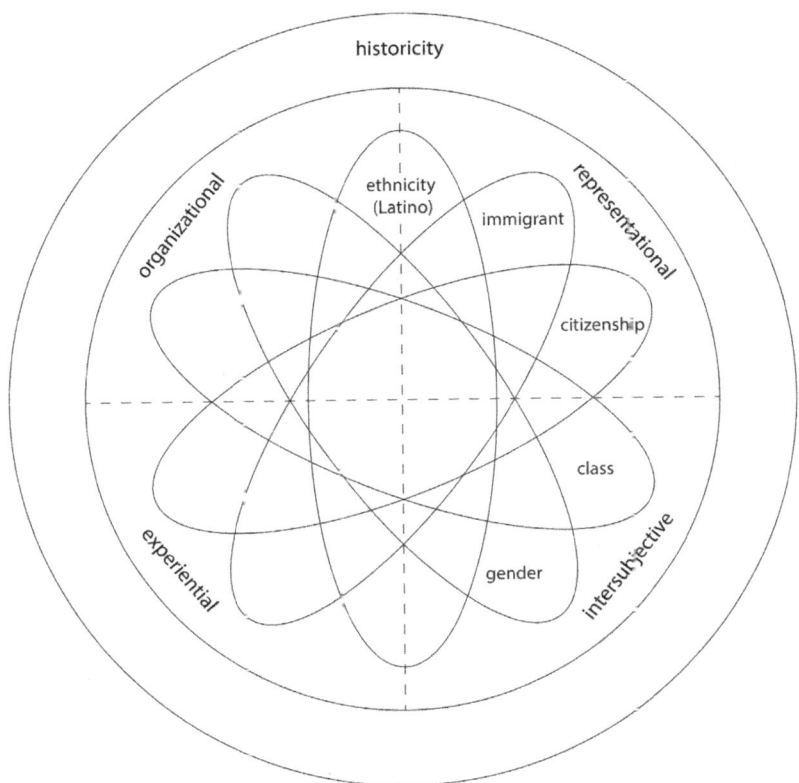

Figure 2.6 Anthias's Multilevel Model of Intersectionality Adapted by Núñez. Credit: Anne-Marie Núñez.

Floya Anthias's (1998, 2013) multilevel intersectionality theoretical framework positions identities as multidimensional, dynamic and influenced by nested contexts of inequitable distribution of power. This framework can be helpful for early childhood teachers to understand young children's identities from an intersectional perspective. Drawing on intersectional scholarship and utilizing Anthias's (2013) theoretical framework, Núñez (2014) explores how this framework can be used to understand how individuals' multiple social identities (e.g., race, ethnicity, gender, etc.) and their relationships with intersecting systems of power in society influence their experiences with educational (in)equity, especially for historically minoritized individuals (see figure 2.6). Drawing from Collins (1990, 2007), she assumes that individuals can simultaneously have marginalized and privileged identities as they navigate different contexts. Núñez's model was developed to capture the complex institutional dynamics of power that perpetuate inequalities in educational contexts. Drawing from sociologist Floya Anthias (2013), Núñez (2014) argues:

Examining power relations in an intersectional manner must involve interrogating how certain social categories are constituted as inferior in comparison to others, how people are framed as part of a larger economic project rather than encouraged to actualize their own self-defined potential, and how resources are distributed in uneven ways to limit the life chances of certain individuals in specific social categories. (p. 86)

With these goals in mind, Anthias's (2013) multilevel intersectionality theoretical framework adapted by Núñez (2014) recognizes that individuals' social identities are not static and at any moment in time, they vary across diverse social contexts.

Drawing from Anthias (1998, 2013), Núñez's (2014) approach outlines the different factors and levels of analysis involved in talking about an individual's identity:

(a) *Social categories* (e.g., race, gender, nation of origin, im/migration status, language, history of colonization, ability/disability, citizenship status, etc.) are understood to be socially constituted and differentially influence individuals' experiences with social power and their positionality within hierarchies.

 The first level of analysis using this framework involves naming the multiple social categories one identifies with, what Crenshaw (1989, 1991) describes as "axes of identity" including such socially constituted categories as race, ethnicity, class, gender, sexual orientation, heritage language, ability, and immigration status and then examining how these social categories relate to one another. Social categories are continuously negotiated in social contexts and influence the social positions, hierarchies, and resources accessible to individuals (Anthias, 2013). Additionally, new social categories are always emerging in society and the social categories an individual identifies with or is attributed with by others can also shift over time.

(b) *Multiple arenas of practice in society* (e.g., organizational, representational, intersubjective, experiential) where the dynamics of identity, power, and history intersect to contribute to inequality within social categories.

 The second level of the framework, or the meso-layer, consists of identifying the domains of power (Dill & Zambrana, 2009) that influence the inequities individuals experience across various social categories. Borrowing from Anthias (2013), Núñez describes four significant domains of power and influence as follows:

- *Organizational.* The formal positions one holds in society in different contexts and the policies and regulations that impact these positions and influence an individual's multiple identities;

- *Representational.* The discourses, images, and texts used in society to signify and communicate ideas about an individual's identities;
- *Intersubjective.* How individuals and groups relate to one another and the influence these relationships have on an individual's opportunities and sense of self; and
- *Experiential.* The narratives people use to talk about their experiences, relationships, and their unique identities.

  These different arenas of influence can work independently or interdependently, which is represented with dotted lines in figure 2.6.
(c) *Historicity,* or the location of social categories and arenas of practice within larger historical contexts (see figure 2.6).

  The third outside or macrolevel of the model represents what Anthias (2013) calls "historicity," defined by Núñez as representing the "broader interlocking systems of economic, legal, political, media, and social power and classification that evolve over time in specific places, as well as social movements to challenge these systems" (p. 89). Historicity reminds us that individuals' social categories, the relationships developed between individuals and groups, discourses and images, and narratives in circulation in society are all influenced by specific historical and political contexts and moments in time.

Using Anthias's (2013) framework as adapted by Núñez (2014) to expand theorizing and discussions about gender in early childhood is helpful for making visible several important ideas for retheorizing gender in early childhood:

- Gender should be considered in relationship with other social categories of identity for individual children;
- Children's lived experiences with gender can reflect experiences of marginalization and/or privilege as a result of many cultural, organizational, political, and historical influences;
- Gender is a deeply individualized experience as each child has different social categories of identity and is differentially positioned within the various intersecting systems of power. Therefore, each child has different points of view about their gender and their own and others' experiences with privilege and social inequalities associated with gender.

Using this framework reveals how intersectionality and important elements of complexity are missing in the previous models of gender discussed above. Next, we provide some examples to make this visible.

Social categories. We could consider each child's *axes of identity*, the social categories they identify with personally or find themselves associated with by others (e.g., ethnicity, race, immigration status, primary language, housing status, etc.), and how they relate with one another, influence the beliefs they develop about themselves and the actions or inactions they take in their everyday experiences. For example, educators might consider how a child's race and immigration status might influence their family's access to and comfort enrolling in an early childhood program. Imagine a young preschool-aged Latinx child, Raul, who is developing an awareness of their gender identity as different from their legal designation living in a low-income family that qualifies for Head Start—an early learning environment where the child could learn about gender diversity through gender inclusive books and curriculum. Yet, Raul, a young TGE child, is unable to participate because Raul's parents, who are undocumented, heard stories of U.S. Immigration and Customs Enforcement (ICE) agents arresting parents (as a first step toward deporting them) after they drop off their children in the morning. Such stories have left Raul's parents too fearful to enroll their child in any government-supported programs.

In contrast, Brianna, a young TGE child born into a white family with parents who are also undocumented as a result of overstaying the time limit of their work visa from Australia—is enrolled in a local parent co-op preschool and attends without any problems or parental concerns. This is because Brianna and her parents are unlikely to experience the same level of surveillance, fear, and community trauma as Raul and other children and families of color routinely do. Although these two children share certain social identity categories (being TGE children living in mixed status families), they have very different positionalities within a society plagued by structural racism (Adams, Bell, Goodman, & Joshi, 2016; Pollock, 2008). The young children and their parents are likely to have very different points of view about gender as they have very different experiences with privilege and marginalization resulting from their social identity categories and the power structures that influence them.

Acknowledging how each individual child's experiences with gender are inter-related with other social categories of their identity *and* how children's association with different social categories of identity affords them (and their families and communities) different access to social positions, hierarchies, and resources (e.g., as seen with Brianna's ability to attend preschool and Raul's inability to do so) is a more honest accounting of the complexity and intersectional understanding of how young children develop social categories of identity including gender.

Arenas of practice. Next, we could identify various arenas of practice where power influences the gender inequities an individual child experiences. For example, we could consider how *organizational* factors (e.g., the child's access to different types of early childhood programs, the program's status/position with the community and/or field, and the organizational policies that influence the teachers' roles and workplace climate within the early childhood program) influence experiences a child has in an early childhood program and the manner in which these experiences impact their developing sense of self including their understanding and feelings about gender. It is likely that the opportunities for children's gender health to be supported would be different for a child whose family only has access to an underresourced childcare program where teacher stress and staff turnover are high and opportunities for teachers' professional development are extremely limited or even nonexistent in comparison to a child who is enrolled in a well-resourced program with an experienced and stable teaching staff who have regularly scheduled opportunities for professional learning and a program-wide commitment to ABE reflected in both policies and practices. Considering how organizational factors can influence young children's access to and experiences with early childhood programs—including the interactions they have that support or hinder their gender health—provides an important lens for understanding how even children with similar social categories of identity can have very different experiences that influence their own identity development.

We could also explore how individuals with different genders are *represented* in the early childhood field including classrooms, schools, and centers. That is, the discourses and images used to describe gender and how power influences this process. For example, the images and labels associated with the words "boy" (strong, active), "girl" (kind, quiet), "men" (controlling, aggressive), "women" (nurturers, maternal), "transgender/nonbinary" (dysphoric, disordered, invisible), and the way these words and what they signify can influence children's understanding of themselves including who they are and who they can become. Or we could ask teachers and others working in early childhood to reflect on how the language and imagery circulated in the news, the media, and among their friends and family members about gender—too often not acknowledging or pathologizing anything outside the binary—influences their own sense of self (their own gender health) and how they might be communicating these feelings to young children.

Intersubjective. We could examine how teachers, administrators, and families think about and interact with children of different genders, especially TGE children. Specifically, how their "image of the TGE child" (e.g., healthy, agentic child who is knowledgeable about their gender identity versus a child with a clinical problem that needs to be "fixed") might impact the quality of the relationships they develop with the children entrusted in their care. Or how the different members of an interdisciplinary team working with a young TGE child and family (e.g., early childhood teacher, school administrator, parent, mental health consultant, and/or private clinician from a gender clinic) relate to one another and the influence this team has on the child's opportunities to experience gender health.

The *experiential* realm would include asking children to tell stories about the wide range of experiences they have and listening carefully to what they share to learn about their multifaceted and intersectional identities including the unique and dynamic ways they talk about their genders. Creating space for children to tell us stories about their lives—and then listening emergently to what they share—provides teachers with rich texts for learning about how children's diverse experiences and relationships influence their unique identities including their relationship to gender.

Finally, *historicity* reminds us that children's social categories of identity, their relationships, and the discourses, images, and narratives in circulation are all influenced by specific historical and political contexts and moments in time. Therefore, a child growing up in 2019 in Oakland, California, where there is a strong, visible, and vocal LGBTQ+ culture will likely have very different experiences related to gender than a child such as Sophie, who was born in 1948 and grew up moving around the world—Italy, Bangkok, Maryland, and Massachusetts—with a father who was a diplomat in the foreign service and a home base in Rockville, Maryland. Because the privileged discourse used to talk about gender and the images and stories available and circulating in society to acknowledge or silence gender diversity change in accordance with specific historical and political moments in time, the date and location of a child's birth, and the political contexts that shape that place and time are additional factors that influence how a child begins to relate to gender in their early childhood years.

As evidenced above, Anthias's (2013) multilevel intersectional framework adapted by Núñez (2014) can be useful for making visible more of the complexities associated with children's intersectional identities. Using the three levels of analysis allows individuals to discuss a more complicated, nuanced, and contextualized understanding of gender in children and how children's understanding of and experiences with gender can be impacted by many factors and contexts that are dynamically shifting across time. Whether identifying micromoments of interaction between a preschool teacher and a young toddler or naming historical changes in signifying TGE individuals (e.g., shifting from "transsexual" to "transgender/gender expansive"), this framework allows for the exploration of a more authentic, tension-laden, and complex discussion of identities for young children than we currently see available in other models representing gender.

This framework is a useful tool for making visible *a foundational contribution of the intersectional gender constellation model*—that intersectional categories of social identity, and their associated interlocking relationships to power and oppression, influence children's experiences with privilege and marginalization which then influence their developing sense of self across all axes of their identity, including gender. In adulthood, this is seen with a white, gay, cisgender male who may experience oppression for being gay, but also benefits from being white and cis male. Inserting intersectionality into a model of gender allows for a more equitable rendering of the ways individual children are differentially positioned within intersecting systems of power and demonstrates why gender can never be represented in essentializing, binarized or linear ways. The only way we can ever truly understand a child's gender is to acknowledge that each child will have different and unique points of view on their own and others' experiences with complex social identity categories including gender because of the many mutually constructing factors that intersect to dynamically and continuously constitute a child's unique lived experiences.

Using Anthias's (2013) multilevel intersectional framework adapted by Núñez (2014) for critical reflection, reflect on the following questions to strengthen your understanding of your own and others' intersectional identities. It is helpful to do this reflective exercise with one or more of your colleagues to create the conditions for epistemic friction to emerge, a critical foundation for transformative learning to happen.

1) *Social categories of identity*
    - Which axes of identity (Crenshaw, 1989, 1991) or social categories do I identity with (e.g., ethnicity, race, immigration status, primary language, housing status, etc.)?
    - Which social categories do others attribute to me? How do I feel about these attributions?
    - How do these social categories influence my beliefs as an early childhood educator? The decisions I make? My willingness to take risks and make changes and/or my preference to "play it safe"?
2) *Arenas of practice* where the dynamics of identity, power, and history intersect to contribute to inequality within social categories
    - *Organizational*
        - What formal position(s) do I hold within an organization, school, and/or program?
        - What is the status of my organization, school, or program within the community and/or early childhood field?
        - What policies and regulations influence my role and responsibilities and the climate of my workplace?
        - How do the policies and regulations of my organization, school, or program impact my position (my role and responsibilities) and my multiple identities (e.g., experience of race, ethnicity, age, gender, immigration status, etc.)?

- How is my formal position influenced by my gender? How are the policies and regulations at my workplace influenced by the gender makeup of the workforce?
- *Representational*
  - What language, images, or texts are used to represent and communicate ideas about me—for example, in conversations, written documents, and social media—as an individual within my organization/institution, school, or program?
  - What language, images, and texts are used to represent and communicate ideas about the group of people who work in the formal position I'm in (e.g., teachers, family childcare providers, professors/instructors, etc.)? What meanings do people associate with these words, images, and texts?
  - What language, images, or texts are used to represent and communicate ideas about the field of early childhood? What meanings do people associate with them?
  - How do the different social categories of my identity (e.g., race, age, religion, etc.) influence the words and images used to signify—represent and communicate ideas about—me? And specifically, how does my gender influence how I am signified?
  - How do I feel and respond to being signified in these ways?
- *Intersubjective*
  - How do I relate to colleagues in my same role both within and outside of my organization/institution, school, or program? Colleagues in different roles? To administrators and/or supervisors?
  - How are these relationships, role models, and/or mentors influenced by my social categories of identity? Specifically, my gender?
  - How do my different relationships (or lack of them) impact my professional opportunities? My sense of self?
- *Experiential*
  - What stories do I tell to talk about my work as an early childhood educator? What experiences do I highlight/share? What do I silence?
  - Who do I share my stories with? Do I tell different stories to different groups of people?
  - How do my stories represent my relationships?
  - How do the stories I tell reflect my multiple identities? What do my stories communicate about my own and others' gender?
  - What do I make visible in my stories about my identity? What do I hide? Why?

3) *Historicity*
  - What politics (e.g., elections, change in leadership, current issues, crises, etc.) are impacting my organization/institution, school, or program?

How are these politics impacting my relationships? The language and images used at my workplace? The narratives or stories being told about the work I do and its value?
- How do my intersectional identities influence my response to these politics? And specifically, how does gender have an influence?
- How is doing my job at this moment in time providing opportunities for me? Limiting me?

To go through the reflection process, first, *answer the questions for yourself* so you gain a stronger awareness of your own identity as this will help you understand the unique and multiple factors that influence your beliefs and practices as a teacher. Share your thoughts with a partner(s). Second, *listen to your partner(s) share their reactions to the questions*. Third, *think together and participate in collaborative dialogue* where the goal is to expand your sensitivity by listening to and learning about others' different experiences and engaging with the heterogeneous perspectives within the group (Medina, 2013). Consider:

- How does an intersectional framework influence how you think about your social categories of identity? Specifically about gender?
- How is this framework beneficial? What is challenging about it?
- How can this framework help you think about gender in new and more complex ways in your teaching?

Fourth, *plan for specific transformative social actions* that can be taken based on what surfaced during the process of critical reflection—both in your solitary thinking as well as your collaborative dialogue with others. Identify new understandings you gained about your intersectional identities and your personal experiences of privilege and marginalization. How can you use this increased self-knowledge to become a more responsive, attuned, and supportive educator, especially for a young child whose intersectional social categories of identity may disadvantage them in early childhood classrooms (e.g., TGE children)? Make a plan for one positive change you can make drawing on your "expanded sensibilities."

Zooming In: Gender as a Constellation

Zooming out and thinking about how gender intersects with other social categories of identity and sources of power and oppression is essential for a contemporary model of gender. Now, we are going to Zoom In and focus exclusively on gender to explain the metaphor of a gender constellation. In doing so, we still recognize gender in the swirl of intersectional and contextual relationships discussed in the previous section at all times. However, we take a moment to think with more specificity about the complexities that need to be acknowledged in theorizing about and discussing gender for young children. While intersectionality can never truly be "set aside," each intersecting area of social categorization and identity power has its own unique characteristics and dynamics. We zoom in now to allow for closer examination of specific elements of the gender constellation model and gender-based identity power and oppression.

The gender constellation model builds on Vade's gender galaxy, Ehrensaft's web and the multiple spectrum models. In the gender galaxy model, each gender was conceptualized as a location in the galaxy. The gender constellation model expands Vade's (2005) model to incorporate the many aspects of gender, including but not limited to those discussed in chapter 1—identity, expression, anatomy, physiology, legal designation, pronouns/language, and attributions. Instead of a person's gender being a single location, we view an individual's gender as a unique constellation, where one can connect the dots of their unique combination of the many different aspects of gender.

Thinking back to Joey and Asha from the gender galaxy, we might imagine that "twirling in sparkly skirts" is a star in the galaxy of gender. Other stars could include having a body part one refers to as their penis, having ambiguous genitalia, being a girl, using the girls' bathroom, using the boys' bathroom, being called "he," being called "she," and being called a "boy." Joey's gender constellation would have lines connecting the stars representing sparkly skirts, having a penis, and using the boys' bathroom. Joey might then draw in a new star labeled "being called Joey." Before Joey was able to tell adults not to say "he" or "boy," those adults may have connected those stars to Joey's constellation, but Joey is working to erase those lines by communicating about the language Joey wants used. Asha's constellation would include stars for the sparkly skirts, being a girl, having ambiguous genitalia, and being called "she." Since she didn't know at first which bathrooms she wanted to use at school, she explored both stars before drawing a line to the girls' bathroom on her constellation. Asha doesn't seem to have strong feelings about which words she wants adults to use when they talk about her genitals so far. Her teachers have told her that, if she decides she likes certain words better than others, she can just let them know.

Joey and Asha's constellations share at least one star (sparkly skirts), but they are also very different (see figures 2.7 and 2.8). Each of them actively works to construct their constellation using the celestial pencil they've been given, the stars they can see from where they are, and the supports they have in their lives that help them reach those stars in the galaxy that resonate with them.

Theorizing from the Edge 89

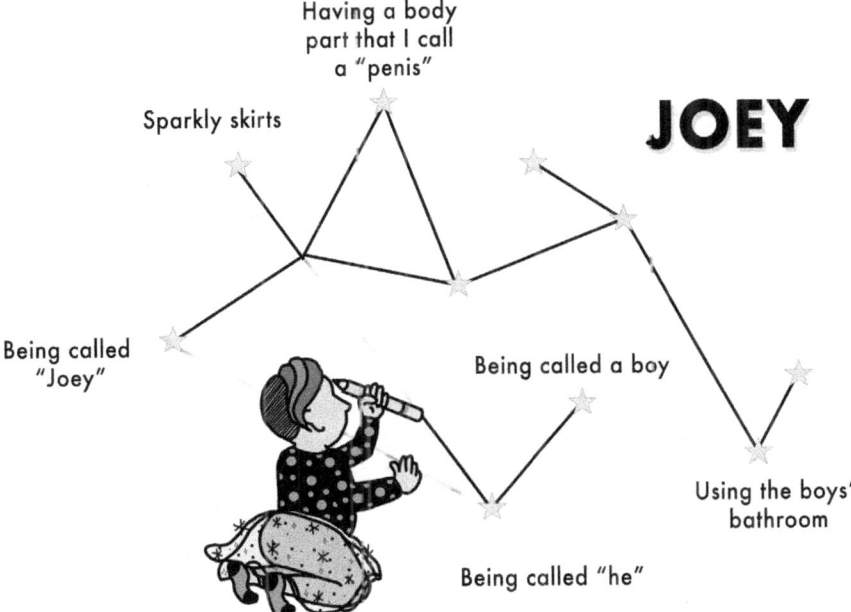

Figure 2.7 Joey's Gender Constellation. *Credit*: Alice Blecker and Jonathan Julian.

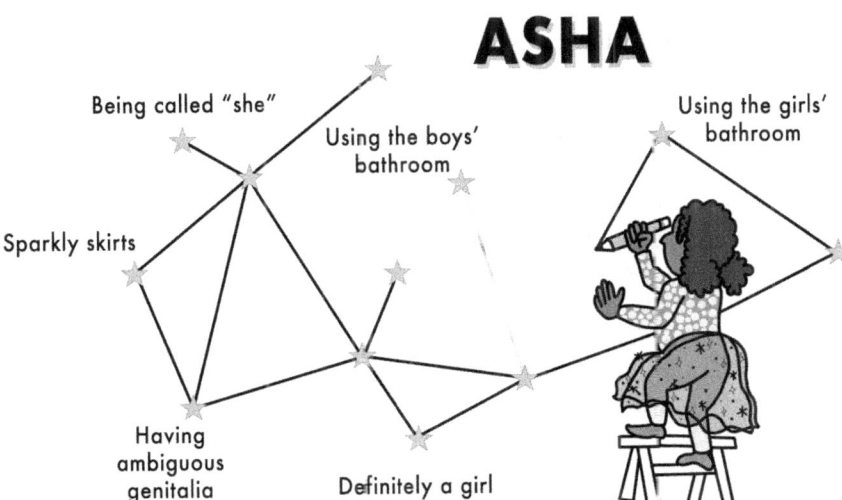

Figure 2.8 Asha's Gender Constellation. *Credit*: Alice Blecker and Jonathan Julian.

As with the gender galaxy, no aspect of gender (identity, expression, bodies, etc.) is placed on a linear spectrum and no attempt is made to quantify them with scales. In the gender constellation model, the various aspects of gender are presented as open-ended and free-floating prompts with infinite possibilities. For example, "my body has _____" allows an individual to give a more nuanced account of their anatomy and physiology than "sex: M/F." There is an allowance for a future star labeled "my body *had* _____" to recognize the journey of a body through a person's life. One might say to a Joey, "When you were born, your body had a penis. The doctor thought you were a boy, because most people with bodies like yours are boys, but only you get to say if you are really a boy or not. Some people with penises are not boys, and some boys don't have penises."

The ability for a child to actively draw their own gender constellation introduces the element of active agency to the gender galaxy idea, as with Ehrensaft's (2016b) web and the act of spinning, but we do not get to draw our whole constellation with total freedom. We do not choose the body we are born into, the society in which that body exists, or any of the adults around us as we begin to develop our gender as young children. We also don't get to choose how people attribute gender to us or treat us based on our genders. Those stars draw themselves into our constellation or are drawn in by others.

When Joey was labeled a boy at or before birth, a gender constellation was already being drawn. By the time Joey was born, several stars relating to anatomy and physiology (among other things) already existed in Joey's constellation. The adults in Joey's life made assumptions based on those body stars and drew lines to stars for *being called "he"* and *being thought of as a "boy."* However, in the constellation model, there is an opportunity for a child to adjust and alter their constellation throughout their life. Some stars that are drawn in for us can be renamed, reworked, or removed from our constellations altogether. Also, as with Joey just wanting to be "Joey," new stars are added to the galaxy every day. The number of stars drawn into a child's constellation by the adults in their life depends on many intersectional factors (e.g., strength of the gender binary and gendered expectations in a family's culture, values, and beliefs). A program that is working toward increased child agency in gender exploration might imagine themselves as giving children access to as much of the galaxy as possible while trying to hand over the celestial pencil to children as early as they can.

Older children, adolescents, and adults draw new stars into the galaxy as well. The expanding lexicon of transgender identities (genderqueer, ambigender, demigirl, transmasculine, and many others) are examples of TGE individuals drawing stars into the gender galaxy when they feel as though none of the existing ones are quite suited to their needs. Some stars in the galaxy may not seem to be related to gender at all, but someone drew them there because it feels like part of gender to that person. For example, a young child who is exploring gender might draw in a star for being a dog in imaginative play with friends. Many TGE children explore and test out gender expressions and identities in play, and pretending to be a dog might be a way that child is exploring being outside their assigned gender and gendered expectations.

Much like the spinning of Ehrensaft's web, children in this model are imagined actively and creatively connecting the dots of their gender to draw their own unique gender constellation. These can shift and change over time or remain relatively fixed in gendered space. Asha might someday want to undergo surgery to affirm her identity as female, shedding the star of ambiguous genitalia for a new star to represent her changing anatomy, or she might shift her identity later in life away from binary "girl" to wanting others to recognize her intersex body as part of her identity. Her constellation is never written in stone. Everything that exists in the infinite galaxy of gender is fair game for a child to use in creating their constellation—to try on and discard, to keep for life, to play with, to learn from, to empathize with, to build upon, or to discover anew—as long as those things are available to children (though nobody has access to the entire galaxy) and as long as children are supported in their gender journeys and explorations as they actively draw their constellations.

Similar to Ehrensaft's (2016b) web, the constellation model recognizes that gender is not constructed alone. In the gender constellation model, children with knowledgeable, supportive, and attuned adult relationships are offered the greatest possible agency over their genders. However, if the adults in a child's life are either unaware of, or unwilling to make available to the child, the vast reaches of the gender galaxy, that child will be limited in drawing their constellation. They will not be exposed to the many diverse stars in the galaxy or informed that they can draw their own, and their attempts at exploration may be, intentionally or inadvertently, reined in by adult interference.

If the adults in Joey's life insist on using "he" and "boy," Joey might give in over time to living in a way that does not feel authentic, a life where Joey doesn't feel *seen or listened to*. Without being given any indication that Joey can have agency over the language that others use, Joey might not ever think to draw in the star labeled "being called Joey" and might not realize that erasing the lines to "he" and "boy" is an option. If Asha's doctor and parents had decided to perform a "normalizing" genital surgery when she was born, she might never even know about her intersex body. She wouldn't have been given the opportunity to possibly draw a line on her constellation to "intersex identity," which could be a strong source of pride and self-empowerment for her.

Some adults know about lots and lots of stars in the gender galaxy but choose to explicitly restrain young children to a very narrow and reductive version of the galaxy—a "girls play with dolls and wear dresses while boys play with trucks and wear pants" binary, prescriptive, and harmful version. Others are simply unaware of the diversity of stars in the galaxy. Both intentional and inadvertent limitations placed on children's ability to create their gender constellations have negative impacts on their gender health, much like Ehrensaft's (2016b) image of interference with a child's web spinning process. The harms that are possible—often epistemic in nature—limit a child's ability to truly know about themself and to communicate about their gender successfully. These harms will be explored in the next three chapters.

Children's relationships with parents and early childhood teachers provide critical contexts where they have their gender agency and gender health supported or inhibited. The adults and peers who are closest to a young child have the most direct and meaningful impact on whether or not children learn to feel empowered and loved in their gender(s) or in contrast, to feel misgendered and constrained in their ability to create their own authentic gender constellation (Ehrensaft, 2016b).

The next section continues the process of "zooming in" by looking more closely at specific forms of gender-based oppression. Making them visible to early childhood teachers is critical as children's agency as active explorers and co-constructors of their individual gender constellations are always influenced by these forces. Working for gender justice involves understanding these sources of oppression and knowing how to reduce their impact.

Three Axes of Gender-Based Oppression

There was a lot of worrying about like "are you going to be normal?" like "this isn't normal," "that isn't normal." And it's like, you're a child playing with toys. How are you supposed to discern everybody's gender dogma from just playing with toys? And you really don't. It just leaves you feeling like you're wrong, you're dirty, you're inadequate as a child. And then you start trying to hide, you know. Everything that they're telling you is like, "you're not supposed to do this," "you're not supposed to do that." And it really robs the joy out of your childhood. And so I feel like my parents tried to take the joy out of the things they thought weren't normal instead of being like, "Okay, well we're just going to have to make sure you're in the right environment for you to be yourself and to flourish," but I feel like they thought that wasn't me. That they were gonna manage to change who I was before it became a problem. (Jen, twenty-four, nonbinary, she/he/they)

In her book, *Whipping Girl*, biologist and transgender activist Julia Serano (2016) describes two interlocking systems of gender-based oppression that both depend on and sustain the gender binary. The first is *"traditional sexism*[5]—the belief that maleness and masculinity are superior to femaleness and femininity" (p. 13, Kindle edition). The second system of power and oppression has had much less worldwide acknowledgment, but it is actually the system that upholds and maintains traditional sexism. Serano calls this system *"oppositional sexism,* which is the belief that female and male are rigid, mutually exclusive categories, each possessing a unique and nonoverlapping set of attributes, aptitudes, abilities and desires. Oppositional sexists attempt to punish or dismiss anyone who falls outside of gender or sexual norms because their existence threatens the idea that women and men are 'opposite' sexes" (p. 13, Kindle edition). Without oppositional sexism, the hierarchy of male/masculine over female/feminine begins to break down entirely. If gender, bodies, and sexuality are all much more complex, full of overlap and gray areas, fluid, and expansive, the traditional sexism model becomes impossible to enforce.

It is important to note that a key aspect of gender that oppositional sexism needs in order to function is the evaluation of whether or not an individual *passes* as binary male or female, whether cisgender or transgender. This part of the power dynamic stems from the ease and certainty with which others can attribute a binary gender to an individual. If a transgender person undergoes medical transition, uses a binary name and pronouns, and is virtually unnoticeable as being transgender unless they choose to share that part of their story openly, they may not elicit oppositional sexism from others.

> *When I meet people for the first time and tell them my name, or when I get carded and someone looks at my license, they see a common female name and a person they perceive as being male, and they say "Wow, you have a really unusual name!" I must have heard that sentence a thousand times, verbatim. Just yesterday someone said that to me, so I told her "I'm transgender" and she said "OH! WOW ... I mean ... You're awesome! I couldn't even tell!" as if being invisible as a trans person is the ideal. I was doing a great job at being trans by not letting anyone know I was trans. (Katie, thirty-four, nonbinary, he/him/she/her)*

The entire plot of the 1994 movie *It's Pat* was based on the fact that the central character's gender was ambiguous, representing those who do not *pass* as a binary gender as not just the butt of a joke, but as actively repulsive and offensive. The movie also highlighted the fact that most people feel entitled to know not just someone's gender identity, but what kind of genitals that person has, when that person is not easily categorized as a binary gender. When an individual steps outside the gender binary, oppositional sexism works to push them back into one gender box or the other. When someone presents as so ambiguous that others are unable to confidently attribute a binary gender to them, it creates a deep discomfort in others that often manifests as an invasive curiosity and a desire to force that person to conform to the rigid standards of oppositional sexism.

A third oppressive hierarchy exists, known as *cissexism* (Serano, 2016). This hierarchy places those who are cisgender above those who are transgender. Cissexism is the oppressive system that places cis men above trans men and cis women above trans women, whether one *passes* as male or female or not. At its essence, cissexism is about one's obedience and compliance with their assigned gender. In the gender binary, power structures are set in place for an individual's life the moment they are first assigned a gender and then enforced through their designations and structural social power.

> *As I walked home, urchins followed me, chorusing, "Disguise! Disguise! Female disguise!" I finally reached my neighbour's house. I had not worn a disguise I said to myself; I had given form to my real feelings. I was unwilling to shed my female clothes and stood for several minutes in front of the mirror. My neighbor rushed in and whispered, "Dorai! Take it all off! I don't want your brothers scolding me!" Reluctantly, I changed into my regular clothes. As I re-emerged in my man's garb, I felt that I was in disguise, and that I had left my real self behind. (A. Revathi, The Truth about Me: A Hijra Life Story, 2010, p. 16)*

Transgender narratives question the idea that one's assignment, and therefore, their positionality in gender power structures, is fixed. A person who is assigned male, who rejects that assignment, and who transitions to living her life as a woman challenges the idea that men are superior to women. Why would a man want to abandon a position of higher status to take up a less powerful position in society? Conversely, someone who is assigned female at birth, who rejects that assignment, and who transitions to living his life as a man evokes the "slippery slope" question of "What if all women do this?" What if, because "woman" is an oppressed category, all women decide to abandon that post for more privileged territory? Who will be left to oppress?

Many variations of this "slippery slope" warning have been used to invalidate transgender identities. In 2014, a post on a social media forum claiming "I sexually identify as an Attack Helicopter. . . . From now on I want you guys to call me 'Apache' and respect my right to kill from above and kill needlessly. If you can't accept me you're a heliphobe and need to check your vehicle privilege. Thank you for being so understanding." went viral—spreading to image memes, blogs, YouTube comments and videos, and other social media platforms.[6] Countless variations exist across the Internet of people claiming to identify as mayonnaise, a subway train, a cheese sandwich, a computer, and other impossibilities meant to mock and invalidate transgender identities. These arguments are often backed up with the false notion that there are only two *sexes* and that the idea of someone self-identifying is simply absurd. Again, the goal of cissexism is to assert that one's formally assigned gender at birth is the ultimate truth of that person's gender.

Serano (2016) places the oppressive force of cissexism within oppositional sexism, but it can operate separately. Brandon Teena, a transgender man, was violently raped and murdered in 1993 by two men who had been his friends until they found out he was not a cis man (Muska, 1999). Brandon Teena had been identifying, living, and passing as a binary man until he was arrested and held in a women's facility, revealing to others in his life that he was not cisgender. Several of the people in his life reacted with outrage, claiming fraud and deception. Some went as far as to say that everything he had ever told them was a lie. This kind of reaction, in which people feel personally offended and lied to upon learning that someone is transgender, stems from the sex-gender distinction and the socially constructed idea that someone is fundamentally and permanently the gender they are assigned at birth, and that a transgender identity is a sham and a lie. The violence against Brandon Teena was not violence against femaleness or femininity (traditional sexism) nor was it violence against him being unreadable or somehow nonbinary or nonconforming to a binary gender (oppositional sexism), as he had been fully accepted in his social circle as a masculine man. This violence was specifically about cissexism as he was discovered to be transgender and not cisgender, which was interpreted as him being a liar. Cissexism is about whose gender is considered real and whose is considered fraud. It is about who properly accepts their assigned gender and who needs to be controlled. Since cissexism can operate separately from both traditional and oppositional sexism, it is considered here as a third axis of gender-based oppression. A multidimensional view of gender-based oppression allows for more nuanced analysis of individuals' experiences than any of the three axes alone.

All three systems of gender-based oppression work to reduce the beautiful complexity of gender—bodies, identities, expressions, and so on—down to crude and controllable categories, over which a hierarchy can be maintained. No hierarchy can be laid over gender constellations in a gender galaxy, but value judgments can be made regarding which gender box is superior, and linear spectrums are always in danger of being superimposed over a fictitious good-bad binary. As such, traditional sexism, oppositional sexism, and cissexism create power structures that continuously work to reduce gender to distinct male and female categories so that binary, cisgender, and male power can be maintained.

Viewing these different structures of social power together, we can see a much more complex model of how society works to categorize, empower, disempower, and place more or less value on individuals' lives based on multiple gendered factors. A cis man who passes easily as male—meaning

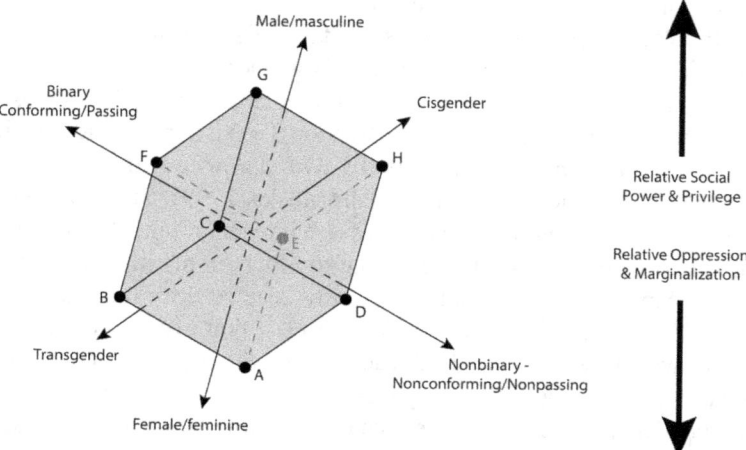

Figure 2.9 Intersecting Axes of Gender-Based Oppression. *Credit*: Katie Steele.

he was assigned male at birth, he identifies as male, he embodies his culture's ideals of masculinity comfortably, and he has never experienced being misgendered—is at the pinnacle of gender privilege and gender identity power (position G in figure 2.9). Conversely, a transfeminine person who does not pass as binary cis female—meaning they were assigned male at birth but do not identify as male, they present as female or feminine but are not read by others as cis female—is on the lowest rung of the gender power hierarchy (position A).

In this diagram, the three axes of gender-based oppression—traditional sexism, oppositional sexism, and cissexism—are represented with their respective positions of power (male/masculine, binary/conforming/passing, and cisgender) on top. The respective positions of oppression/marginalization (female/feminine, nonbinary/nonconforming/nonpassing, and transgender) are at the lower end of each axis. Holding two of the three positions of power (positions C, F, and H) theoretically corresponds to relatively more power and less oppression than holding only one (positions B, D, and E), though the formula is never so simple.

The real-life enactments and experiences of these forces of power and oppression are not distinctly quantifiable or plottable on a coordinate system in the way it is depicted here. Instead, we present them in this manner to highlight the false binaries and dualities that drive gender-based forces of social power, oppression, and control. Additionally, this represents *only* gender-based power and oppression. When the many other dimensions of social identity categories are considered (e.g., intersections with race, class, and ability/disability, etc.), this model becomes even more complex.

For example, a transfeminine person of color is statistically more likely to experience social identity-based oppression including gender-based violence than a transfeminine person who is white because of the additional impact of structural racism. In a study of antitransgender fatal violence over the period of 2013 to 2018, the Human Rights Campaign (2018) found that almost 90 percent of all victims were trans women, 80 percent of all victims were trans women of color, and 69 percent of all victims were black trans women (p. 62). The intersection of traditional sexism, oppositional sexism, cissexism, and racism is a very dangerous place to live.

One's position within these three interlocking systems of gender-based social power can shift and change throughout their life, and the fact that social power is *social* and depends on other's perceptions of an individual further complicates the operation of such power. In discussing gender-based power and privilege, it is common to hear questions like "Do trans women have male privilege?" and the answer is that it is just not that simple. All three axes of gender-based power and oppression must be considered, as they do not operate independently of each other. A transgender woman may start her life with a certain amount of social identity power simply because she is assumed to be cis male at birth, despite the fact that she will likely experience a significant amount of gender-based oppression throughout her life for expressing any amount of femininity (traditional and oppositional sexism) and for being trans, if and when she comes out (cissexism). She may be encouraged academically in ways that children assumed to be female are not, while simultaneously experiencing severe bullying for any presentation of femininity. Her voice may be heard while she is being perceived as a male in ways it will be silenced when she is perceived as a woman, and especially as a trans woman.

> *There's no question that I notice, in my professional life, sitting around in meetings. And it's exactly the same sort of meetings I had before when I was a guy. Back then, things would come up, I'd throw some idea in, and everybody would be like "oh yea, that's interesting. . ." Now I do the same thing, but no one hears it! (Sophie, sixty-eight, trans woman, she/her)*

Similarly, a transgender man may experience traditional sexism as a child assumed to be female, but then receive an amount of social identity power upon embracing masculinity and maleness. He may be bullied as a child for being a "tomboy" and not fitting nicely into a binary female box under oppositional sexism, while also benefiting from a more masculine presentation and being encouraged in math and science classes where more feminine children are discouraged.

While most people are cisgender and do not experience cissexism, cisgender individuals who defy gender norms in any way are likely to experience social pressures encouraging them to return to their rigid binary box (oppositional sexism). Cultural messages embedded in the social imagination, such as "boys don't cry" or girls should "act like a lady," encourage everyone, cis or trans, to uphold the gender binary and the rigid nonoverlapping boundaries between the "opposite" genders.

In their earliest years, young children begin observing the world and learning about oppressive and hierarchical social dynamics related to gender and other social categories of identity. Studies have shown that children as young as preschoolers reproduce such social power dynamics during play and other interactions with each other (Grieshaber & McArdle, 2010; Zosuls, Ruble, Tamis-LeMonda, Shrout, Bornstein, & Greulich, 2009). They are learning these dynamics both from the structures of the society and culture in which they live and from individuals in their lives who are reproducing and reinforcing these hierarchies.

When a caregiver takes a child to buy clothing, oppositional sexism is structurally represented by the clothing being physically separated in the store into boys' and girls' clothes. Oppositional sexism may be subconsciously enacted by the caregiver walking the child to one of those sections without reflecting on the fact that they are limiting a child's gender expression opportunities based on binary cisgender assumptions. Traditional sexism is commonly represented in children's clothing when T-shirts for boys show empowering messages that depict them as superheroes, while T-shirts for girls highlight their physical appearance or attractiveness to boys. Cissexism and oppositional sexism may be actively enacted if the child expresses a desire to peruse the clothing on the other side of the store yet the caregiver refuses to entertain the idea. All three axes of gender-based oppression may be represented if the child is one who was assigned male at birth, but who wants to shop in the section identified for girls, and the caregiver responds negatively with messaging that also devalues femininity or femaleness ("you're not a sissy, why do you want to look over there?").

EMBRACING GENDER AS AN INTERSECTIONAL GENDER CONSTELLATION

Every child arrives in early childhood classrooms with their own intersecting identities and social categories, with their own positionalities and experiences of power, privilege, and marginalization. It is possible that the only social category that all the children in a given class have in common is their age group. Working for gender justice for young children requires teachers to regularly Zoom Out to view a child's whole self—their diverse social categories of identity and the organizational, representational, intersubjective, and experiential arenas of practice as well as the historical and political contexts that impact how they experience these different "axes of their identity." The gender constellation model acknowledges the important influence of these interlocking and mutually constructing aspects of young children's lives and communicates that *an important part of understanding young children's gender is recognizing that gender is best understood "in relationship to" versus in isolation from children's diverse experiences and dynamically evolving, complex and uniquely constructed identities.*

The gender constellation model also communicates that working for gender justice involves teachers in the process of Zooming In to develop day-to-day strategies for supporting individual children to be respected as agentic beings with the ability to create their own gender constellations. ECE classrooms cannot be places of liberation or environments that support gender diversity until teachers learn about the social norms and the various forms of oppression that exist to maintain the hegemony of the gender binary. ECE environments should be the places where children can be themselves and flourish. Learning about various forms of oppression, and how they operate in the lives of young children is important for teachers committed to changing their beliefs and teaching practices that reinforce the status quo. The gender constellation model envisions teachers supporting the gender health of all children as they continuously learn more about how to make a wider range of stars visible and available to children so they can actively and dynamically construct authentic individual gender constellations.

PATH TO GENDER JUSTICE

One significant hurdle to approaching any justice work is the impossibility of reaching a perfectly just world. As such, the approach to gender justice presented in this book and embedded in the intersectional gender constellation model starts with a *commitment to the nonideal*—an image of a future that contains friction, that is constantly readjusting to new information, that strives for better rather than best. We draw from Medina (2013) who breaks this commitment into three parts: particularism, empiricism/fallibilism, and meliorism. The commitment to *particularism* involves valuing the specifics of a given situation over lofty ideals or generalizations (p. 11). Given the intersectional and contextualized view of gender presented, there can be no singular path to justice for all TGE young children. What works in one country, city, or program may be entirely irrelevant in another. The needs of a single transgender child will be affected by many intersectional factors and so cannot be assumed to match the needs of another transgender child, even in the same classroom. A commitment to particularism is a commitment to recognizing that individuals of different genders experience the world differently, are treated differently, and need differing strategies to achieve justice, and that intersectional identities and circumstances will also play a part in creating those strategies.

Committing to *empiricism* and *fallibilism* is committing to try strategies until finding what works, but not assuming that a successful strategy will necessarily succeed again next time. According to Medina (2013), "there is never final and absolute proof of the correctness of our norms, for our norms can only be backed up by how they impact the actual experiences of those affected by them" (p. 12). It is often the response of cisgender individuals who want to be good allies and advocates for the TGE community that they want to help but are scared of saying or doing *the wrong thing*. A commitment to empiricism and fallibilism accepts that there will be an amount of trial and error in the process of working towards justice, but that the possibility of getting it wrong is not an excuse for not trying.

Finally, the commitment to *meliorism* is the commitment "to making things better without being shackled to any particular picture of 'the best'" (p. 12). Committing to meliorism requires that one does *something* to improve the lives of TGE individuals, even if it is not within their power to fix everything for everybody or to do anything perfectly. The dovetailing concern with not wanting to "get it wrong" is wanting to get it perfectly right. Both fears can leave one paralyzed or at least complacent with *how things are*. A commitment to meliorism is a commitment to both not settling for how things are nor delaying action until the perfect solution is found, but rather always aiming for making things *better*.

NOTES

1. See http://www.transstudent.org/gender/.
2. In Their Own Words, Beyond the Binary. See: https://yr.media/interactive/in-their-own-words-beyond-the-binary/.
3. In Their Own Words, Beyond the Binary. See: https://yr.media/interactive/in-their-own-words-beyond-the-binary/.
4. In Their Own Words, Beyond the Binary. See: https://yr.media/interactive/in-their-own-words-beyond-the-binary/.
5. We use the term *sexism* here despite its inextricability from the false concept of categorical *sex* to provide some consistency with the vast body and history of academic and colloquial discourse on *sexism*, of which this examination is a part. However, the three forms of gender-based oppression presented here should be thought of as just that: *gender*-based, with *gender* considered in all its complexity.
6. See: https://knowyourmeme.com/memes/i-sexually-identify-as-an-attack-helicopter.

Chapter 3

Testimonial (In)justice

Establishing Credibility in an Early Childhood Context of Identity Prejudice

Having developed a model of gender that centers child agency and the voice of the child (including all the varied languages of young children), we must turn to ourselves as listeners, receivers, and perceivers of the messages that children share with us about their unique gender constellations. The kind of listening this requires, though, is one that includes a commitment to being changed by what we hear. Davies (2014) tells us,

> Listening is about being open to being affected. It is about being open to difference and, in particular, to difference in all its multiplicity as it emerges in each moment in between oneself and another. Listening is about not being bound by what you already know. It is life as movement. Listening to children is not just a matter of good pedagogy; encounters with others, where each is open to being affected by the other, is integral, I will suggest, to life itself. (p. 1)

Further, when we have heard what a child has said to us, we must ask ourselves, "Do I believe you?" Radically extending credibility to all young children and young TGE children especially, is a responsibility of early childhood educators driven directly by the imperative to *do no harm*. As Rebecca Solnit (2015) notes, "Credibility is a basic survival tool" (p. 5).

In her 2005 book, *Playing it Straight,* Mindy Blaise builds an enlightened description of the role of the child in actively using "gender discourses to construct themselves as girls or boys, or . . . something in between" (p. 183). We learn how, over the course of one school year, Blaise supports a class of kindergarteners to observe and discuss gender roles, discourses, expectations, power structures, and identities. Blaise challenges ideas of gender as either an innate biological trait or as a learned social construct. She frames gender as a much more complex and dynamic idea involving the agency of the child to create their own gender within social, biological, and power structures they perceive around them. She works with the children and the teacher of the class to confront problematic normative discourses around masculinity and femininity throughout the year. She uses samples of children's conversations, play, and questioning to demonstrate children's "serious, complex, and important gender work" (p. 45), rejecting the idea of children's gender exploration as simply cute and meaningless. However, even in this groundbreaking study, Blaise may still be subconsciously influenced by negative images of young children and/or transgender individuals.

Three of the chapters in Blaise's book each focus on a single child, presenting rich and vivid characterizations of the three children throughout the year. One of these children, Madison, is described as "an 'atypical' girl who defies gender norms" (p. 127) and who is "confident about her female identities and is able to create alternative ways of being within these" (p. 187). Madison does seem to confidently cross gender borders within the culture of the classroom—playing with groups of both boys and girls. Madison, whose mother is an advocate for women's equality, often points out gender dynamics in the classroom that are unfair to the girls. Blaise views these qualities as being part of Madison's confidence in enacting femininity.

However, Madison is also regularly observed insisting on playing male roles (sometimes as a dog) in dramatic play, saying things like "I hate being a girl" (p. 150) or "I like to be a boy" (p. 154), and mentioning sometimes imagining having a penis (p. 155). Blaise examines Madison's behaviors—playing actively, getting dirty, engaging in aggressive imaginary play with boys—in the context of being outside of *hetero*normativity (including entertaining questions of lesbian narratives not brought up by Madison), but she does not examine them through the lens of *cis*normativity. Blaise frequently describes Madison as creating new ways to enact femininity and as having "multiple gender identities" (p. 129), but to Blaise, these are multiple ways of being female and do not include any possible male identities. Blaise recounts one exchange during dramatic play between Madison and Anne, in which Madison is a boy and Anne is his mother:

Anne: (Pulls a long necklace and bracelet out of a jewelry box, holding them up in the air and swinging them back and forth) I bought this . . . for a present for y::o::u.
Madison: Yuck! (Grabs the jewelry out of Anne's hand and throws the bracelet into the kitchen area) I'm not a girl. I am *not* a girl! These are girl things and I don't wear them. (p. 147)

In Blaise's analysis, Madison is using masculinity to access power in this interaction. She acknowledges that Madison is "contesting her gender," but then remarks that "By throwing the bracelets into the kitchen area and saying 'yuck,' she is marginalizing a particular form of femininity" (p. 147). It is noteworthy that, according to Blaise, Madison rejects *femininity*, remakes femininity in many ways, or even enacts a form of masculinity at times, but never quite rejects *femaleness* as identity. She even goes as far as to hint that Madison identifies as a boy, but only in the context of the scene being acted out. When dramatic playtime is over, Madison is still seen as a girl. Based on the picture painted by Blaise, Madison has considerable agency over gender expression, but it seems like the agency stops there.

Outside of dramatic play, Blaise questions Madison about playing a boy in the scene, saying, "But you're a girl" and eliciting the response "But I hate being a girl" (p. 149). Madison has not left the male narrative behind when the scene ended, but the analysis is that Madison is "creating new feminine discourses that are liberating" (p. 150) as Madison has described the things boys can do that are cooler than things girls can do. In a later discussion of gender with Blaise and a few female classmates, Madison says, "When I went to the bathroom I saw a boy part right on my private part. So I think I'm a boy. I think I was just imagining it. Because my eyes were closed" (p. 155). This comment surprises two of the other children, and one asks to hear the playback from the tape recorder—something the children have been able to do with Blaise researching in their classroom—but Madison changes the subject quickly. Blaise's identifies this as a moment of social risk, noting Madison's quick subject change, but it does not seem to register as a possible transgender narrative.

Of course, we can't know exactly how Madison identifies, nor was it Blaise's job to excavate a definitive gender identity from this child. However, we are inspired to wonder what kind of constellation Madison might draw, if given access to the entire gender galaxy and the chance to hold a celestial pencil. It is quite possible that Madison might align more with a masculine or male identity than with the female one assigned at birth, if given the opportunity and agency. Of course, its also possible that Madison isn't trans, and it is still extremely important to support and affirm gender-expansive children who want to break the rules of gender but have no interest in identifying differently than how they were assigned, as Blaise worked hard to show. However, its difficult to imagine a five-year-old who *is* trans communicating their identity more clearly than with statements and expressions like Madison's. One of the most fundamental parts of being human is our capacity for language—including "the hundred, the thousand languages, symbols, and codes we use to express ourselves and communicate" (Rinaldi, 2001, pp. 80–81)—and our ability to convey very specific pieces of knowledge, thought, belief, and experience to one another. But what does it take for a voice to be *heard*?[1]

The various intersecting systems of identity-based oppression might be imagined as volume knobs, turning up the volume of the voices of those who hold relative social power and turning down the volume of those voices who are oppressed—lower and lower with each intersecting marginalized identity a person holds. The aggregated result is a society in which some types of voices take up significantly more cultural space, are given more credence and credibility by the nature of their being louder and more commonly heard, and are used to narrate the stories that everyone is expected to identify with, while other voices are effectively and completely drowned out. It creates a society, also, in which most people's ears become sensitive to hear some voices and not others, even when those marginalized voices are screaming as loud as they can. As with Blaise, we can have just and equitable goals in our work with children and actively strive for attuned and responsive relationships with them, but some voices are simply harder to hear by the nature of their having been historically devalued and discredited.

TESTIMONIAL INJUSTICE: SCREAMING LOUD AND NOT BEING HEARD

This systematic and persistent diminishment of certain voices is the phenomenon which Miranda Fricker (2007) describes as *testimonial injustice*—"the injustice that a speaker suffers in receiving deflated credibility from the hearer owing to identity prejudice on the hearer's part" (p. 2). The two main components of this phenomenon are *credibility judgments*—assessments of how much we can trust a given person on a given subject in a given situation—and *identity prejudice*—a prejudice against a certain social category, and by extension, its members.

Credibility Judgments

As people exchange thoughts, beliefs, stories, knowledge, and ideas between themselves, instantaneous judgments are made by the *hearer* (the person receiving the information) regarding the credibility of the *speaker* (the person sharing it). We ask ourselves, "how much can I trust this person about this subject under these circumstances?" (Fricker, 2007). Fricker argues that extending credibility and trust to someone requires an assessment that two attributes are present—sincerity and competence. If a coworker tells us that a child has just been injured and needs a bandage, we are likely to believe them. Perhaps we've worked together for some time and know they are competent in caring for children with minor injuries, and we can't see a reason why our coworker would be insincere about something like that.

Most of the time, we make our credibility judgments subconsciously and instantaneously during conversations. There is little need to stop and scrutinize the situation to determine just how credible our coworker is in communicating that a child was injured. However, the actual process is complex and requires us to read countless cues to determine if we believe someone to be credible (Fricker, 2007). If the same coworker had been laughing when they made their statement, we would have made a qualitatively different instantaneous judgment of the credibility of the statement. Perhaps we would assume a less serious interpretation of the word "injured." It is beneficial to us to be able to read these cues accurately and use them swiftly and without conscious intervention in making credibility judgments (Fricker, 2007). If the child is significantly injured, we don't have time to waste interrogating our coworker to determine their trustworthiness in that moment.

Fricker (2007) tells us that the cues we are reading and using to make our credibility judgments are learned social signals informed by our experiences and positionality in different privileged and marginalized groups. Sometimes, though, our social positionality leads us to make inaccurate credibility judgments. In most white and Western cultures, eye contact during conversation is a physical cue of one's sincerity, respect, and attention, but in many other cultures (e.g., many Indigenous cultures in the Americas) children learn to convey those things to adults by averting their eyes (Rogoff, 2003). If a white teacher subconsciously interprets a Navajo child's lack of eye contact during their interactions as some kind of reduction in the child's sincerity in what they are communicating, that teacher is liable to unduly deflate any credibility judgments made for this child. The subconscious nature of credibility judgments allows us to move along through our day without spending half of it scrutinizing everyone's credibility, but the process of making those judgments is vulnerable to inaccuracy due to our social positionality.

Identity Prejudice

In the previous example, the reduction of credibility afforded the child was the result of a cross-cultural misinterpretation. However, if enough white teachers misperceive enough Indigenous children as insincere and not credible, a negative cultural image of Indigenous children as being deceptive and untrustworthy could form and begin to circulate. If this negative identity-based image got enough social traction, then even teachers who *know* that Navajo children avert their eyes to show respect might reduce their credibility judgments of the Navajo children in their class. In building her concept of *testimonial injustice*, Fricker (2007) asserts that negative identity-based stereotypes, especially in the form of cultural images of marginalized groups, can insinuate themselves into our subconscious and deflate our credibility judgments of individuals who belong to those social categories. This is especially true when those negative images impact our subconscious assessment of one's trustworthiness—competence and sincerity. Perhaps Fricker's (2007) most important point about these images is that they operate below the level of one's articulated beliefs about the social categories in question and below the level of conscious involvement in forming one's credibility judgments.

These negative images of marginalized groups are subconsciously used as cues—along with all our regular cues—in determining someone's trustworthiness, and our credibility judgments are reduced not because a speaker is demonstrating any signs of untrustworthiness, but because they belong to a particular marginalized social category (Fricker, 2007). For example, in a culture where women are viewed as intuitive thinkers and men as rational thinkers, a woman in a high-level math degree program may experience testimonial injustice when presenting her work, being perceived as less credible than her peers not because she is actually less competent or sincere in her studies and performance, but simply *because she is a woman* (Fricker, 2007). Her peers and professors don't have to consciously believe that women are less capable of high-level math and logical, rational thinking for their credibility ratings to be unjustly reduced. They only have to live in a culture that paints women as intuitive and as less capable in those capacities than men.

In the case of Madison, Mindy Blaise is a feminist and poststructuralist thinker who is examining gender inequities using queer theory. She positions young children as complex thinkers and constructors of identity. She certainly does not consciously view Madison as incompetent or insincere, based on her descriptions and analyses. Madison is taken as credible and is heard in many contexts, but when Madison says, "I'm a boy," Blaise seems to be hearing something else—a refutation of available feminine discourses, an undermining of heteronormativity, but never that Madison might just *be* a boy. Something unseen is deflating Blaise's subconscious judgment of Madison's credibility in claiming "I am a boy." Blaise takes Madison seriously, in that Blaise considers Madison's expressions and gender explorations to be serious gender work, but she does not take Madison literally. We are compelled to ask the question, what if Madison was being both serious *and* literal? Blaise's work with Madison had the specific stated intent of working toward gender equity, and her own articulated beliefs about gender are relatively progressive and empowering for young children. And yet, her extension of credibility and trustworthiness to Madison stopped just shy of considering the possibility that Madison was *literally* a boy. If Madison *was* trying to express a transgender identity, that attempt was met with a testimonial injustice.

We argue here that young transgender and gender-expansive children live at the intersection of two marginalized social categories—young children and TGE individuals—and the negative cultural images of both groups interfere with adults' abilities to truly and authentically *hear* the voices of young TGE children. These negative images insinuate themselves into the subconscious of all members of a given society in which they circulate, and they can disrupt genuine attempts at attunement despite one's conscious intentions and beliefs.

Negative Cultural Images of Young Children

In chapter 1, we introduced several images of the child which are prominent in early childhood education due to the privileging of developmental theories and Western perspectives (Dahlberg, Moss, & Pence 2013; File, Basler Wisneski, & Mueller, 2012). Murris (2018) proposed six images of young children, which are embedded in Western early childhood practice. Here we examine the ways these six images preclude our ability to make just and equitable credibility judgments of young children by attacking their competence and sincerity.

Murris's (2018) "developing child" who is immature and needs guidance is incompetent—not yet fully formed into an agential and self-aware being. The "ignorant child" who needs instruction because they lack experiences is incompetent—simply not yet knowing or understanding about the world. The "evil child" who needs discipline is insincere—not yet having learned how to follow a moral compass. The "innocent child" who needs protection and experience is both insincere and incompetent—perhaps cute and sweet, but not serious or experienced. The "egocentric child" who must be enculturated by elders to learn to exist with others is both incompetent and insincere—unaware of how the self relates to society and with self-centered motivations which may undermine their reliability. The "fragile child" who needs protection and is easily damaged is incompetent—not able to handle complexity, their own or the world's (Murris, 2018).

If our credibility judgments of children are being subconsciously influenced by these kinds of images, then we will not be able to honor a child's voice when they tell us who they are. If José, assigned male, spins around in a dress and says, "I'm a girl!" we don't need to know exactly what José means by that statement, but we need to be *capable* of hearing anything that José *might* mean. If we subconsciously view José as "innocent" and "developing" and "ignorant," we might understand that moment to be a moment of innocent joy and expression by a child who simply does not yet understand the difference between boys and girls or a child who is just in the act of pretending. We may respond with a smile and an affirmative, "You look great!" and then ask José to take the dress off and line up with the boys to go to lunch. Our credibility judgment, in that case, was diminished by our image of the child as not fully formed and as not an expert of their own experiences.

A single claim like this does not warrant so much credibility that we demand the child pick a new name, change pronouns, and then line up with the girls for lunch (perhaps we need better ways of lining up for lunch). But if we subconsciously view children as too incompetent or insincere to claim a transgender identity with any credibility, we will undoubtedly subject the transgender children in our care to persistent testimonial injustice.

Negative Cultural Images of Transgender People

Even if a teacher is not consciously wondering if a child is expressing a transgender identity, transgender and gender-expansive narratives and themes in young children might evoke cultural images of transgender people in one's subconscious credibility judgment processes, and so they are examined here.

Media portrayals of both real and fictional transgender people frequently discredit trans identities—attacking both competence and sincerity. Specifically examining media representations of trans women, Julia Serano (2016) argues that there are two prevailing archetypes: the "deceptive transsexual" and the "pathetic transsexual" (p. 36, Kindle version).[2] According to Serano (2016) the deceptive trans person is one who *passes* as binary and cisgender. She notes that this archetype is often used in fictional stories as a plot twist when the "truth" of their deception is revealed, citing such movies as *The Crying Game* and *Ace Ventura: Pet Detective*. The underlying implication of this plot twist is that the trans person is fundamentally the gender they were assigned at birth, and the audience and other characters have been fooled.

This deceptive trans person narrative—cutting directly at transgender sincerity—can result in violence, as with the 2002 murder of Gwen Araujo by two men who found out she was transgender a few months after they had had a sexual encounter with her. According to one of the murderer's lawyers, the "discovery that he had unknowingly engaged in homosexual sex incited revulsion and rage in him" (Lee, 2008, p. 515). In a news article by Vicki Haddock (2004), the defense attorney in the case was quoted as saying, "This didn't occur because [perpetrator] had a bias. It happened because of what Eddie [Gwen's birth name] had done." The interpretation of their sexual encounter with Gwen as homosexual implies that Gwen was lying about who she *really* was, and therefore the violence was her fault. Another article about the murder claimed that Gwen had tricked the men into having sex with her, and that by not disclosing her transgender identity what she did was "just as bad as rape" (Calef, 2002, cited in Vade, 2005, p. 288).

The cultural image of transgender identity as deception is so pervasive and insidious that it has many times been effective in at least reducing the charges and sentences of those who have perpetrated violence against trans individuals simply for their being trans (Woods, Sears, & Mallory, 2016).

The image is one in which transgender individuals cannot be trusted. They are deviant, conniving liars. Supporters of the bathroom bills examined in chapter 1, aimed at preventing transgender people from using the restroom which most closely aligns with their gender identity, often invoke the transgender-identity-as-deception trope as an argument in their favor by claiming that the movement for transgender safety in restrooms is just about "men in dresses" who want to harass and assault women and children in women's rooms. Texas Senator, Ted Cruz, stated "men should not be going to the bathroom with little girls"[3] in support of laws requiring individuals to use the restroom that corresponds to the legal designation on their original birth certificate.

The image of transgender women as just men in dresses, lying for personal and immoral gain at the expense of others might be evoked in an early childhood classroom via an adult's credibility judgment of a young TGE child. Imagine Ahmed, assigned male, who usually plays and sits with the girls in the class, doesn't like rough and tumble games with boys, and wants to join the girls any time the class is divided by gender. A teacher who has been exposed to images of the deceptive transgender identity—where identity is just a disguise used for nefarious and possibly perverse goals—might subconsciously (or consciously) question Ahmed's motives for wanting to socialize with the girls. The credibility judgments made in observing Ahmed's behavior are unjustly deflated. Perceiving this behavior with heterosexual overtones, the teacher might scold Ahmed for always trying to flirt with the girls or for invading the girls' privacy when they are talking together. But if Ahmed actually just identifies more with the girls and with the ways the girls in the class socialize, the message received is that Ahmed has done something wrong and shameful—Ahmed's identity and affinity for female social interaction is, therefore, cast as wrong and shameful. This image also aligns with the "evil child" and "egocentric child" images examined already (Murris, 2018).

The second archetype that Serano (2016) describes—the pathetic trans woman—is similarly pervasive and works to undermine the credibility of transgender and gender expansive people, though from the side of competence rather than sincerity. The pathetic trans woman trope depicts a hopelessly masculine person with obvious beard stubble and over-the-top masculine mannerisms wearing an ill-fitting dress, bad wig, and poorly applied make-up. This trans person, as opposed to the deceptive trans person, is "generally considered harmless" (p. 38), as her failure to achieve any amount of believable femaleness proves she is not a real threat to the gender binary. This portrayal is "meant to demonstrate that, despite her desire to be female, she cannot change the fact that she is really and truly a man . . . the audience is encouraged to respect [her] as a person, but not as a woman" (p. 39). It is noteworthy that there are far fewer depictions of a pathetic trans man than a pathetic trans woman. There is nothing *pathetic* about a woman wanting to be a man if men are categorically superior under traditional sexism, but a man wanting to sacrifice his superiority to become a less-valuable woman is seen as just that—pathetic.

The pathetic trans woman archetype discredits transgender narratives by creating an image of a tragic boy or man who *desires* to be a girl or woman but sadly can never reach that dream because "his" body dictates who "he" will always be deep down. Whereas the deceptive transgender narrative reduces trans identities to lies, the pathetic transgender narrative reduces trans identities to *desires for the impossible*. The failure of the pathetic transgender person to enact their gender respectably paints an image that erodes any assessment of competence—thus limiting the credibility one can extend to this caricature.

Thinking back to José, who was spinning around in a dress and telling us "I'm a girl!" the image of the pathetic transgender person might be evoked in one's subconscious—viewing José in a way that might even elicit a hint of pity. "Poor José is always dressing up like a girl. He really just doesn't understand. He's going to have a hard time learning that he has to toughen up and act like a boy." This pathetic transgender image couples with the developing, ignorant, innocent, and fragile child images (Murris, 2018). José is treated as cute and sweet but is seen as not competent and is not taken seriously—not heard. If José was expressing a piece of self-knowledge in that moment, then José has experienced testimonial injustice proportional to how important that knowledge is to them.

Negative Cultural Images of Transgender People in Medical and Psychological Fields

Jack Drescher (2014) argues that the inclusion of transgender identities under various labels in the World Health Organization's *International Statistics Classification of Diseases* from the 1960s and the American Psychiatric Association's *Diagnostics and Statistics Manual* (DSM) from 1980, both to the present day, has created a stigmatized cultural image of transgender identities as a mental *disorder* or *illness*—a defect or dysfunction. The removal of homosexuality from the DSM-II in 1973 was shown to significantly reduce stigmatization and pathologization of nonhetero sexualities. A similar effort has been made to remove transgender identities from diagnostic references, but the requirement of a diagnosis to access medical interventions for gender transitions (e.g., hormone therapies, surgeries) has led to TGE narratives continuing to be pathologized, though the definitions have evolved considerably in the last few decades (Dresher, 2013).

The image of transgender individuals as mentally ill or disordered has a negative effect on the assessment of one's competence and therefore one's credibility. If associations are drawn to delusion or psychosis or other stigmatized mental health conditions, the transgender person may be seen as lacking touch with reality. In this image, trans identities and narratives become medicalized delusions. Indeed, "conversion" or "reparative" therapies to "cure" a transgender person by convincing them to live as and accept their assigned gender were the norm for many years, though they have now been banned in many places and proven to be extremely harmful to one's mental health (Ehrensaft, 2011, 2016b).

Negative Cultural Images of TGE Children and Youth

The medicalization and pathologization of transgender identities has not been restricted to adult transgender individuals. The DSM-5 (American Psychiatric Association, 2013), the most current version, includes the diagnosis of *gender dysphoria*—"a conflict between a person's physical or assigned gender and the gender with which he/she/they identify"—with different required criteria for children, adolescents, and adults. This diagnosis is a significant improvement on previous diagnoses in which TGE experiences were classified as identity disorders (Drescher, 2014). Since identity disorders are considered to be permanent, but gender dysphoria is described more as a temporary mental state, the image of being inherently defective or deficient is alleviated to some extent.

However, the description of gender dysphoria creates an image that has become quite common in discourses of TGE children and youth by using terms like "conflict" and "distress" (American Psychiatric Association, 2013). Olson-Kennedy and Tando (2018), both licensed social workers who work with transgender youth, express that it has long been a trend in the field of behavioral health to look for signs of distress in a TGE child before initiating some form of intervention, even if "intervention" means something as simple and impermanent as trying out different pronouns, clothing, or names for a child (Olson-Kennedy & Tando, 2018). Since one of the major driving factors for gender dysphoria remaining in the DSM at all is for transgender youth and adults to be able to access medical interventions using health insurance (Dresher, 2013), the criteria is written to establish a threshold far above the level at which early childhood teachers should be operating in their commitment to supporting children's needs.

The image of the transgender child or youth as being significantly distressed is pervasive—especially with assumptions that the child will act out, will be visibly angry or will be depressed (Olson-Kennedy & Tando, 2018). One mother of a transgender child told Tando she had brought her daughter to another counselor who would not diagnose her with gender dysphoria because she was not distressed enough. This lead Olson-Kennedy and Tando to ask the question, "How much distress is enough distress?" and, perhaps more importantly, do we want to force children into distress before we are willing to listen to them?

While the images of children and transgender people examined so far have directly discounted the speaker's sincerity or competence, this image works slightly differently by setting the bar for "sincerity" at *externally visible pain or distress*. Ehrensaft (2016b) advocates for a lower bar than distress, with her "motto of 'insistent, persistent, and consistent'" (p. 56) to distinguish between children who are just playing and exploring with gender and children who are likely to be transgender. In working with parents who are unsure whether their child is simply playing with expression or is actually identifying as a gender other than their assigned one, Ehrensaft (2016b) advises that transgender children are often *consistent* (showing gender expansive behaviors from very early ages and then continuing to do so), *insistent* (accompanying behaviors with early verbal declarations, "not just once in passing but over and over" [p. 57]), and *persistent* (not relenting in their gender expressions and identities in the face of cisnormative expectations and assumptions).

However, Tando (2018) remarks that the child who was denied a diagnosis of gender dysphoria had been *persistent* and *consistent* for five years prior to seeing that counselor. She just wasn't *insisting*. Children who internalize their distress and withdraw, rather than acting out and shouting loud, are not seen or heard as being distressed or *insistent* and can be overlooked by parents, teachers, and clinicians who think they are just "doing fine" (Olson-Kennedy & Tando, 2018). The parents of a transmasculine adult reflect back to their child about his gender presentation and lack of visible distress in early childhood and adolescence:

> *You never ACTED uncomfortable, so it must have been really difficult if you were uncomfortable to not show it, or if you did show it, we didn't pick up on it. We had two kids to watch, and you were good. We didn't have to pay too much attention to you. We had to worry about your brother with his depression. You never went through that. (Janelle, mother, cis woman, she/her)*

> *Looking back, you weren't really emotive. You kept to yourself a lot. You were the ideal child from the perspective that you came home, you did your homework, we never had to discipline you about anything. I never knew about the problems you had in high school. I don't think even mom knew because you kept it to yourself. What we saw was a quiet studious child who really didn't seem to have a hard time doing what we expected her to do. It wasn't until later that I realized there were issues. I wish I had been more observant to realize it. I don't know what I would have done but I would have spent more time talking to you about it. (George, father, cis man, he/him)*

Janelle and George knew their child hated girls' clothes and supported his agency in gender expression as much as they knew how. What they didn't know at the time was that their child *was* in distress and even considered suicide in high school. If the image of the transgender child requires visible distress or insistent messaging to be interpreted as sincere and not just "innocent child" playfulness, then transgender children who do not throw temper tantrums over gendered experiences, who do not insist, and who internalize and withdraw after the first time they are shamed are at great risk of experiencing persistent and systematic testimonial injustice. Their voices are softer and gentler to begin with, and they are likely to go completely unheard.

Do you have a message for teachers about how to welcome kids of all genders? (Luke, transgender preschool teacher, he/they)

Definitely listen to what kids tell you and help out if a kid needs help. (Tobble, seven years, he/him)

Cultural Images of Both Young Children and Transgender People as Less Than Fully Human

Both social categories—young children and transgender people—are, differently, viewed as less than fully human in common social discourses. These images undermine a TGE child's competence and deflate credibility judgments made about them. The image of children as "becomings" rather than "beings," as biologically incomplete adults-in-the-making who are dependent on adults for an expression of personal agency, is pervasive in privileged early childhood developmental theories and practice (Murris, 2013). How can someone make bold claims about their gender if they are not even a fully developed person yet?

Images of transgender people as less than human are many and varied, drawn by the insults routinely slung especially at those who do not *pass* as binary and/or cisgender. A YouTube video posted in June of 2016 by POPSUGAR Entertainment entitled *The Number of Transgender People Killed So Far in 2016 Will Make Your Heart Sink* shows the names and photos of some of the trans women of color who were murdered along with several chilling statistics about violence against the trans community.[4] In the comments posted on the video, the transgender people who are honored in it are called freaks, pedophiles, perverts, scumbags, abominations, degenerates, and shape shifting demons, just to name a few. The murder of transgender people is referred to as pest control, as heartwarming, and as deserved. Many commenters felt that the number was not nearly high enough.

[In] Boston, I was shooed out of the women's restroom. There was a lot—it was really hard. I was told point blank by a professor, "what are you doing in this program?" I was called "freak" by professors and told to get out of their classrooms. (Ikaika, trans and māhūkāne, he/him)

The images of transgender people as subhuman creatures who do not deserve to live are held consciously and openly by many people in western society, as evidenced by their willingness to make comments such as those mentioned above. Even without holding such beliefs consciously, the imagery can impact adults' ability to see the full humanity of a TGE child or, conversely, to imagine that a child they know and care for could be trans. How can someone whose life is valued as less than fully human be seen as competent and credible? How could a child who has already been embraced as fully human be one of *those* children?

THE HARMS OF TESTIMONIAL INJUSTICE

According to Fricker (2007), there are several types of harm that can be caused by testimonial injustice. There is the purely epistemic harm of knowledge offered and not received—damage done to the integrity of the shared knowledge base of the community in which testimonial injustice is happening. This is part of the way that hegemonic discourses are able to dominate the field of what counts as "truth"—precluding marginalized voices from contributing to public knowledge—and it leads to more testimonial injustices in the future, as the dominant narratives are fortified with every dissenter who is silenced. The more TGE voices in early childhood that go unheard, the more *unheard of* it will be for a two- or three-year-old to credibly claim a trans identity and live authentically outside of cisnormative discourses. However, the harms that are done directly to a child are the ones we will examine here, as they are the ones that teachers have the most opportunity to avoid.

To Fricker (2007), the primary harm of testimonial injustice is that the "subject is wronged in her capacity as a giver of knowledge" (p. 44). This harm is epistemic in nature—one's literal testimony is taken as unworthy of belief or trust or credibility. The message to the child is that they are somehow deficient in their capacity to *know*. When a child presents a piece of their knowledge and they are not heard, or worse, they are "corrected" and redirected, it can undermine their confidence in themself as a knower—one of the secondary harms of testimonial injustice (Fricker, 2007).

In a single instance of testimonial injustice, a child might lose confidence in the specific piece of knowledge they were attempting to share at the time (Fricker, 2007). Imagine two-year-old Noah, assigned male and identifying male, being drawn to a pair of shiny pink leggings in a store and taking them off a shelf to show his father. Noah's father says, "Put those down. Those are for girls." Noah, who trusts his father, is forced to contemplate the dissonance he is left with—"I am a boy who likes pink leggings, but pink leggings are for girls." Of the two things Noah thinks he knows—that he is a boy and that he likes leggings—he is more confident of the former, and he has had lots of reinforcement about his being a boy so far in his life. So if he is to trust his father, Noah might start to lose confidence in his knowledge of himself as someone who likes shiny pink leggings and wants to express himself by wearing clothing like that.

Fricker (2007) notes that "Many definitions and conceptions of knowledge cast some sort of epistemic confidence as a condition of knowledge" (p. 49). That is to say, if Noah loses enough confidence in knowing that he likes pink leggings, he ceases to *know* that he likes them. He might *want* to like them, or *remember* liking them before, but if he isn't confident at all, he can't really *know* that he likes pink leggings. A piece of knowledge is lost.

Now consider the case of persistent and systematic testimonial injustice owing to negative identity-based prejudices, which reduce other's credibility judgments for a given person, which is the central case as defined by Fricker (2007). A TGE young child is both a gender transgressor and a very young child everywhere they go and is likely to evoke the negative images examined in this chapter in many adults on many occasions throughout their earliest years. They are at a high risk of experiencing frequent testimonial injustices, especially in regards to their attempts to communicate about their gender, as those interactions will evoke both cultural images of young children and of transgender people more broadly. The subject of such a repetitive undermining of their capacity as a sharer of knowledge "may lose confidence in her general intellectual abilities to such an extent that she is genuinely hindered in her educational or other intellectual development" (Fricker, 2007, pp. 47–48). Fricker (2007) notes that this kind of prolonged attack on one's intellectual confidence can have far ranging and lifelong ramifications.

One of the most salient ways that this erosion of epistemic confidence can manifest is in its interference with the process of knowledge construction which Bernard Williams (2002) calls *steadying the mind*. Steadying the mind, according to Williams, begins not with something known already, but with a wish. He notes, "It is far from being true that every thought swimming around in one's mind is already the content of a belief as opposed to some other mental state such as a guess, a fancy, or (very importantly) a wish" (p. 82). In this process, Williams posits that our wishes are often uncommitted in their destinations until they are tried and tested through conversations with trusted others, in which we have an interest in being trusted as well, where they may be sorted roughly into beliefs or desires. While interacting with someone we trust and wanting to maintain that trusting relationship, we are motivated to express things which we *believe* to be true, whether or not we *know* them to be true yet. To Williams (2002), we are all constantly in the process of trying wishes out on one another, receiving feedback regarding what we can give a trusted other to believe, so that we can believe it ourselves

Hal, 3, is playing by himself in a sandbox. Luke, a teacher, sits nearby. "I'm a kitten," Hal suddenly announces. Luke responds, "Hello kitty." Hal pauses, then continues: "I'm a flying kitten." The teacher replies, "Ah, a flying kitten." After another pause, Hal adds, "I'm a flying kitten named Felix." The teacher smiles. Hal is often a flying kitten named Felix. "I'm a flying kitten named Felix who's a girl. A girl kitten." Hal looks up at his teacher, a grin spreading wide across his face. Luke smiles back and comments, "I see. You're a girl kitten named Felix. How do you fly?" Hal lifts his elbows: "See my wings?"—and flies off (cited in Pastel et al., 2019)

In this scenario, Hal is engaging in the process of steadying the mind, testing wishes out on Luke to see what things might be possible in this interaction. By listening, smiling, and reflecting Hal's wishes back to Hal, Luke has indicated that, in this space, Hal is welcome to be a girl kitten named Felix who can fly. There may be other interactions where Luke asks Hal not to be a kitten or not to fly. Williams (2002) argues that those wishes that are truly impossible are bound to remain mere wishes. Wishes that are possible, but require some amount of commitment, may become desires. Beliefs, however, are "answerable to the world" (p. 134). That is, one must find them to be not just possible someday or somehow, but already true in some way that is convincing to the believer. This could mean believing that a ball covered by a cup still exists even when it is not visible because it is there when the cup is removed again, or it could mean believing in a higher power because of the symmetrical beauty one sees in a single leaf. As Williams (2002) notes, there is a social interest in finding some agreement on what is believable, and so testing wishes on trusted others is one way of seeing if they are convincing enough to be believed.

Hal's wishes to be a kitten and to fly will be tested both by whether any trusted others can be made to believe in them and also by their demonstrable possibility in the world. It is unlikely Hal will end up believing that he is literally a kitten or that he can fly (at least in the way imagined above). Hal's other two wishes, though—being a girl and being named Felix—*are* possible outside of hegemonic cisgender narratives. Luke's response to Hal can be affirming—conveying that these wishes *are* worldly possible, and it is only Hal's motivations and internal leanings that will determine whether they become desires or beliefs or are left as mere wishes. Or Luke's response can be one of testimonial injustice—unjustly reducing his credibility judgment of Hal's declarations due to privileged cisnormative discourses and prejudiced images of young children and TGE people, and by doing so, strongly discouraging Hal's wishes from becoming beliefs.

Williams (2002) argues that steadying the mind is not just how we come to generate knowledge about the world, but it is a fundamental process by which we come to know and generate knowledge about ourselves and how we fit in to certain social categories or identities. By learning from and with trusted others about the ways in which people relate to and associate with each other, we steady our sense of self in a way that fits within the available social categories. Fricker (2007) argues that persistent and systematic testimonial injustices interfering with one's process of steadying the mind undermines one's ability to form authentic social identities.

Imagine Luke had responded differently to Hal. Let's say Luke allowed for Hal to be a flying kitten named Felix, but then said, "You can be a kitten, Felix, but you are a boy." Then imagine all of Hal's trusted others—parents, friends, other teachers, grandparents—had responded similarly by making it clear that Hal's wish of associating with the social category of "girl" was not considered by trusted social others as worldly possible. Hal's confidence in even the *possibility* of knowing or believing themselves to be a girl is eroded each time Hal is not offered credibility in claiming the identity of "girl." Indeed, the relegation of transgender narratives to the realm of wishes and desires is present in the negative cultural images of transgender people and in the upholding of the sex-gender distinction—painting the flawed image of *sex* as worthy of belief, but *gender* as a tragically fanciful wish (the "pathetic" trans person) or a desire that is fundamentally a lie (the "deceptive" trans person).

So Fricker's (2007) primary harm of testimonial injustice—being wronged in one's capacity as a giver of knowledge—can result in further secondary harms. Specifically, the person offering knowledge can literally lose that piece of knowledge if they are not afforded enough credibility to maintain confidence in what they know. They can also suffer prolonged deterioration of their epistemic confidence more broadly, if testimonial injustice is persistent and systematic. And the final epistemic form of harm from testimonial injustice is that the child can be marginalized in their capacity to form authentic and empowering social identities.

Fricker (2007) argues that another type of secondary harm is caused by testimonial injustice because one's capacity as a knower is essential to one's value as a human. So, to be wronged in one's capacity as a knower is to be dehumanized. Fricker (2007) claims that when a testimonial injustice occurs, "what the person suffers from is not simply the epistemic wrong itself, but also the meaning of being treated like that" (p. 44). To unjustly judge a person as not credible or trustworthy in their efforts to share knowledge, and particularly their efforts to share knowledge about themself, is to treat that person as less than fully human. Fricker (2007) claims that this kind of dehumanization can be profoundly humiliating, especially if witnessed by others, even if the underlying epistemic harm is relatively minor.

Shame researcher Brené Brown (2015) defines shame as "the intensely painful feeling or experience of believing that we are flawed and therefore unworthy of love or belonging" (p. 69). The child who is precluded from forming one or more social identities in a way that is authentic, and who is treated in a manner that undermines their humanity, is likely to experience a sense of shame. Brown (2007) believes that "many of our early shame experiences, especially with parents and caregivers, [are] stored in our brains as traumas" (p. 89), including small and quiet everyday experiences of shame. When young children have traumatic experiences in their earliest years, and they do not have supportive relationships with adults who can buffer their stress (as many times it is their adult caregivers who are the *source* of the stress), the impacts can be significant and lifelong. When children endure repetitive, persistent, and significant stressors—for example, being continually misgendered by adults and peers in all communication and interactions on a daily basis—the impact can lead to alterations in the very neural tissue and architecture of their growing brains and impair their ability to learn and pay attention, to cope with daily stressors, and to self-regulate their emotions and behavior, consequences that can endure throughout their lives (Nicholson, Kurtz, & Perez, 2018; Perry, Pollard, Blakely, Baker, & Vigilante, 1995; Schore, 2003). Further, when very young children experience trauma, as they grow up they often feel the trauma was their fault. This can lead them to develop an internal narrative of self-doubt and shame where they tell themselves that they are not lovable.

> Children who have been harmed in the context of a relationship can only be healed in a relationship. You will never truly change a child's heart without first establishing a relationship of trust and unconditional acceptance. (Sorrels, 2015, p. 48)

If there is persistent and systematic testimonial injustice that is specifically related to a child's expressions and communications about gender (or even just one memorable instance), we believe that the shame a child experiences can be internalized in a way that is significantly detrimental to one's gender health and emotional health overall and can result in a child hiding their authentic gender from others, and possibly from themselves. Steele (2016) completed a Participatory Action Research study with three other TGE adults, reflecting on personal experiences of gender in childhood together and in personal journals, as well as by contacting family members to ask about their experiences of participants' gender during childhood. The most prominent themes to emerge from the study were of shame and hiding, beginning in participants' earliest memories. Persistent testimonial injustice, which dehumanizes TGE children, could work to create and/or exacerbate these feelings in young TGE children, forcing them to internalize shame about their genders and to live inauthentically by hiding who they are.

PATH TO TESTIMONIAL JUSTICE

The path to testimonial justice for TGE children begins first with a radical commitment to trust children even, and perhaps especially, when we feel uncomfortable or uncertain about the direction their gender journey is going. The process of uncovering our biases, reflecting on our own privileged and marginalized intersectional social categories, and learning to *hear* the voices we have historically not heard is continuous, and dramatic change in our subconscious behaviors will not happen overnight. In this section, we present three practical strategies for beginning to avoid incidents of testimonial injustice for the children in our care.

Epistemic Resistance and Counterstories

One thing we can do immediately on starting our path to testimonial justice for TGE children is to reflect on the stories that do and do not get told in our classrooms and environments, the images that are and are not visible. As noted in *Anti-Bias Education*, "What children do *not* see in the classroom teaches children as much as what they do see" (Derman-Sparks & Olsen Edwards, 2010, p. 43). By intentionally introducing empowering picture books, persona dolls, images, and other representations of a diversity of genders that specifically and openly include transgender individuals, intersex individuals, and people who do not fit the gender binary, we resist allowing cisgender narratives to become normalized and hegemonic in our classroom culture.

In introducing counterstories and TGE narratives, it is important to be intentional and thoughtful about which stories to introduce and how. Pastel (2018) offers several points to consider in selecting gender expansive children's literature. He notes that some available children's literature depicting TGE characters focuses only on storylines of bullying and struggle. We do not need to assume a fragile child image by withholding these stories from children, but it is important to balance these stories out such that *most* of the narratives that depict TGE characters focus on the positive aspects of gender diversity and show characters who are given agency over their gender identities, expressions, and the language used for them. Otherwise, the TGE narrative may become synonymous in children's minds with the narrative of bullying and struggle.

Pastel (2018) recommends looking for literature that *meaningfully* portrays characters with gender identities, expressions, and bodies that transgress binary gender norms as well as revealing other intersecting social identities and categories—body sizes, skin color, abilities, family culture, and so forth. Similar principles can be used in seeking visual imagery (e.g., pictures, videos) to expose children to TGE narratives. Additionally, books should have strong plots (that are not only about gender), resist stereotypes, and should have other characteristics that make for quality children's literature in general (e.g., compelling imagery and rich language) (Pastel, 2018). Persona dolls can also be used to explore gender actively with children, to work through questions and topics that arise in the class and among the children, and to give depth to TGE characters and their intersecting identities. Bringing these counterstories into the learning environment creates more space for children to confidently use their own voices to express and explore gender in new ways.

Caution should be taken to avoid the pitfalls of what Derman-Sparks and Olsen Edwards call *tourist curriculum* or "a teaching approach to diversity that visits 'other' people's ways of life—that is, ways that differ from the dominant culture" (p. 48). These pitfalls are *tokenism* (using a single image or story to represent all TGE people), *trivializing* (reducing the diversity and variety in the TGE community to a narrow view of gender expansiveness, such as pronouns), *misinforming/misrepresenting* (offering inaccurate, outdated, or inauthentic representations of TGE people, such as suggesting that all trans people feel as though they were "born in the wrong body" and will need surgery), and *stereotyping* (depicting all TGE people as the same and in negative, exaggerated, and/or dehumanizing ways) (Derman-Sparks & Olsen Edwards, 2010). Curriculum that falls into these pitfalls, or that introduces TGE lives as a brief departure from the norms of daily routines to learn about "other" people, will do little to sensitize children or adults to the marginalized experiences of TGE people. In fact, it may do even more harm, as it further "normalizes" dominant cisgender narratives and experiences (Derman-Sparks & Olsen Edwards, 2010).

Finally, teachers need to consider their own need to hear diverse and resistant counterstories of transgender and gender expansive people. Seeking books, documentaries, articles, blogs, and vlogs can be relatively accessible ways to find authentic transgender voices sharing about their experiences. Teachers can also seek out professional development opportunities that focus on gender diversity. Intentionally seeking out voices of those with markedly different experiences from our own increases our exposure to, and hopefully comfort with, epistemic friction. As Medina (2013) reminds us, epistemic resistance and counterstories "enable subjects and communities to detect and sensitize themselves to their blind spots and shared self-ignorance" (p. 176). By becoming more attuned and sensitive to TGE narratives in all arenas of our lives, we will become more attuned and sensitive to the voices of TGE children, and less likely to miss or dismiss the knowledge they share with us.

I would always stop and look at the ties, I was obsessed with ties. And I don't know if my grandmother—if it was because we would watch a lot of Marlene Dietrich films together or other German films from the 30s and 40s, but I remember obsessing over this Mossimo tie of all things, I still have it to this day. And my grandmother caught me looking at these ties when I was like thirteen and she goes, "Do you really like that?" And I said "Yes," I said, "It's really beautiful but it's very expensive." Cause we didn't have much money and it was a little bit pricier of a tie, I think it was like fifteen dollars or something. And my grandmother goes, "then I'll buy it for you." And I was so gracious and we get to the checkout line and my mother comes up and goes, "What's this tie doing here? That's not dad's style," referring to my grandfather, and my grandmother just said, "This is for Anna." And my mom threw this fit in the middle of the checkout area, "I can't believe you're wearing c—why would you want to wear a tie? I can't believe that you'd want to do this. Why are you doing this to me?" She became incredibly dramatic, and my grandmother turned to my mother in German and just said, "Hold your tongue, I'm buying the tie and that's it," and gave this look to my mother, like she was my age being put in her place. And I wore that tie in my high school graduation, I wore it to every single big event, I still have it, I still wear it, you know. It was a moment of being seen and heard. And this was before I think I had gender really worked out."(Ikaika, trans and māhūkāne, he/him)

Consciously Adjusting Our Credibility Judgments

Since our processes of making credibility judgments of others typically happen below the level of consciousness, we must consciously practice intervening in those judgments (Fricker, 2007). As we work to increase our own exposure to diverse gender voices and narratives, to sensitize and attune ourselves to authentic TGE experiences, and to uncover the negative cultural images of young children and TGE people which have affected our credibility ratings in the past, we cannot assume our subconscious processes will automatically adjust. We must actively practice noticing when we seem to be deflating a credibility judgment for a child, whether in the moment or in mindful reflection afterwards. Then, Fricker (2007) argues, we must actively, consciously, and intentionally adjust our credibility judgment upwards. She notes, "There can be no algorithm for [one] to use in determining how much it should be revised upwards, but there is a clear guiding ideal. The guiding ideal is to neutralize any negative impact of prejudice in one's credibility judgments by compensating upwards to reach the degree of credibility that would have been given were it not for the prejudice" (Fricker, 2007, p. 92). Recalling gender fluid Oak, from chapter 1, and one of his teachers, David:

As a staff, people were at different places in their ability to handle a gender fluid child. David is in his mid-fifties, cisgender, and had the hardest time with it—I remember one statement he made about how it was hard to call Oak "she" when he was always playing with his penis!

David was not viewing Oak's requests to be called "she" with credibility because his idea of gender and pronouns was informed by the gender binary and assumptions about bodies. He may have been affected by some of the negative cultural images of children, imagining Oak to be ignorant of the "facts" about gender or just still developing and in need of guidance. To support Oak better, David would need to acknowledge the fact that he was not extending complete trust to Oak and to work each day to find ways to offer Oak as much trust and credibility as he could. This exercise takes practice and must follow Medina's (2013) principles of a commitment to the nonideal:

1. *Particularism*—David's efforts to *hear* Oak need to be focused on the particular needs Oak is expressing. What types of communication does Oak use that David has the hardest time hearing? How much does Oak *want* to be believed and taken seriously?
2. *Empiricism/fallibilism*—David must make efforts to adjust his credibility judgments and then respond to feedback from Oak by noticing what strengthens the trust between them and what makes Oak withdraw or rebel.
3. *Meliorism*—David must commit to doing *better* to trust and support Oak, without getting stuck worrying about how to do it perfectly.

The strategy of consciously intervening in our credibility judgments of children requires critical self-reflection, planned ways of responding to children who we realize we have a hard time *hearing*, and a willingness to engage in a process of trial and error with the child to achieve a greater degree of attunement and, therefore, testimonial justice. The mindful reflection process introduced in chapter 1 can be very helpful for teachers to anchor this strategy to a cycle of observation and reflection.

Emergent Listening

In her 2014 book, *Listening to Children: Being and Becoming*, Bronwyn Davies describes her concept of *emergent listening* as not just being open to hearing and learning about a child's perspective, but "being open to being affected" (p. 1). When one engages in emergent listening, one comes out the other side of the interaction as a different person than who they were before—they are changed by listening to others. According to Davies (2014), emergent listening differs from what she calls *listening-as-usual* which is about listening to categorize what is heard into what is already known. Listening-as-usual, as implied in the name, is the typical state that one occupies in day-to-day life, and not unreasonably. Much of the information one receives and processes in a day is not revelatory (e.g., information about the weather, pleasantries with coworkers) and can be reasonably processed using what one already knows and by employing one's standard subconscious tactics of credibility judgment. However, when that mode of listening becomes the only mode one employs, learning and growth and creativity are stifled, and open-mindedness becomes impossible (Davies, 2014).

> *Mostly I liked when they're calling me by the pronouns I was hoping that people would. Yeah, it made me happy. (Oak, eight years, answering "what made me feel supported" in preschool)*

Davies (2014) recognizes that, because listening-as-usual is dependent on utilizing relatively stable ways of thinking and understanding that have been cultivated in the hearer, emergent listening "involves working, to some extent, against oneself, and against those habitual practices through which one establishes 'this is who I am'" (p. 21). In the context of testimonial injustice, this can include challenging the negative identity-prejudicial stereotypes and images that have taken hold in one's conception of their own self-identity.

In his work with Oak, David might have to reflect on his own conception of himself as a man. If his idea of maleness is deeply invested in anatomy, Oak's expressions of femininity and usage of "she" and "her" while having a body that David sees as male might challenge David's own construction of himself. He may have to pause and ask himself, "If my body doesn't make me a man, then what does?" or "What does it mean to me to have anatomy like mine? And what parts of my identity does my body inform?" If David has never thought deeply about his own gender constellation, then he may learn something about himself by listening *emergently* to Oak. If David enters into interactions with Oak unprepared or unwilling to learn anything or change any of his beliefs about gender and/or young children, he risks creating situations of testimonial injustice for Oak by using listening-as-usual practices that will reproduce cisnormative narratives and silence Oak's voice.

We cannot help but enter into encounters with others carrying all of our past experiences, understandings, assumptions, prejudices, and bodies of knowledge with us. However, we can actively and consciously enter into encounters with others with a willingness to leave those encounters having been changed by them. According to Davies (2014), emergent listening "means opening up the ongoing possibility of coming to see life, and one's relation to it, in new and surprising ways. Emergent listening might begin with what is known, but it is open to creatively evolving into something new" (p. 21). David might begin by reflecting on how he relates to his own body, and then, by listening emergently to Oak, discover that there are other ways one might relate to their body even if they have a body similar to David's.

Importantly, Davies (2014) notes, young children are often already engaged in emergent listening, as they are dynamically and creatively and seriously exploring and discovering the world around them. In fact, it is the assumption of an educational space that children (or students) arrive in the space willing to leave having learned something (or having been changed/affected). If teachers are affected by the cultural image of the teacher-child relationship as knowledge giver to knowledge receiver, then the child might be the only one in the interaction who is willing to learn. If a cisgender teacher interacts with a TGE young child about gender, and only the child is listening emergently, then only the child will leave the encounter changed. If that teacher enters that encounter carrying only cisgender ways of understanding gendered experiences and images of TGE children that are not empowering, it is unlikely that the child will be changed in a way that is supportive of their gender health.

Teachers must practice emergent listening *with* children, allowing all parties to learn from and affect one another in whatever empowering ways *emerge* in the interaction. They must be attentive during those interactions to the credibility judgments they are making, and work against the subconscious impact of negative cultural images of young children and TGE people on their credibility judgments as children explore and communicate about gender. We must radically trust young children as they provide testimony to their lived experiences, their assessments of the galaxy of gender, and their ways of identifying themselves within it.

NOTES

1. We use terms like *voice*, *speaker*, and *hearer* in this text, as they are the terms used by the scholars we draw from. However, we want to recognize two significant limitations to this terminology when interpreted in a limited way—the erasure of D/deaf and mute individuals and the exclusion of the many ways that very young children can communicate nonverbally. All uses of terms related to voice, language, communicating, and hearing are intended to be interpreted broadly to include all forms of communication between people.

2. The word "transsexual" has fallen largely out of favor in the trans community. It is not generally used in this book, as it has a history of being used to distinguish trans bodies from trans identities via the sex-gender binary. However, it is the word that Julia Serano uses to describe herself, and it is used here to honor her agency in self-identifying.

3. See: https://talkingpointsmemo.com/livewire/ted-cruz-supports-hb2-north-carolina.

4. See: https://www.youtube.com/watch?v=NmjFC6ES7bc&t=1s.

Chapter 4

Hermeneutical (In)justice

Rendering Lived Experience as Visible Truth for Young Children

We did a three-part collaborative inquiry [in response to a trans student] where we had about twenty minutes per staff meeting over three staff meetings. [At the first meeting, we explored our own genders. At the second meeting, we talked about the student. I started by sharing observations.] One of my observations was that we were all noticing that she felt more comfortable wearing "girls' clothes." She liked wearing dresses, she liked wearing heels and makeup, she really had like a high femme presentation that she was going for. She had long hair. She would also have a hard time putting on clothes that weren't gender affirming in those ways. So, if she got dirty or had an accident or something and there wasn't something that was pink or purple or a dress she didn't want to wear it and she would get really like resistant and emotional about it. I said, "Ziggy, do you like when people call you he or she?" And she said, "yes." But also she lit up. It never occurred to her that [choice of pronouns] was something she could ask for, that it would be respected. I could tell that "she" being added to the equation felt really good to Ziggy . . . and I just watched Ziggy's face light up when I used female pronouns for her. So then I had a conversation with Ziggy to ask if she wanted me to talk to other teachers about using "she." That got her really excited.

(Toby, transgender preschool
teacher, he/him in conversation
with Ziggy, four years, she/her)

In order for testimonial injustice that is based in negative images of gender-expansive people to occur, a child must at least try to communicate about their gender in a way that is intelligible to the hearer. The child's behavior must be able to evoke those negative images in the subconscious mind of whomever they are trying to talk to or reach. But what happens if a child can't even begin to make sense of what they are experiencing because they have been given no words, no images, no stories, no role models, no icons, no songs, no picture books, no cartoons, no shared social contexts, and no other tools of understanding and interpreting their experiences to be able to grasp what they are thinking and feeling about gender? When a child is so utterly at a loss in trying to understand their gendered experiences that they are unable to even attempt to communicate about those experiences, or their attempts to communicate are unintelligible or uninterpretable to those around them, they are experiencing *hermeneutical injustice*.

> To put it simply, I feel like a girl trapped in a boy's body, and I've felt that way ever since I was 4. I never knew there was a word for that feeling, nor was it possible for a boy to become a girl, so I never told anyone and I just continued to do traditionally "boyish" things to try to fit in. When I was 14, I learned what transgender meant and cried of happiness. After 10 years of confusion I finally understood who I was. (Suicide note of Leelah Alcorn, seventeen, transgender girl, she/her [Alcorn, 2014])

HERMENEUTICAL INJUSTICE: HAVING NO WORDS TO SHOUT OR MIRRORS TO SEE ONESELF

"[H]ermeneutics is the art of understanding and of making oneself understood" (Zimmermann, 2015, p. 2). As a formal field of philosophy, hermeneutics is often concerned with the interpretation of texts, especially religious and legal texts, but it is also about everyday understandings and interpretations. There is nothing about a yellow equilateral triangle with one corner pointing down that inherently means "danger" or "warning." That meaning has been culturally bestowed, and when someone from a culture where warning signs are displayed on such yellow triangles sees one of those signs and knows there is some kind of hazard in the area, they are employing hermeneutical tools of interpretation to come to that understanding.

Hermeneutical tools are the means through which we come to understand our lives, our social relations, and our worlds and the means through which we share our understandings of those things with each other. Drawing on Heidegger, Zimmermann (2015) claims that "language is not a tool to name objects in the world but the very lens through which we understand the world and ourselves" (p. 37). When *language* is understood to include not just verbal expression, literal stories and narratives, and discreet words but the "hundred languages of children" (Malaguzzi, 1994)—drawing, dancing, smiling, crying, tactile exploration, painting, play, and more—our working definition of *hermeneutical tools* is then all the forms of language and representation which are used in making internal sense of our lives in a shared social context, in making shared sense of ourselves to others, and in making sense of others within ourselves.

All of the cultural images examined in chapter 3 are examples of hermeneutical tools—means of understanding young children and TGE people—and specifically, they are hermeneutical tools which have been asymmetrically shaped by cisgender adults as evidenced by their negative ways of perceiving young TGE children. The interpretation of a child making eye contact with an adult speaker as a sign of respect is a hermeneutical tool which privileges Western ways of understanding and representing respect, whereas the interpretation of a child averting their eyes as a form of respect is a hermeneutical tool that has been marginalized and colonized in much of Western society.

When a child puts on a tiara and another child calls them a princess, the first child might smile because that's what they wanted to convey. Since they both know stories about princesses wearing tiaras, the tiara is interpreted and endowed with shared social meaning drawing on those stories. If two children want to "play house" by pretending to be adults doing day-to-day things at home, they may come to that imaginative exercise with different ideas of what happens in a house or a home because their families and home lives may be very different. They may need to negotiate a shared understanding of what the scene will be, who will play what role, and how they will interact together. While they may have to work to find or create shared understandings on which to build their dramatic play, they are both drawing on narratives they share with their respective families or communities and their interpretations and understandings of what they experience where they live.

However, when certain social groups have more power to create and disseminate hermeneutical tools that are relevant to them and their experiences than other groups, an imbalance of social understanding is formed (Fricker, 2007). Sometimes this imbalance is so great that certain social groups have so few hermeneutical resources that they are left trying to understand their experiences through the lens of the dominant group's narratives and images, which are inherently inadequate for understanding that marginalized group's unique experiences (Fricker, 2007; Medina, 2013). As cisnormative and heteronormative discourses are privileged and majoritized, they "systematize and frame" how we interpret and make meaning out of gendered behaviors, interactions, signifiers, and representations (Foucault, 1980; MacNaughton, 2005, p. 20), while leaving transgender and gender-expansive ways of understanding and interpreting out of view and out of general circulation. Let's revisit Jen's experiences of being told that playing with dolls would make him gay:

If anything, you would have thought that like . . . I don't know, Barbies are like the epitome of the female form or whatever, and that should be encouraged to be like "Yeah!" but no, they were like "Here, play with these WWE toys" like with these jacked dudes. (Jen, twenty-four, nonbinary, she/he/they)

Heteronormative and cisnormative ways of interpreting and making meaning out of a TGE child's expressions, behaviors, identities, usage of language, explorations, and experiences will inevitably misconstrue and distort that child's lived realities and truths. Without knowledge of and sensitivity to counternarratives that might interpret Jen's playing with Barbies as a healthy exploration of gender expansiveness and femininity rather than a warning sign of possible homosexuality and disordered gender development, an adult working with her would be hermeneutically insensitive (Medina, 2013) or unable to understand Jen's narratives in ways that are authentic to Jen. Without a way of understanding Jen, they might not be able to empathize with the shame she might feel by having a heteronormative and cisnormative interpretation overlaid on her experience and understanding of herself.

Hermeneutical injustice exists when there is a gap in a society's, culture's, community's or classroom's collective hermeneutical resources or shared tools of social interpretation (e.g., stories, role models, personal dolls, terminology, and images), and that gap exists in just exactly the place where a marginalized group's unique experiences lie (Fricker, 2007). The effect of this hermeneutical gap is that it, "prevents them in particular from making sense of an experience which it is strongly in their interests to render intelligible" (Fricker, 2007, p. 7). Fricker (2007) argues that there may be times in which there is a hermeneutical gap that doesn't rise to the level of injustice but could be described as epistemic bad luck. She offers an example of someone who suffers from a disease which has not yet been discovered—leaving that person and their doctors unable to explain or treat the symptoms. This person is certainly hermeneutically disadvantaged, as it is in their best interest for there to be an explanation for their condition, a way of understanding their experience. However, a hermeneutical *injustice* is present when the gap in collective hermeneutical resources stems from identity-based prejudices and the relative powerlessness of particular social groups in contributing to collective hermeneutical resources in the first place (Fricker, 2007)—for example, if the disease described above primarily affects an economically disadvantaged social group that is underrepresented in the medical and legal fields and has, therefore, received little scientific attention or research funding.

In the quotation at the start of this chapter, Leelah Alcorn described finally understanding who she was simply by being given a word for her experience. Until that point, she had struggled to anchor her experiences in any kind of shared understanding or interpretation of gender that she had been given access to, and so she had settled for an ill-fitting understanding of who she was that was based in how other people understood her—as a boy. Similar to William's (2002) concept of steadying the mind, one can often only make sense of something if it can be put in a shared social context. It wasn't until Leelah was given a word, a signifier, a name for her experience that allowed her to communicate it to others that she was truly able to understand herself.

> *I definitely identified with a tomboy identity as a gender. I think I learned that word from my grandmother. I heard my mother use it in a negative way—and my grandmother just said, "Oh it's just a matter of fact," you know, without that kind of stigma attached to it. And I think I was probably six, maybe seven. . . . Later I used it for myself. Probably when I was around eight—when I tried to play on the playground, like at recess and stuff, I remember wanting to play a version of football or murder ball and the boys being like, "You can't play you're a girl." And I'm like, "No, but I'm a tomboy. It's okay" and they're like, "Yeah, okay I guess." (Ikaika, trans and māhūkāne, he/him)*

For Ikaika, the signifier of "tomboy" gave access to a new shared social understanding of how one can be a girl. A girl who was a *tomboy* was held to different social expectations and, importantly, had different kinds of social identity power—accessing a space that otherwise excluded girls—than a girl who was not a *tomboy*. The *tomboy* signifier also came with the potential for social stigma, which Ikaika was entirely cognizant of, as he was able to recall feeling a negative connotation from his mother but a neutral nonchalance from his grandmother. Ikaika was able to evaluate both the social benefits and risks of being understood as a *tomboy* and came to understand himself that way at that point in his life because it fit better than just being signified as *girl*.

If one is given no words or images or other tools to use in interpreting and understanding their experiences, they may be effectively unable to do so (Fricker, 2007). Moreover, if one is struggling to even comprehend their experience internally, they are very unlikely to be able to communicate about it effectively to someone else, and especially to someone who does not share those same experiences. As Medina (2013) points out, "It is not the same to try to make sense of one's experience to oneself, to others within one's group or in the same predicament, or to others who do not share the experience in question. And when it comes to hermeneutical gaps, it is crucial to pay attention to the communicative processes in which subjects *struggle to make sense to themselves* of what they cannot yet communicate to others, especially to those others who do not share their predicament" (p. 98). In this quote, Medina is shedding light on the particular difficulty experienced by an individual, whose marginalized experience is not yet fully understood even to themselves, trying to communicate about that experience to someone who cannot relate, let alone comprehend.

Without a signifier like *tomboy* Ikaika would have struggled to convince the boys to let him in to their games. Being understood by them to be a girl, he was, by their rules, not allowed. Ikaika may have tried to express being a different kind of girl: "No, but I'm . . . like . . . different. I'm kinda like a boy, you know? It's okay." A *tomboy* is a signifier with a shared social meaning, whereas Ikaika's struggle to make meaning of his gender—which he himself was still trying to understand—could easily be laughed off by a group of cisgender boys who have never struggled to understand their genders. "Eww! Does that mean you have a penis? A girl with a penis! That's gross! Haha!" A cisgender adult listening in might tell the boys they have to let a *girl* play, but they are unlikely to interpret Ikaika's belabored attempt at expressing an affinity with maleness for what it is.

Cisgender individuals have had their own privileged and majoritized experiences of gender validated as "truths" and as common-sense knowledge for their entire lives. As listeners, cisgender adults have few hermeneutical resources to call on to assist a TGE child in rendering their gender-expansive experiences intelligible in empowering ways. Instead, they are left with their own cisgender ways of understanding to interpret the child's attempts at communication. Conversely, a TGE child working to express their experiences of gender to a transgender adult is likely to find greater ease in developing shared language and effective modes of communicating that are affirming of the child.

A young TGE child attempting to communicate about their gender to a cisgender adult may struggle in ways that make the child seem confused, conflicted, or otherwise ignorant about gender (as interpreted by the cisgender adult) as a result of the child not having access to any gender-expansive language, role models, imagery, narratives, or other tools of understanding gender beyond the binary. This kind of muddled attempt at communicating can then result in a hermeneutical injustice being compounded by a testimonial injustice, as the person they are trying to communicate with would likely deem them to be incompetent on the subject and therefore not credible (Fricker, 2007; Medina, 2013).

We will follow Marcel and Grace, from our mindful reflection example, for a while to see hermeneutical injustice in action. Marcel often expressed a desire to be a mother and would pretend to be pregnant, and this imaginative play was frequently discredited and discouraged by Grace, the teacher. Marcel's own understanding, or understanding-in-the-making, of that imaginative play is unknown. Marcel may have been using *mother* and *father* as signifiers and representations of femininity and masculinity, drawing on the narratives of their home life and their role models of female and male identities. When Marcel says, "Yes I can be a mother. I don't want to be a father. No fair!," they might be saying they don't want to grow up to be a man in the same ways their own father enacts masculinity. Perhaps Marcel is trying to imagine other ways to be male and masculine or a way to be a feminine male. Or perhaps Marcel is exploring a female identity by playing female roles in imaginative play. There are countless gender-expansive interpretations of Marcel's behavior. However, by being fixed on an interpretation of *mother* that is tied to a binary understanding of gender as dictated by one's body and the perceived physiological impossibility of Marcel becoming pregnant, Grace interprets Marcel's behavior as being ignorant or confused about bodies and gender, and she feels compelled to "correct" Marcel's play and "teach" Marcel a hegemonic cisgender understanding of femaleness and motherhood and of Marcel's immutable positionality as a boy. It is only through critical reflection that Grace is able to pause and consider alternative interpretations of Marcel's play, asking herself what the behaviors might mean *to Marcel*.

Marcel isn't able to elaborate much on wanting to be a mother, aside from saying that Grace's perspective was not fair. Not having the right tools to understand and express what one is going through (e.g., not knowing any TGE people, stories, or vocabulary), or using tools that are not understood or respected by dominant discourse (e.g., Marcel's use of imaginative play to challenge certain conceptions of gender), can result in one being misunderstood, dismissed, redirected, and offered alternate explanations that don't authentically represent one's experiences. The child may be forced to try to accept those alternate understandings of their experiences because the interpretive tools they need just don't exist or aren't available to them. Marcel might give up on playing female roles in play if those interactions are interrupted, discouraged, and discredited enough times. Since Marcel may have been using those play experiences to make sense of their internal feelings of gender, and the message conveyed by Grace was that those feelings are wrong and the "correct" understanding is that Marcel is a boy, Marcel might start trying to understand how to be a boy in a way that does not elicit the same kind of redirection. Marcel is doubly wronged by first not having access to hermeneutical tools that would make gender diversity and expansiveness normalized (hermeneutical injustice) and second by being deemed incompetent in their attempts to make sense of their gender through play (testimonial injustice). Indeed, José Medina (2013) argues that "testimonial injustices become not simply likely, but almost inescapable when the persistence of hermeneutical gaps renders certain voices less intelligible (and hence less credible) than others on certain matters, and their attempts to articulate certain meanings are systematically regarded as nonsensical (and hence incredible)" (p. 96).

According to Fricker (2007) hermeneutical injustice is not enacted by an individual in the same way as testimonial injustice. For testimonial injustice, there is a hearer who gives an unduly deflated credibility judgment to someone who is trying to communicate with them. The hearer enacts the testimonial injustice. However, for hermeneutical injustice, Fricker (2007) describes the unequal participation in the creation of hermeneutical tools (e.g., story books, fairy tales, cartoons, and other ways Marcel and Grace could have learned about diverse kinds of *mothers, fathers,* and other gender signifiers) as the background condition for the injustice, but the injustice itself is only realized "in a more or less doomed attempt on the part of the subject to render an experience intelligible, either to herself or to [another]" (p. 159). Marcel's gender exploration through play (an attempt to render an internal experience of gender intelligible), in a classroom with a teacher who could only understand *mother* to mean *person who can get pregnant,* was the moment the hermeneutical injustice manifested. However, Fricker (2007) argues that, since neither Marcel nor Grace created the background condition, neither of them enacted the injustice. The "blame" is diffused across systemic and structural conditions of hermeneutical disadvantage. However, we propose two ways that an individual can act which we argue constitute an enactment of hermeneutical injustice by an individual.

Enacting Hermeneutical Injustice through the Reproduction of Hegemonic Ways of Interpreting

When someone is attempting to communicate about a marginalized experience to someone who does not share that experience, the listener may attempt to preempt the story being told with their own hegemonic and distorted interpretation of the marginalized experience, often for their own benefit (whether they know they benefit from this act or not) (Medina, 2013). In her reflection, Grace was able to identify being uncomfortable with watching Marcel pretend to be pregnant. By telling Marcel "You are a boy and only girls can be mothers," this discomfort was relieved for her because she was able to use her own understandings of gender to explain Marcel's behavior. However, her increased comfort came at the expense of Marcel's agency in gender expression and exploration and in meaning-making through play. Grace's cisnormative ways of understanding signifiers like *mother* and *boy* were enforced through her social identity power (as being older and cisgender) and organizational power (as a person with authority over Marcel), disrupting and silencing Marcel's attempt at understanding an internal experience of gender.

In Fricker's (2007) conception of hermeneutical injustice, there is simply a void in a society's or community's shared hermeneutical tools in the place where a particular marginalized experience exists, such that *nobody* in the society or community can effectively make sense of it. This may be true in the case of the person suffering from the undiscovered disease—both patient and doctors lack the tools to make sense of the situation. The patient is clearly harmed more by the gap in hermeneutical tools than the doctors, but all parties are perplexed. However, Medina (2013) argues that, in true cases of hermeneutical injustice cause by identity-based prejudice and oppression, such a gap cannot be sustained without the marginalized experiences becoming distorted and obscured in dominant discourses. That is to say, the gap is filled with ways of understanding marginalized experiences that are asymmetrically shaped by dominant discourses in ways that maintain the unequal balance of power.

If there simply were no shared ways of making sense of transgender lives, then transgender people would just fill that gap, and cisgender people would then have ways of seeing and hearing and understanding those experiences that are empowering and authentic because they would have come from people with lived experiences. However, instead of a gap or void, there is already a collection of hermeneutical tools created by hegemonic cisgender discourses and "naturalized" as truth and common knowledge which misconstrue and misrepresent transgender experiences. All of the negative cultural images of transgender people examined in chapter 3 are examples of hermeneutical tools—means of interpreting and understanding transgender lives and experiences—which have been generated by cisgender discourse and which distort cultural understandings of transgender experiences. The medicalized and pathologized transgender person as in the DSM, the deceptive and pathetic transgender archetypes (Serano, 2016), and the images of transgender people as less than fully human are interpretations of transgender experiences which emerge out of hegemonic cisnormative discourses that preempt, obscure, and obstruct authentic accounts of TGE experiences which would otherwise destabilize cisgender truth claims such as a binary system of gender or a concept of "biological sex." In this way, not only are marginalized voices and stories kept out of general circulation, but when members of marginalized groups attempt to bring their voices to the center, they find there are already other explanations for their experiences which oppose their authentic views and maintain hegemonic understandings as truth.

Medina (2013) challenges Fricker's idea that a hermeneutical gap will render a marginalized experience unintelligible by all parties. Grace was not completely without a way of understanding Marcel's behavior. There were narratives and images available for Grace to draw on in making meaning of the situation (e.g., pregnancy as a prerequisite of motherhood, assumptions about bodies labeled *boy* which preclude one from participating in either pregnancy or motherhood, the pathologization of transgender narratives that led to her thinking there was something "wrong" with Marcel, the ignorant or developing or fragile child who needs to be enculturated and protected). The conflict with Marcel arose because all of the hermeneutical resources at Grace's disposal were cisnormative and heteronormative narratives which ignore or denounce intersex bodies and trans identities and childist narratives that position the child as not yet being a complete human.

Marcel was not displaying behavior that was so foreign or confusing or unknown as to leave Grace stumped in the way that the doctors were for the patient with an unknown disease. There *was* a lack of *empowering* hermeneutical tools that would have affirmed and supported Marcel, but Grace subconsciously filled that void with her own cisnormative ways of interpreting Marcel's gendered behavior. At the start of Marcel's play, there was a space for meaning-making that could have been affirming of Marcel's gender exploration—offering access to the entire galaxy of gendered stars—but that space was filled instead with rigid limitations and explanations that put a stop to generative meaning-making through play. In this way, Grace was writing Marcel's story and drawing Marcel's gender constellation, instead of letting Marcel doing it.

This preempting and commandeering of Marcel's story need not be conscious or intentional for Grace. In fact, Medina (2013) contends that members of privileged groups, by the nature of having their own experiences and ways of knowing consistently validated and reproduced throughout their lives, develop an insensitivity to counternarratives such as Marcel's and also an insensitivity to their own hegemonic discourse as being a *discourse* at all, rather than simply being the *truth*. As a cisgender woman, Grace has never had to question many of her beliefs and understandings about gender, and it did not occur to her to open her mind to counternarratives until she saw how hurt Marcel was by her actions. She certainly had no conscious intent to cause Marcel harm. In fact, she was motivated by wanting to protect Marcel by presenting what she believed to be the truth to a child she perceived as being confused. In fact, it was only in realizing that she had hurt Marcel that she stopped to interrogate her perspective at all.

It is this obscurity of the self and insensitivity to the experiences of marginalized others that necessitated a portion of this book be dedicated to *unlearning* before relearning about gender. In reviewing her notes, Grace realized that she had been routinely silencing Marcel's gender exploration for quite a while before she paused to reflect on what Marcel might be trying to communicate. She had been insensitive to Marcel's pain until it reached a boiling point of sobbing and insisting on the possibility of being a mother. Medina (2013) argues that the kind of insensitivity to and ignorance of marginalized experiences which "protects privilege and hides complicity with oppression is motivated by the *need not to know*, which in turn is directly related to the *need to know* of those negatively affected by the injustice or of those genuinely interested in fighting it" (Medina, 2013, p. 109 citing Bernasconi, 2007).

For Grace, a compassionate teacher who cares about the children she works with, to carry on believing what she had always believed about gender, she *needed not to know* that she was hurting Marcel by insisting on a cisnormative understanding of gender in the classroom. Marcel's pain had to be obscured from her consciousness—by viewing Marcel as the fragile child she was protecting or as the disordered gender transgressor who needed to be taught the truth for their own good—for her to continue feeling she was doing her duty as an educator to do no harm. Once Marcel's pain became overwhelmingly evident to Grace, she found herself motivated by the *need to know* more about gender expansiveness in order to genuinely support Marcel without doing harm. She could also see that Marcel *needed to know* more about gender in order to find ways to make meaning of their internal experiences of gender.

Grace started to realize that she had signified Marcel as a *boy* and that, to her, that signifier was incompatible with the signifier of *mother.* As she brainstormed alternative interpretations of Marcel's behavior, learned more about Marcel's gender exploration at home, and consulted a trusted colleague to get another perspective, she realized she had a lot to learn. TGE narratives for young children had been completely hidden from her sight, as a cisgender woman who aligned with dominant discourse. She also realized she had a lot to *unlearn,* as she discovered that she had been preventing Marcel from offering counternarratives into the classroom because she already had negative cultural images of gender bending behavior in young children solidified in her mind (e.g., feeling like something was *wrong* with Marcel). Most importantly, Grace realized she was hurting a child, and she decided it was worth her feeling uncertain and uncomfortable if it meant she could figure out how to be supportive of Marcel instead.

Becoming actively engaged in the liberation of TGE children requires first unlearning the cisnormative interpretations of bodies and genders that uphold the gender binary and marginalize counterstories and then learning new ways of understanding the complexity of gender and one's relationship to it. This process is distinctly hermeneutical, as it involves a reinterpretation and a renewed attempt at meaning-making of something that has been taken for granted, but it also begins to touch on the idea of resistance which will be discussed in greater detail in the next chapter. Marcel's insistence on wanting to be a mother introduced a counterstory into the classroom—one in which a child assigned male could become a mother. It put a familiar face on the concept of *transgender* for Grace, who had only ever thought of the idea in the abstract and from a deficit perspective. It caused Grace to question her beliefs as pillars of truth and to make space for other possible truths.

In seeking gender justice and in doing no harm to young children, it is our responsibility to avoid silencing counterstories that question what we know about gender and reproducing privileged truth claims that distort and obscure the lived experiences of TGE children. While Fricker (2007) does not recognize an agent as being responsible for enacting hermeneutical injustice, we argue that the person who (consciously or unconsciously) preempts or disrupts a child's attempts to make meaning of and interpret their own gendered lives and experiences by presenting cisnormative ways of knowing as stable and unquestionable truths is enacting hermeneutical injustice and has a responsibility to interrogate their assumptions in order to more fully support and affirm the children in their care.

This is no small task.

Paulo Freire (2018), conceptualizes oppression as a "dehumanized and dehumanizing totality" (p. 47), meaning that all parties lose some amount of humanity in the process of oppression. He claims that "Whereas, the violence of the oppressors prevents the oppressed from being fully human, the response of the latter to this violence is grounded in the desire to pursue the right to be human. As the oppressors dehumanize others and violate their rights, they themselves also become dehumanized" (p. 56). Freire is pointing out that, as acts that are dehumanizing are not, themselves, humane, someone who oppresses another must do so by sacrificing a piece of their own humanity. Grace began to feel this tension when she saw how hurt Marcel was by being silenced and "corrected"—running away and sobbing, insisting on a different way of understanding than the one Grace had presented. Grace began engaging in mindful reflection of her actions because it hurt her to see how she had hurt Marcel but doing so was not easy for her.

> Discovering himself to be an oppressor may cause considerable anguish, but it does not necessarily lead to solidarity with the oppressed. Rationalizing his guilt through paternalistic treatment of the oppressed, all the while holding them fast in a position of dependence, will not do. Solidarity requires that one enter into the situation of those with whom one is solidary; it is a radical posture. (Freire, 2018, p. 49)

We see Grace going through this process of discovering the harm she has done to Marcel, experiencing the guilt of the impact of her interventions. She is exploring the tensions between a path of seeing something *wrong* with Marcel's gender exploration and wanting to protect Marcel using a cisnormative idea of truth and a path of allowing Marcel the space and freedom to explore gender in ways that make her uncomfortable. The former path seeks to reduce Marcel's outward behavior enough to ease the discomfort it seems to cause for others. The latter path, a radical act of trusting in Marcel, seeks to center a marginalized expression of gender so that the entire hermeneutical atmosphere may become more just and equitable. It requires a group effort of holding tension and discomfort while working together to generate a new way of making meaning of Marcel's gender explorations, allowing Marcel to guide the direction of the narrative.

Enacting Hermeneutical Injustice through the Intentional Limitation of Hermeneutical Tools

In some parts of the world, the hermeneutical gap for understanding and interpreting transgender and gender-expansive lives and experiences may still be almost entirely filled with cisgender interpretations. However, in much of the world, the language exists, TGE lives are becoming more and more visible, and transgender activists are working to increase cultural understandings of TGE experiences. Most of the world is beyond the point of having *no* publicly available hermeneutical tools for transgender and gender-expansive individuals to use to interpret, understand, and communicate about their experiences in ways that are empowered by first person perspectives. Yet, many TGE individuals, such as Leelah and Sophie, are not introduced to those resources until adolescence or even long into adulthood. The second way that we propose an individual can enact hermeneutical injustice is in the intentional withholding of the empowering and affirming hermeneutical tools that *do* exist from those who are in the most need of them (regardless of the intention behind this withholding).

In May of 2019, the Rocklin School District outside of Sacramento, California passed a new curriculum in compliance with a 2011 CA law (FAIR education act; Morrar, 2019) mandating that public schools do more to represent the historical contributions of underrepresented groups, including those of the LGBTQ+ communities. The curriculum specifically focuses on exposing children, beginning in the second grade, to examples of influential figures in history and society (e.g., scholars, authors, scientists) who are or were transgender and/or nonheterosexual and acknowledging their LGBTQ+ identities when talking about their contributions to society, thus offering children positive images of queer and trans people. It is not a curriculum designed to teach children about gender or sexual orientation, just to show them that LGBTQ+ people are beneficial members of a diverse society.

The curriculum sparked a parental protest that kept 700 children home from school in a district of roughly 12,000 students (Broverman, 2019). Many of the parents spoke out that they were not against the representation of LGBTQ+ figures in history, but that they were against the curriculum starting in the second grade. One mother interviewed claimed that research states that children that young are "not developed to handle such in-depth world sexual views." These parents felt that seven- to eight-year-old children were too young to even know that LGBTQ+ people exist and contribute positively to society. Based on a 2017 CDC survey of adolescents' self-reported gender identities, approximately 1.8 percent of adolescents in the United States identify as transgender (Center for Disease Control and Prevention, 2018). By that figure, we can estimate that around twelve or thirteen of the children who were held out of school over the implementation of this curriculum and around 200 of the children in the whole district will grow up to identify as transgender, if they don't already. These children are receiving messaging from these protests that they are too young and immature—developing, innocent, and fragile child images—to be allowed to have positive role models who they can relate to in their gender exploration. Kelly, a transgender preschool teacher, believes representation is vital:

What does a gender inclusive classroom look like? I think, well, I liken it to looking at people who look like me. And so, like growing up in the South and being Black and not having Black teachers, and learning about the civil war, and not explicitly saying the confederacy was bad. I remember the one Black teacher I had in third grade, she introduced me to my Black self in a very rooted way. She said, "Kelly, you are going to learn this Black history, and you're going to win this Black history contest we're having. Where you have to talk about all of these Black entities and what they did." And so I memorized what everybody did, and it was just, like, I can call names now and I know what they did. And I stayed stuck on that forever, and it was because of her. And so I think when you can introduce individuals who have a like-minded perspective and/ or they show a possibility for something else. Or kids can see themselves in the image of someone else, and the essence of them, then that's helpful.

Not seeing queerness, not seeing gender nonconformity. Not seeing those things was really hard and isolating. And so, I think in the classroom, if I had to choose some elements that would be helpful for a gender inclusive education, it might start by representation. Who is in the classroom? Who's teaching? Who's writing curriculum? Like just the basic who's in the room? (Kelly, transgender preschool teacher, he/him)

In their 2014 article, *The Big Freakout: Educator Fear in Response to the Presence of Transgender Elementary School Students,* Elizabethe Payne and Melissa Smith discuss the findings of their qualitative study of twelve educators and administrators who were working directly with at least one transgender student in an elementary school in the United States. The major themes that they found in their data are all related to educator fear—fear of being ill-prepared and uninformed, fear of having no clear policies or procedures, fear of both disclosing and *not* disclosing the presence of a transgender child in the class or school, fear of community backlash for supporting a transgender child in elementary school, and fear of disrupting the image of childhood as an "innocent space" that is free from discussions of "sex, sexuality, or gender" (p. 401).

As Payne and Smith (2014) note, this image of an innocent space (and an innocent child) that does not acknowledge those topics exists despite "the pervasive celebration of heterosexuality [and cisnormativity] in early childhood and elementary classroom activities (e.g., pretend weddings, gendered play areas—kitchen and dress-up corner vs. the building-block center) and stories of princesses awaiting princely kisses" (Payne & Smith, 2014, p. 401; see also Allan, Atkinson, Brace, DePalma, & Hemingway, 2008; DePalma & Atkinson, 2009; Surtees, 2005). The conflation of the concepts of gender, sexuality, and an idea of categorical sex makes it impossible for educators to imagine discussing a transgender identity without introducing themes of sexual activity, which are deemed inappropriate for young children (Payne & Smith, 2014). Recalling Jen, whose interest in dolls was perceived as a warning sign of homosexuality in a child who was assigned male, genderexpansive behavior is often discouraged out of the fear of its association with sexuality, and particularly nonhetero sexuality. As Payne and Smith (2014) note, "Transgender children introduce the body—and, implicitly, sexuality—into the classroom" (p. 401), and teachers fear both that they will spoil the innocence of the child and the space by engaging in conversations with children about transgender identities and bodies and that they might be at risk of personal attack from community members if their advocacy work becomes public and is viewed as spoiling that innocence (Payne & Smith, 2014).

However, we argue the withholding of such conversations and narratives from young children amounts to an enactment of hermeneutical injustice by creating an insulated space where there is a gap in allowable hermeneutical resources, which specifically harms TGE children, who are then unable to make sense of their experiences of gender. Children like Leelah Alcorn, without a signifier for their experiences, are forced to try to fit themselves into images and narratives that do not adequately represent them, and they are left feeling the dissonance of that poor fit and the isolation and shame of believing that they are somehow the cause of the discomfort. By actively avoiding discussions of gender diversity (e.g., diversity of bodies, identities, expressions, and language), teachers are working against the values and ethics of their professional work by doing harm to children like Leelah. This withholding does not achieve the imagined result of reducing child confusion. It does the opposite—creating unnecessary confusion for TGE children while solidifying the beliefs of cisgender children in the gender binary, such that they will continue to reproduce those narratives throughout their own lives.

Preschool is not too young for children to pick up on hegemonic and oppressive ways of interpreting gender-expansive behavior and to start reproducing those narratives. Without counterstories of empowered genderexpansive experiences to create resistance against cisgender hegemony, those dominant discourses are naturalized and internalized by all children, and they become the lens through which cisgender, ipso gender, and transgender children interpret gender expansiveness. The message conveyed by withholding gender-expansive narratives but not cisgender ones is that cisnormative behaviors are innocent or neutral, but gender-expansive behaviors are not.

In order to have agency to authentically draw their own gender constellation, a young TGE child would need to dismiss all the cisgender narratives around them and cisnormative interpretations of their own internal experiences. They would have to attempt to create their own counterstory entirely unaware that counterstories already exist, which could help them find their authentic gender narrative with less struggle and distress. Through the use of resistant imaginations, described in the next chapter, many transgender children and adults do exactly that, and have throughout history. If this were not the case, there would still be no names or narratives for trans lives and experiences.

Medina (2013) notes that there may be "hidden communicative processes and embryonic formulations of meaning even in the most adverse hermeneutical contexts" (p. 100). Meaning, even in a situation where a transgender child is regularly subjected to negative images of transgender people and has no access to empowering hermeneutical resources (e.g., positive images of transgender people, counterstories to disrupt the gender binary), that child may still find the strength to imagine a life in which they can embrace their gender and live authentically and in which they are not viewed as deceptive, pathetic, or disordered for doing so. Many transgender youth now find support and hope in online communities when they don't have support in their families, schools, or local communities (Stryker, 2008; Ehrensaft, 2016b). Marginalized groups have always found ways to connect and interpret their experiences in private, often under the threat of violence from their oppressors, as in groups like the Black Panthers, meetings like feminist speak-outs, or tucked-away social spaces like gay bars (Medina, 2013). However, forcing TGE children to make meaning out of their gendered experiences in secret or in private by explicitly withholding the hermeneutical tools that they could use to interpret their genders in empowering ways places an unjust and unnecessary burden on those children. Additionally, as shame tends to breed in secrecy (Brown, 2012), forcing TGE narratives out of shared discourse could lead the child to become shameful of their gender, and the consequences for the children who are not able to surmount the obstacles of shame and secrecy to find their truths are too great to risk.

> *I don't feel like I ever had anything explicitly stated that it was wrong, but I could feel that, like, I'm just gonna keep this to myself. I'm just gonna keep this to me, and I'll play these little fantasies in my head when I'm alone. This is what I'm thinking, and this is what I'm like, but I'm not gonna tell anybody because it's probably not good. And then I just started spending a lot of time alone. (J-Wo, thirty, she/her)*

THE HARMS OF HERMENEUTICAL INJUSTICE

Many of the same kinds of harm that were examined in chapter 3 as resulting from testimonial injustice can also be caused by hermeneutical injustice (Fricker, 2007), though the point of entry of the injustice into a child's experience is slightly different in hermeneutical as opposed to testimonial injustices. Whereas Fricker (2007) describes testimonial injustice as a situation where "someone is wronged in their capacity as a giver of knowledge" (p. 7), hermeneutical injustice is described as a situation where "someone is wronged in their capacity as a subject of social understanding" (p. 7). When the two coexist, as they often do, hermeneutical injustice is often the precondition for testimonial injustice—one's voice is not heard because one's experiences are not considered in the generation of social understanding (Medina, 2013).

Fricker (2007) proposes that the common epistemic thread of the harms of the two kinds of injustice is the "prejudicial exclusion from participation in the spread of knowledge" (p. 162)—in both instances, one is prevented from contributing to public discourse and collective resources of interpretation and understanding due to their membership in a particular marginalized social category. Both injustices can lead to the epistemic harms of the loss of epistemic confidence, the literal loss of pieces of knowledge that one could otherwise have obtained or created, and the loss of the opportunity for genuine and authentic self-knowledge and understanding. A TGE child who is not offered empowering TGE narratives or images, but who sees cisgender stories and cisgender interpretations of gender expansiveness all around them will struggle to understand their experiences in ways that are affirming. Again, we can see this struggle in Leelah's words:

> *I feel like a girl trapped in a boy's body, and I've felt that way ever since I was 4. I never knew there was a word for that feeling, nor was it possible for a boy to become a girl, so I never told anyone and I just continued to do traditionally "boyish" things to try to fit in.* (Leelah Alcorn, seventeen, transgender girl, she/her)

Hermeneutical injustice may not always produce the same feeling of being treated subhuman that testimonial injustice does, as the enactment of hermeneutical injustice—through preempting and distorting marginalized interpretations and through the withholding of empowering hermeneutical resources—is less direct and more obscure to the child than testimonial injustice. However, many cases of testimonial injustice occur to individuals who already understand their experiences in their own authentic ways but are wronged in their attempts to communicate those understandings (Fricker, 2007). Hermeneutical injustice, on the other hand, by definition occurs before a child fully understands their own experiences, and so it's impact on processes such as steadying the mind and identity formation can be profound (Fricker, 2007). Fricker (2007) argues:

> In certain social contexts, hermeneutical injustice can mean that someone is socially constituted as, and perhaps even caused to be, something they are not, and which it is against their interests to be seen to be. Thus . . . they may be prevented from becoming who they are. (p. 168)

In the case of Sophie, born in 1948 and growing up in many countries and cultures around world, not knowing any words for transgender experiences, having no images to identify with, and never being given "permission" to simply think of herself as a woman, she spent nearly sixty years living her life "as a man" because she had no way of understanding that there were any other options. By being socially constituted as a man, she did everything in her power to constitute herself in that way, and when she was permitted to constitute herself on her own terms, sixty years of womanhood came pouring out of her all at once.

It is through the courage and voices of individuals like Sophie, Leelah, Jen, Ikaika, and every other transgender and gender-expansive person who is powerfully speaking their truth, that more TGE children are finding the stories and images they need to understand their genders earlier and earlier in life. We believe that no child should be forced to wait to discover who they are or to construct themselves in inauthentic ways for the comfort of those around them, especially when the hermeneutical resources exist today to help them discover themselves authentically now.

PATH TO HERMENEUTICAL JUSTICE

The path to hermeneutical justice for TGE children begins with a radical commitment to give children the hermeneutical tools they need when they need them. Teachers must be committed to helping each child understand their own gender on their own terms. This requires actively seeking images, stories, role models, language, and other interpretive tools that are relevant and affirming for a child's gender health and journey, regardless of the obstacles to doing so. In this section, we present three practical strategies for beginning to fill in hermeneutical gaps with empowering and affirming ways of understanding, interpreting, and representing gender diversity.

Overcoming Hermeneutical Gaps by Struggling with Children

Since the nature of hermeneutical injustice is such that TGE children are bound to struggle in their attempts to render their gender-expansiveness intelligible (Fricker, 2007), teachers are presented with a choice in how they respond to the struggling child. They can offer blanket explanations that are based in cisgender interpretations. As we have seen, this path will lead to a compounded testimonial and hermeneutical injustice. They can let the child continue struggling alone because they, themselves, don't have all the tools to accurately or adequately interpret the child's experiences. Or they can struggle *with* the child in generating new ways of understanding that feel empowering and affirming for the child.

Fricker (2007) describes the need for "an alertness or sensitivity to the possibility that the difficulty [a speaker] is having as she tries to render something communicatively intelligible is due not to its being a nonsense or her being a fool, but rather to some sort of gap in collective hermeneutical resources" (p. 169). If a child says, "I'm a sister, but I'm a *boy* sister!" we can interpret this statement as nonsense or the child as ignorant or simply undeveloped in their understanding of gender. If we do one of those things, we are likely to interject our own ways of understanding into whatever the child was trying to say, "That doesn't make sense. Only girls can be sisters." Or we can extend the benefit of the doubt that the child has something important and meaningful to convey, but they lack the tools to say it in a way we understand right now.

This alertness and sensitivity to a child who is struggling to express something without the tools to do so must be developed against the impact that negative cultural images of the child have on our subconscious (e.g., the ignorant or developing child images) which might predispose us to view the struggling child as foolish or incompetent. As with conscious credibility judgment adjustments, teachers must intentionally practice noticing children's communicative struggles through observation and reflection.

Once a teacher has identified that a child is struggling to express something about their gender because they do not have the right hermeneutical tools, they can choose to allow the child to continue struggling alone, which is better than enforcing a cisnormative interpretation on the child, but even a teacher who is also lacking the tools to understand a TGE experience can choose, instead, to engage in *emergent listening* with the child—working to *hear* the child through the static of the hermeneutical disadvantage. In this way, Fricker (2007) says one can "help generate a more inclusive hermeneutical micro-climate" (p. 171). This may mean making up new words or labels that feel affirming for the child, sitting in uncertainty together and letting the child know that uncertainty is okay, or otherwise ensuring the child that they are not in their struggle alone.

In her 2016 book, *The Gender Creative Child*, Diane Ehrensaft lists several gender identities that children in her gender clinic have come up with to describe themselves. One child, who presented as a boy from the front, but who had a long braid with a bow hanging down their back told Ehrensaft,

"I'm a Prius . . . I'm a boy in the front, a girl in the back. A hybrid" (p. 36). Another told her, "You see, you take everything about gender, throw it in the blender, press the button, and you've got me—a gender smoothie" (p. 40). If given the opportunity and a supportive and attuned adult who is willing to listen emergently, young children will find ways to communicate about and represent their gender even without the words and narratives being used by TGE adults and adolescents.

It is important to note that teachers should not struggle *for* the child, searching for ways to explain the child's behavior and experience that make sense to themselves. They might have their own meaning making to do, to learn about what the child's gender exploration means to them, but the struggle they must engage in to relieve the hermeneutical injustice is one in which they struggle *with* the child to find ways for the child to understand their gender on their own terms. Committing to hone one's alertness and sensitivity to TGE children's hermeneutical disadvantage and to struggling *with* children to help them create their own tools of interpreting their experiences will help fill the hermeneutical gaps with affirming and empowering tools of understanding TGE young children.

Recognizing and Resisting the Exclusive Reproduction of Cisgender Ways of Knowing and Interpreting

Whether or not a teacher recognizes that a child is struggling to make sense of their gender, they must reflect on their own beliefs and assumptions about gender to avoid reproducing oppressive and hegemonic narratives instead of listening to the child. This is another phase of unlearning and learning, another opportunity for mindful reflection.

As it can be incredibly difficult to see the things we take for granted as "truth" or common sense—like a fish becoming aware of the water they swim in—the process of noticing when we are reproducing discourses that have been naturalized and privileged requires a commitment to the nonideal (Medina, 2013). Returning to Grace and Marcel, Grace has already started down this path with the plan she laid out in her mindful reflection.

1. *Particularism*—Grace has begun reflecting on Marcel's intersectional life and learned more about Marcel's gender exploration at home, humanizing Marcel as a unique and whole person.
2. *Empiricism/fallibilism*—Grace's decision to pause and reflect on Marcel in the first place was because she realized her effort to offer support had backfired and hurt Marcel. She is using that feedback to adjust her manner of responding to Marcel's gendered play moving forward and can continue to adjust based on how Marcel reacts.

3. *Meliorism*—Grace is definitely not entirely comfortable with her plan. She still has a lot to learn about gender, and she doesn't know exactly the right way to approach supporting Marcel. But she knows she has to do *something* differently, because she cares about Marcel and wants to be a supportive and trusted teacher.

In Grace's reflection notes, she spells out the cisnormative assumptions and interpretations that are negatively impacting her relationship with Marcel and her ability to be supportive (e.g., believing there is something *wrong* with Marcel). Although she has not yet fully shed those assumptions and beliefs, she is willing to sit with discomfort and resistance by learning more about gender diversity while testing out a new approach to supporting Marcel. There will undoubtedly be moments when Grace subconsciously forwards cisgender truth claims in her work with Marcel, but she is practicing and engaging in cycles of reflection and action.

Resisting the "Fragile Child" Image and Trusting Children with Complexity and Diversity

The best way that teachers can address hermeneutical injustice is to work to prevent it from manifesting in the first place. By actively educating themselves on gender diversity and by listening to transgender voices on how best to support transgender children, they can prepare themselves to see and hear TGE children more authentically. Furthermore, by actively and intentionally bringing in transgender and gender-expansive narratives, images, persona dolls, and other representational and interpretive tools for expressing and understanding TGE experiences in an affirming light right from the start with our youngest children, teachers can prevent TGE children from having to grow up trying to make sense of their genders through a cisnormative lens in the first place.

> *Young children can conceptualize a grand theory—like what are pronouns? what is gender? (Mitali, intersex teacher and trainer, they/them)*

This act takes courage, as Payne and Smith (2014) note that many teachers fear backlash from parents, administrators, or their communities for proactively supporting transgender young children in their programs. It also requires a radical shift away from viewing early childhood as an "innocent" space (in which TGE narratives are considered taboo) by recognizing that young children have diverse bodies and genders already and that withholding affirming information from them can lead to shame and confusion (Payne & Smith, 2014; Brown, 2012).

The considerations for bringing TGE voices into the classroom that were explored in chapter 3 are the same for doing so here. As Rudine Sims Bishop (1990) says, "When children cannot find themselves reflected in the books they read, or when the images they see are distorted, negative, or laughable, they learn a powerful lesson about how they are devalued in the society of which they are a part" (p. 2). She tells us books (and other representations in classrooms) can act as mirrors and that all children deserve the opportunity to see themselves reflected. A commitment to eliminating hermeneutical injustices for TGE young children requires teachers to overcome their fears of backlash and to bring diverse gender narratives into their classrooms even before they know whether or not they have a TGE child in their program, because *all* children benefit from epistemic resistance and counterstories that normalize gender diversity.

Chapter 5

Resistant Social Imaginations

Striating Paths for Gender Liberation in Early Childhood Classrooms

Vibrant and courageous imaginations are required in order to liberate us from the constraints of the gender binary. As Gene Wilder (1971) sings in *Charlie and the Chocolate Factory*, "There is no life I know to compare with pure imagination. Living there, you'll be free if you truly wish to be." Though early childhood education can be a field that is filled with imaginative individuals, children and educators alike, we all have limitations to what we can and are willing to imagine. Each of our imaginations inform and are informed by what Medina (2013) describes as the social imagination. He tells us,

> Through practices of resistance we can learn to go beyond the strictures of inherited cognitive and affective habits, and we can learn to envision new cognitive-affective attitudes and orientations towards others. Both our ability and our inability to relate to others (and to particular aspects of ourselves) is mediated by the social imagination, the kind of imagination that opens our eyes and hearts to certain things and not others, enabling and constraining our social gaze. We all have responsibilities toward the pluralization of this social gaze so that we can collectively produce a kaleidoscopic social imagination, a fluid way of imagining ourselves and others in which patterns of relations are constantly emerging and vanishing, seamlessly and ceaselessly, with some relational possibilities giving way to others, constantly resisting the ossification of our categorizations. (p. 22)

Medina's (2013) image of patterns of relations—social categories, signifiers, striations, and hierarchies—as being constantly shifting and changing, settling into new equilibriums before rearranging once again is one explored by many scholars (Davies, 2014; Bergson, 1998; Deleuze & Guattari, 1987; Williams, 2002). The idea they all share is that, as social beings, we need some shared ways of understanding how we relate to each other, where our affinity groups fit into the larger society, and where we have commonalities and differences but also that those delineations cannot become too deeply ingrained or they risk being oppressive and prescriptive, reducing us to our signifiers rather than allowing us to use signifiers as productive ways of finding community and celebrating differences.

Bernard Williams (2002) asserts that we need relatively steady ways to relate to one another to develop cooperation and trust between individuals and within communities and societies. He also recognizes two problems with our tendency to draw lines around ourselves in that pursuit:

> One is a political problem, of finding a basis for a shared life which will be neither too oppressively coercive (the requirement of freedom) nor dependent on mythical legitimations (the requirement of enlightenment). The other is a personal problem, of stabilizing the self into a form that will indeed fit with these political and social ideas, but which can at the same time create a life that presents itself to a reflective individual as worth living. (Bernard Williams, 2002)

For too long, the binary hierarchies of adult-child, teacher-student, and male-female have dominated general discourse, becoming the "oppressively coercive" kind of striations which Williams (2002) warns against—dictating narrow ways of being a child, a teacher, a boy, a girl, a man, or a woman. The way forward, to a new and more free and just equilibrium, requires what Medina (2013) calls a *resistant social imagination*—one that uses diverse experiences, stories, and counterstories to continuously and critically assess what *is* and what is *possible,* using feedback from the world as we shift it to ensure we are moving in the right direction. That is, Medina (2013) does not advocate either for a world of "pure imagination" as Gene Wilder sings about or for a world based strictly in previously established ways of knowing and being, but rather a world where imagination and experience inform one another in continuous cycles of reflection and reimagination. Medina (2013) argues that "our experiences are expanded and critically assessed in and through the imagination" but also that "our imagination has to be constantly interrogated by the actual experiences of those affected by the practices and institutions we set up" (p. 7).

The world of "pure imagination," which is what Williams (2002) describes as being "dependent on mythical legitimations" (p. 201), is the world where liberation is born—freeing us from coercive and oppressive social striations. However, it is also the world that is used violently and satirically against efforts to expand our notions of gender—the world where someone insists that they can identify as an "attack helicopter" and demand that society accept that identification. Without the limitless world of imagination, marginalized groups would be doomed to accept their subjugation, unable to imagine a different world in which there was justice and equity. However, there are limitations to what we can, or more precisely, what we are willing to imagine (Gendler, 2000).

Yale Philosophy professor Tamar Szabó Gendler (2000) explores the outer reaches of imagination and the factors that prevent us from imagining certain things when she notes, "I have a much easier time following an author's invitation to imagine that the earth is flat than I do following her invitation to imagine that murder is right" (p. 58). Gendler (2000) argues that we are *capable* of imagining both impossible and immoral things, but that we are often *unwilling* to imagine the latter.

Grace struggled to imagine Marcel as a mother because she believed something was *wrong* with Marcel's gender exploration. It wasn't that she *couldn't* imagine Marcel as a mother, it was that she didn't *want* to do so because it challenged her moral compass. Being affected by cultural images of TGE people depicted as deceptive and morally deviant, and by images of the child as evil and egocentric, Grace feels a moral imperative to limit her imagination and Marcel's imagination, in turn.

Gendler (2000) goes on to examine the difference between *belief* and *make-belief,* arguing that we can decide to *make believe* in something we find morally questionable, as long as we are not being asked to consider *believing* in it. This is a conscious choice we can make—allowing something into our imagination despite our moral objection to it. For Grace, this might be a first step in her work to support Marcel—allowing that Marcel can *pretend* to be a mother in imaginative play, without yet entertaining the idea that Marcel could actually *be* a mother in real life. It is harder, Gendler (2000) argues, to decide to *believe* in something we still find morally wrong. For Grace to take the next step in supporting Marcel, she needs to interrogate her current set of beliefs and assumptions which are casting a moral shadow over Marcel's gendered exploration in her mind. She will not be able to accept Marcel's authentic gender expressions, except in limited imaginary contexts, unless she is able to realign her moral compass.

For those who struggle to *believe* in the necessity of breaking down the gender binary to allow for more diverse gendered experiences and narratives, critical examination of whether one holds a moral opposition to gender expansiveness is required. What negative social images of TGE people have become part of our internalized beliefs about gender? Is there really anything immoral about Marcel's play? The introduction of diverse gender counter-stories, which depict examples of loving and honest and human transgender individuals and which create liberatory resistance and allow lived experiences to expand one's imagination, is required.

A more honest accounting of the moral implications of the gender binary itself is necessary as well. As Williams (2002) points out, we must develop patterns of social relation that offer *every* child a path that they believe is "a life worth living" (p. 201).

> *The life I would've lived isn't worth living in . . . because I'm transgender.* (Leelah Alcorn, seventeen, transgender girl, she/her)

Leelah was one of far too many children who, when presented with the static and unyielding gender binary, decided death was preferable. And so, we are compelled to ask where there is greater moral peril—a world of gender diversity, which will be uncomfortable for many as we re-stratify our social categories and understandings of ourselves, or a binary world of gender, comfortable to most, but fatally intolerable for some?

PATH TO JUSTICE THROUGH RESISTANT SOCIAL IMAGINATION

> *I think in the olden days girls were only allowed to wear dresses and boys were only allowed to wear pants. But now if you're a boy you're actually allowed to wear dresses 'cause it doesn't matter what you wear just by your gender. 'Cause you can't choose what you wear just because you're like a boy or a girl, it doesn't really matter. You could just pick any clothes you want.* (Oak, eight years)

Medina (2013) states, "The imagination can be both empowering and disempowering. It can create and deepen vulnerabilities, but it can also make people stronger and able to resist . . . *resistant* ways of imagining can contest exclusions and stigmatizations, and they can help us become sensitive to the suffering of excluded and stigmatized subjects (p. 252). He reminds us that we each have the capacity to imagine—in empowering, disempowering, stigmatizing, and resistant ways—and we also have a collective social imagination—a shared capacity to wonder, propose, create, and deny. If either becomes stagnant, ossified, or overly homogenous, injustices occur. We must develop resistant imaginations—individually and collectively—which refuse to remain stationary and continuously adjust to accommodate infinitely diverse counterstories that sensitize us to the unique experiences of marginalized members of our society.

By centering the voices of children in our stance of imaginative resistance, we can both reconnect our own imaginations to the perspectives of being a young child and connect our imaginations anew to each of the unique and intersectionally diverse perspectives presented by the children in our care. By listening emergently to children, we can find areas of our imagination which have congealed or hardened, and their voices can help us loosen and reinvigorate.

To Oak, a time of rigid restrictions based on gender are the "olden days"—part of a previous pattern of social relations, a pattern that is no longer of use to us moving forward because we can imagine a more just way of relating to each other. In this section, we will examine the steps and strategies that teachers can employ to imagine resistantly with children about a more sensitive, open and just future.

The Ethical Responsibility and Professional Commitment to Resistantly Imagine

As early childhood professionals, we have made commitments to the children we serve—to offer them respect, dignity, worth, agency, voice, and belonging. Above all, we made a commitment to doing no harm. In order to genuinely foster a resistant imagination, individually or collectively, we must interrogate our own willingness to imagine epistemic justice for young TGE children. Gendler (2000) sheds light on the first place we must look to discover any roadblock we may have to a resistant imagination that works toward gender justice for all children—our own moral compass.

Through critical reflection and epistemic friction through collaborative dialogue, we must interrogate negative cultural images and stereotypes that are affecting our image of the TGE child in a way that poses a *moral* objection to radically trusting those children. The evil child and ego-centric child images may lead us to hold a morally superior conception of ourselves in our relation to children. Are we willing to release that idea? The images of transgender people as deviant, deceptive, and disordered may lead us to want to steer a child away from such a morally suspect path. Can we humanize and reimagine the transgender individual as real and whole and honest and worthy of empathy?

Through cycles of mindful observation, reflection, reimagining, acting, and receiving feedback, we can unearth any moral objections we may have to developing active, liberatory, and resistant imaginations. Then, one by one, each objection must be held up against the implications of maintaining a binary system of gender, in which some children cannot imagine a life worth living. We believe this process will assist teachers in recalibrating their own moral compasses, and as Freire (2018) argues it will restore humanity to both the TGE child and the teacher who had previously been unable to see the child's suffering.

Resistantly Imagining the Image of the Child

As the multiple images of the child as immature and ignorant generate reciprocal images of the adult as mature and knowledgeable, we cannot re-*image* children without reimagining ourselves. Through critical reflection, we can examine each negative image of children (developing, ignorant, evil, innocent, egocentric, and fragile) and the reciprocal image of adults (complete, knowledgeable, just, wise, altruistic, and strong). With a critical friend, examine each reciprocal pair of images. Reflect on the ways the image of the child is placing limits on epistemic trust and disrupting attuned relationships. Consider each image of the adult, asking critically how much of your identity as an early childhood professional is shaped by that image. How much of your *self* is bound up with being an epistemic authority in your work with children?

Only after thoughtfully examining these images, and their embeddedness in our own conception of ourselves, can we resist—struggling against the self—by consciously reimagining children as equal epistemic agents and ourselves as partners in co-constructing knowledge with them. Epistemic justice for young TGE children is not possible without resistantly imagining children as the epistemic authority of their own lives and experiences, and doing so requires relinquishing our own positions of epistemic authority.

Resistantly Imagining Gender

> *Gender is who, how you identify yourself with being. There are many different genders. Basically I don't know how much genders there is, there's probably a lot. Definitely a lot. I don't know, like, the exact number. (Tobble, seven years, he/him)*

Western society is going through an exciting time of gender upheaval and rebellion. The binary striations which have hardened in the social imagination and been enshrined in laws have been intolerable for too many for too long. Gender is in flux. As Davies (2014) notes, "[C]ommunities cannot exist without some striations and will always tend toward re-striating and re-territorializing both action and thought, as powerful alliances form and re-form. At the same time, a community's power to endure comes from multiplicity, from encounters, from an always-emergent openness to the not-yet-known. . . . Ethical practice in this sense is not so much tied up with regulation and repetition (though it is partly that), but with the practice of listening for that which cannot yet be said" (p. 11). This pattern of re-striating and re-territorializing is neither new nor unique to gender. Trans and gender expansive people have collectively developed a lengthy list of new gender identities, with new ones coming out all the time. Some advocate for abolishing gender, while others advocate for expanding it infinitely.

We expect re-striation, a new equilibrium at some point in the future before that, too, gives way to resistant imaginations. However, we, like Tobble, are not in a position to guess how many genders there will be. In fact, we don't believe anyone who has been completely enculturated in the gender binary from birth will be the proper authority on where to draw the next set of (temporary) lines. What we do know is this: two is not enough.

For the rest, we are turning to children, who have not yet been ossified by binary thinking. Early childhood teachers are a critical inflection point in the greater social movement for gender justice. By listening emergently to children as they design gender constellations that this world has never seen before, we can support them in writing counter-stories that are not hindered by epistemic doubt or preempted by oppressive and limited ways of imagining. We can help them develop epistemic confidence and strong voices, voices that refuse to allow gender to be colonized by binary ways of thinking.

For me, it's very de-colonial to say, "you can't own gender," you know? It's like, you can't own land. You can't own water. Why? Why would you want that? You know? This is an idea we can share with everybody. Why would you want to own it? What value does that have? I don't understand, you know? (Ikaika, trans and māhūkāne, he/him)

Through critical reflection, we can interrogate the need to *own* gender, to territorialize it, to reproduce it in children and ourselves in stable, possessive, and hegemonic ways. By acknowledging our current point in the Western history of gender as simply a routine re-striation, we can let go of any need to either maintain the binary of the past or to dictate the resettling of the future, for the former has been proven to be unjust and the latter is not our work to do. Through resistant imagination and emergent listening with children, we can support them in redefining gender in increasingly pluralistic ways that are sensitive to continuously more counterstories.

Resistantly Imagining Early Childhood Classrooms

We also need to resistantly imagine early childhood classrooms that embody all of the ideals we desire for gender liberated experiences for young children. Caring environments that center epistemic justice as the nucleus from which all life in the classroom generates. Spaces that acknowledge and respect children as credible knowers capable of communicating about their authentic life experiences and internal wisdom. Communities that trust children to sculpt, paint, draw, dance, sing, play and use all of their hundred languages (Edwards, Gandini, & Forman, 2011) and more to create unique gender constellations in an ever expanding sky.

Encian Pastel, a transgender preschool teacher (he/they), offers a window into what such spaces could and should be for young children, families, and their teachers. Pastel resistantly imagines what early childhood classrooms could look like with teachers who practice radical listening, disrupt practices that reinforce gender-related oppressions and encourage young children to explore, create, experiment, erase, disrupt, resist, subvert, reclaim, reimagine, and exist among diverse gender possibilities.

Pastel resistantly imagines the physical use of space for an early childhood setting to be liberatory. He envisages *intentionally planned and arranged environments for young children that disrupt and obscure binaries* of all types both inside and outside the classroom and support children to be their "free-est selves."

> *I'd be really curious to talk to someone with an architecture background . . . about how the physical layout of space supports a gender-liberation lens . . . I know there has been a feminist architecture movement. I don't know if this has been applied to ECE. But there's a way that our spaces influence our thinking—and so much of gender-liberation is about expanding out of binary thinking. So I'm imagining a space that blurs binaries by design—inside/outside, light/dark, gross motor and fine motor! One of the self-segregation points we often see is girls at the art table and boys on the climbing equipment and bikes, right? So intentionally having large materials to work with at the art table, materials that require some wrestling and muscle power to get them into the shape you want . . . and levers and buttons and things on the climbing structures. Ropes, strings. Velcro attachment pieces.*
>
> *I imagine there's a connection between all the right angles and our linear thinking. So, a gender liberated environment for young children would be a space with curves. We would see natural elements in the playground—hills, slopes, meandering paths and waterways, circular and spiral shapes, plants and trees and stones. A sense of wildness, within a container of safety. I also think my program would mash up simple and glam. Imagine in the circular multilevel tree house the rope bridge connecting different platforms would be pink and some of the climbing rocks would be covered in glitter paint.*
>
> *Everything that nurtures spiritual intelligence, creative growth, unique personalities is going to support gender liberation because gender liberation is, at its heart, about being your free-est self, letting your body move how it wants to move without the constrictions gender roles place on our bodies and brains.*

Pastel resistantly imagines classrooms where *the use of pronouns is very thoughtfully considered*. He knows that every time teachers, parents, and other children use a pronoun, they are making a statement about gender. Usually a "this is what gender I think that person is" type of statement. And, typically, without verbal confirmation that this pronoun is used by the individual. He owns that he is guilty of this habit too. He often assumes that people use the pronouns he hears others using to describe them, which tend to follow gender presentation cues. He is also aware that no matter how often he tells the children in his class, "you can't tell someone's gender just by looking at them," he, their parents, other teachers, and everyone they meet everywhere are attempting to do just that. So how can he—through his resistant imagination—address these realities and imagine otherwise? He explains what he thinks about for early childhood classrooms where teachers understand the serious connections between pronouns and developing identities for young children.

> *First, really getting solid about whether I know someone's pronoun preference before picking "he" or "she" for them. Asking out loud to the kids, "I wonder how so-and-so knew to say "she" for that person?" Switching up pronouns with some adults who don't have a preference. Using gender neutral pronouns more often in stories and for stuffed animals and with dolls because when we had a child who switched pronouns, it became a lot of pressure on that child for us to always be asking their pronouns and using different pronouns, which would of course spark the curiosity of the other kids and draw a lot of unwanted attention on the one gender fluid child. Creating a linguistic precedent for pronoun and gender flexibility is what I imagine.*
>
> *I also think we would have periodic circle time activities where children have an opportunity to share what pronouns they want to be called, within a fun structure or game, so that there was an easy way for children to try on new identities without having to take the first initiative and broach the subject on their own. This would also reinforce the idea that gender identity can change and flow.*

Pastel resistantly imagines *how materials can support liberating and opening up ideas about gender.* He describes a cross between natural materials and "glam." Early childhood classrooms would include materials that are hard to categorize, blur binaries and are organized in flexible and dynamic ways.

> *Shiny capes, sequins-covered tunics, taffeta, velvet, silk scarves and fabric pieces; dress-up that blurs male/female divisions. Lots of animal pieces—ears and tails as well as full body suits. Unclear-what-it-is, interesting bodysuits. Programs can totally do princess dresses and construction worker vests as long as they also have more gender-flexible options mixed in and as long as staff are careful about supporting exploration. The program I'm envisioning, I wouldn't call the dress-up gender-neutral but I would strive for gender-expansive. And hard to categorize. Young kids are figuring out categories to order the world and cementing these categories. I imagine teachers constantly helping kids to widen these categories, broaden them, categorize without relying on those binaries that make everything easier to comprehend.*
>
> *In the spare clothes closet, there would be different styles of underwear mixed together, different styles of socks—short socks and knee socks—mixed*

together. Different styles of pants, leggings, skirts, and dresses mixed together and different styles of shirts perhaps separated into short sleeves and long mixed together with more dresses.

Pastel also resistantly imagines early childhood classrooms having *excellent libraries with a range of books that have a balance of characters with different social identities, including trans and nonbinary genders.* Teachers in these classrooms would supplement the rich body of literature available to children with oral storytelling.

Pastel resistantly imagines early childhood environments that include teachers, administrators and staff who are gender expansive to reinforce to children, families and the community, the program's core value for gender diversity.

Gender expansive teachers, please! I believe this makes the single biggest difference for our kids. Also, gender responsive staff.

Pastel resistantly imagines early childhood programs, schools, and centers that provide *multiple access points for parents and families to investigate their own assumptions about gender* and reflect on what they are passing down to their children.

Parents and families would receive accurate information from teachers and administrators and they would have opportunities to practice language and responses that support a gender liberation lens. Teachers would know the school's values and use them when bringing up conversations about gender with parents and family members. I imagine teachers asking such questions as: Are we creating a safe space for children to learn and grow? Social safety is important, and teachers would emphasize this in their conversations. Are we honoring diversity or committed to social justice? I envision programs that see supporting everyone as part of their work and want to change their practices, paperwork, and communication to be more inclusive.

Finally, Pastel resistantly imagines early childhood teachers and staff who are *willing to engage in deep self-reflection to examine their assumptions about gender* (also about race, class, and other social identities). Teachers and staff who are committed to implementing the four anti-bias education goals[1] (Derman-Sparks & Olsen Edwards, 2010) in their programs given how critical they are to a gender liberation program. And teachers and staff who are continually examining how the children are responding to their teaching and classroom practices and considering transformative social actions they can take in working towards more gender liberated practices. Teachers who use their reflection to identify and disrupt gender-based oppression that shows up in many ways throughout the classroom, including examples like the one below where Luke reflects on his interaction with Ajay, a three-and-half-year-old child in his class. Luke considers how changing the way extra clothes are organized in his classroom could increase opportunities for young children to experiment with gender more freely. Thinking back to a moment when Ajay was looking through a cabinet of extra clothes, Luke's use of critical reflection brought into view how a classroom practice—separating dresses and skirts from pants and shirts—while an efficient sorting process for the teachers, also functioned to reinforce the reproduction of oppositional sexism. In freezing a moment of his practice to deconstruct the power structures at work, Luke noticed an opportunity where he could make a small change in his practice to disrupt gender-related oppression and liberate young children's options for gender exploration. He explains:

Ajay, 3.5 years (he/him) did not have any clean clothes to change into so I let him look and choose an outfit from our cabinet of extra clothes. He was attracted to something on the pants shelf with bright polka dots which I took to be leggings but when I pulled it out, it was a dress. I said, "Oh, it's a dress. Do you still want to wear it?" and he very enthusiastically did. It fit him well, with ruffles at the shoulders, and I commented on the polka dots, making sure not to comment on the fact that he was wearing a dress for the first time I'd ever seen. Once it was on, he strode out from the bathroom onto the patio, where everyone else was already eating lunch, and announced, "Look at me, everybody!" I wish I had caught everyone's reactions instead of heading inside to deal with the wet clothes. . . . Thinking back on this, I wonder if Ajay would have found the dress if it hadn't been mixed in with the pants. To an adult, this makes them much easier to find when requested. But I wonder if we lose opportunities for experimentation when we separate dresses and skirts from pants and shirts. (Luke, transgender preschool teacher, he/they)

Like Pastel, Luke continually uses a resistant social imagination to inspire and strengthen his commitment to work for gender justice with the young children in his care. Your resistant social imagination may share some overlap with Pastel's and it will undoubtedly depart in significant ways—reflecting healthy epistemic frictions—as his imagination is but one window into the infinite possibilities that exist on a journey toward gender liberation.

Every educator has their own resistant imagination that will contribute to our collective social imagination. *But how to commence such a significant and deep-rooted journey?*

- *Start by noticing gender in your teaching.* Conduct a self-study of your practice. Try to go a whole day without using any gendered words (e.g., he/she, boy/girl, mother/father). Adults are usually amazed at how pervasive gender is in our daily lives and how difficult it is to avoid labeling ourselves and others within a binary system of gender. Notice when and how gender comes up and in what contexts. Notice activities, statements, and thoughts that reinforce gender-based forms of oppression—traditional sexism, oppositional sexism, and cissexism. Look for the use of language, images, transition routines or other classroom management practices that direct, constrain and assume what girls/boys "do," "are like," "wear," "want to be," and more. Notice how your language and practice may be structured explicitly to divide children into two categories (e.g., lining up by boys and girls, separating boys and girls in bathroom facilities or in the extra clothes bins you pull down for them after a messy day of art or outdoor play).

- *Document what you notice.* Start a journal with your observations and thoughts about gender's role in your practice. Videotape yourself working with children to be able to look more closely at how gender is showing up and the hermeneutical tools they have access to in order to explore and communicate about gender in the classroom. Or if you do not work directly with children, videotape yourself when you talk about children (e.g., if you are a professor or researcher working in the field of early childhood) and engage in the same type of critical examination of the way you conceptualize and talk about gender. Create a personal inventory of when, where, and how gender exists in your practice.
- *After creating a record of your observations, start reflecting on what you have seen. What assumptions about gender frequently go unquestioned?* Do you communicate that children need to have agency over their gendered behavior, activities, expressions, and identities? Do you recognize that diverse gender expressions and identities need to be visible to children in meaningful ways?
- In addition to this reflective approach to recognizing that gender identity and gender attribution play a role in your work, leveraging the gender constellation metaphor, consider how you can become more attuned to the children and families in your early learning community. *Approach children's identities with curiosity.* Recognize that the only way to have an idea of what is happening within anyone's gender constellation is to radically and emergently listen to them. What are the children concerned about? What are they sharing about their identities? What cultural ideas are coming up in their interactions, conversations, and play? Are they changing, confronting, or debating these ideas? What questions are they asking about gender or identity? What statements are they making about gender or identity? When are they silent? What happens when you ask them questions about gender?
- *Start practicing some of the changes you would like to make.* It is important for all educators to remember that gender justice work is challenging and requires a long term effort. This is why understanding and committing to

the principles of the nonideal are so important. It is essential to focus on the concrete realities for children by observing them closely and listening to what they are saying. These observations can guide educators to small and specific changes they can try out to see if they make an immediate and positive impact for a specific child (e.g., a smile, an expression of safety and belonging, an interest to look through a new book placed on the bookshelf). Children communicate whether our efforts are making things better or when we are not yet listening and hearing in the ways they need us to.

Teachers will undoubtedly discover that young children are much more easily liberated from the forces of gender oppression—and the assumptions and expectations they influence—than adults are. When children are imagined to be agentic, sincere, and competent knowers, and adults acknowledge the limitations of their own knowledge and perspectives, they can learn from children's open-mindedness and blooming imaginations and stretch themselves to new understandings about the complex galaxy of gender.

To an adult who has grown up in the gender binary, meaningful and systemic change can seem daunting and perhaps impossible. Indeed, a single act of imaginative epistemic resistance in the direction of gender justice will not generate the seismic shift that is needed. However, Medina (2013) tells us that "When acts of resistance are not simply isolated instances without repercussions, but they become the chained actions of individuals and groups linked through social networks, these acts of resistance become *echoable*, that is, they acquire a repeatable significance and, therefore, they are memorable, imitable, and have the potential to lead social change" (p. 225). By working with critical friends, by incorporating diverse and pluralistic perspectives of adults and children, by committing to a nonideal and iterative process of cycles of reflection, experience, and imagination, and by bringing this work with us every day to the transformative space of early childhood education, we have the capacity to create just such a seismic shift.

NOTE

1. "Goal 1: Each child will demonstrate self-awareness, confidence, family pride, and positive social identities.

Goal 2: Each child will express comfort and joy with human diversity; accurate language for human differences; and deep, caring human connections.

Goal 3: Each child will increasingly recognize unfairness, have language to describe unfairness, and understand that unfairness hurts.

Goal 4: Each child will demonstrate empowerment and the skills to act, with others or alone, against prejudice and/or discriminatory actions." (Derman-Sparks & Olsen Edwards, 2010, p. xiv)

Conclusion

At the heart of the early childhood field are several core values and professional commitments that guide teachers' work with young children and their families:

- Respect the dignity, worth, and uniqueness of each child.
- Respect diversity in children.
- Affirm children's identities.
- Value and nurture children's voices.
- Foster children's agency as a human right.
- Create a sense of belonging for children.
- Nurture deep, caring, human connections.

We are also ethically and morally obligated to *do no harm*.

Young TGE children exist at the intersection of several forms of epistemic injustice. As young children, they suffer from adults' identity prejudice and false associations with naivety, immaturity, and shortcomings of credibility. And TGE children, like transgender people of all ages, find their voices are inaudible in a world that reifies heteronormativity and cisnormativity. Children gain awareness of their gender identities early in life. Many toddlers and preschool aged TGE children are doing their best to share their authentic truths with adults and, despite their best efforts to be seen and heard, far too many experience moments of psychic disequilibrium with teachers who describe a world that they are not in.

> *I do not want to explain myself to others over and over again I just want to be seen. (S. J. Miller, 2016, p. 1)*

Leelah Alcorn saw hope in places like schools—she saw the impact a teacher could have in a child's life when that child had no one else. "Gender needs to be taught about in schools," she wrote, "the earlier the better."

The earlier the better. As early childhood educators, we are best positioned to listen to Leelah's voice. The type of listening where we are open to being affected. The type of listening where we are not bound by what we already know. The type of listening where we will take risks to reformulate, think deeply about, reimagine, and shift our perspectives (Medina, 2013).

Teachers can drive imaginative resistance in bold protests that insist this world is not one they endorse *as is* (Gendler, 2000). They can engage in epistemic disobedience and delink from dominant knowledge projects, deconstructing and dismantling practices that ignore, exclude, and harm TGE children. Using resistant ways of imagining gender inclusive early childhood environments—"where it is safe to be non-, ambiguously, or multiply gendered" (Scheman, 1997, p. 133)—they can journey toward epistemic justice for young TGE children. For all teachers, but especially individuals who are in positions of relative safety and gender privilege, a commitment to improve gender justice will begin with an intimate turn inward to critically examine the "costs of their comfort" (Medina, 2013).

> What is needed is a kaleidoscopic consciousness that remains forever open to being expanded, that is, a subjectivity that is always open to acknowledge and engage new perspectives. (Medina, 2013, p. 224)
>
> *All the boys in the class, they mostly don't really wear dresses and I was afraid they might laugh at me for being a little different from them. But just because you're different, doesn't mean people laugh at you. Like just because I have blue eyes and you have brown eyes, doesn't mean you can just laugh at me, because I'm here right now. And my mom has brown eyes, and we love each other. And we're not laughing at each other and sleeping in separate rooms without saying goodnight. (Oak, eight years)*

It is through an ongoing commitment to critical reflection and collaborative interaction with diverse others that teachers will move from resistant imaginations into transformative social actions in their classrooms to improve testimonial and hermeneutical justice for TGE children. Radically listening to children and affording them credibility as knowers who are sincere and capable. Providing children with access to cultural tools that help them name and understand their lived experiences and provide mirrors to reflect back to them a respect for their sense of being. Informing collective understanding by circulating empowering knowledge about gender diversity. These are the epistemic levers teachers will use to build empathy, respect, and belonging—a kaleidoscopic consciousness (Medina, 2013)—for TGE children in their early childhood classrooms. Environments where children of all genders can wear dresses without being afraid because they are seen, heard, and loved for exactly who they are and trusted to create their unique gender constellations that shine bright in the sky for everyone to see.

References

Adams, M., Bell, L. A., Goodman, D., & Joshi, K. (2016). *Teaching for diversity and social justice* (3rd ed.). New York, NY: Routledge.

Ailwood, J. (2011). It's about power: Researching play, pedagogy and participation in the early years of school. In S. Rogers (Ed.), *Rethinking play and pedagogy in early childhood education: Concepts, contexts and cultures* (pp. 19–31). New York: Routledge.

Alcorn, L. (2014, December 31). *Listen to Leelah Alcorn's Final Words*. Retrieved from Slate: http://www.slate.com/blogs/outward/2014/12/31/leelah_alcorn_transgender_teen_from_ohio_should_be_honored_in_death.html.

Allan, A., Atkinson, E., Brace, E., DePalma, R., & Hemingway, J. (2008). Speaking the unspeakable in forbidden places: Addressing lesbian, gay, bisexual and transgender equality in the primary school. *Sex Education, 8*(3), 315–328.

American Psychiatric Association (2013). *Diagnostic and statistical manual of mental disorders (DSM-5)* (5th ed.). American Psychiatric Association.

Anthias, F. (1998). Rethinking social disvisions: Some notes towards a theoretical framework. *Sociological Review. 46*(3), pp. 506–535.

Anthias, F. (2013). Intersectional what? Social divisions, intersectionality, and levels of analysis. *Ethnicities 13*(1), 3–19.

Anzaldúa, G. (1990). Haciendo caras, una entrada. In G. Anzaldua (Ed.), *Making face, making soul: Creative and critical perspectives by feminists of color* (pp. xv–xxviii). San Francisco, CA: Aunt Lute Books.

Balsam, K. F., Huang, B., Fieland, K. C., Simoni, J. M., & Walters, K. L. (2004). Culture, trauma and wellness: A comparison of heterosexual and lesbian, gay, bisexual, and two-spirit Native Americans [Special issue]. *Cultural Diversity & Ethnic Minority Psychology, 10,* 287–301. http://dx.doi.org/10.1037/_099-9809.10.3.287.

Barad, K. (2007). *Meeting the universe halfway: Quantum physics and the entanglement of matter and meaning*. Durham, NC: Duke University Press.

Bergson, H. (1998). *Creative evolution*. Mineola, NY: Dover Publications, Inc.

Bernasconi, R. (2007). On needing not to know and forgetting what one never knew: The epistemology of ignorance in Fanon's critique of Sartre. In S. Sullivan & N. Tuana (Eds.), *Race and epistemologies of ignorance* (pp. 231–239). Albany, NY: SUNY Press.

Bishop, R. S. (1990). Mirrors, windows, and sliding glass doors. *Perspectives: Choosing and using Books For the Classroom, 6*(3) https://scenicregional.org/wp-content/uploads/2017/08/Mirrors-Windows-and-Sliding-Glass-Doors.pdf.

Blackless, M., Charuvastra, A., Derryck, A., Fausto-Sterling, A., Lauzanne, K., & Lee, E. (2000). How sexually dimorphic are we? Review and synthesis. *American Journal of Human Biology: The Official Journal of the Human Biology Association, 12*(2), 151–166.

Blaise, M. (2005). *Playing it straight: Uncovering gender discourse in the early childhood classroom.* Routledge.

Bonilla-Silva, E. (2013). *Racism without racists: Color-blind racism and the persistence of racial inequality in the United States.* Lanham, MD: Rowman & Littlefield Publishers, Inc.

Bornstein, K. (2013a). *Gender outlaw: On men, women and the rest of us.* Routledge.

Bornstein, K. (2013b). *My new gender workbook: A step-by-step guide to achieving world peace through gender anarchy and sex positivity.* New York, NY: Routledge.

Braidotti, R. (2013). *The posthuman.* Cambridge: Polity Press.

Brill, S., & Pepper, R. (2008). *The transgender child: A handbook for families and professionals.* San Francisco, CA: Cleis Press, Inc.

Broverman, N. (2019). Hundreds of parents pull kids from school to protest LBGTQ curriculum. https://www.advocate.com/news/2019/5/08/hundreds-parents-pull-kids-school-protest-lgbtq-curriculum.

Brown, B. (2007). *I thought it was just me (but it isn't): Making the journey from "what will people think?" to "I am enough."* New York, NY: Penguin.

Brown, B. (2015). *Daring greatly: How the courage to be vulnerable transforms the way we live, love, parent, and lead.* New York, NY: Penguin.

Brown, E., & Mar, K. (2018). Culturally responsive practice with children of color. In C. Keo-Meier & D. Ehrensaft (Eds.), *The gender affirmative model: An interdisciplinary approach to supporting transgender and gender expansive children* (pp. 55–69). Washington, DC: American Psychological Association.

Brown, K. M. (2004). Leadership for social justice and equity: Weaving a transformative framework and pedagogy. *Educational Administration Quarterly, 40*, 79–110.

Budge, S. L., Orovecz, J. J., Owen, J. J., & Sherry, A. R. (2018). The relationship between conformity to gender norms, sexual orientation, and gender identity for sexual minorities. *Counselling Psychology Quarterly, 31*(1), 79–97, doi: 10.1080/09515070.2016.1214558

Burman, E. (2008). *Deconstructing developmental psychology* (2nd ed.). London: Routledge.

Butler, J. (2004). *Undoing gender.* New York: Routledge.

Campbell, S., Smith, K., & Alexander, K., (2016). The gender factor: Continuing the dialogue. In R. R. Scarlet (Ed.), *The anti-bias approach in early childhood* (pp. 41–50). Sydney, AU: MultiVerse Publishing.

Cannella, G. S., & Viruru. R. (2004). *Childhood and postcolonization: Power, education, and contemporary practice*. New York: Routledge Falmer.

Center for Disease Control and Prevention (2018). Youth risk behavior surveillance – United States, 2017. *Surveillance Summaries, 67*(8). Retrieved from https://www.cdc.gov/healthyyouth/data/yrbs/pdf/2017/ss6708.pdf.

Chapman, V. L. (2003). On "knowing one's self" selfwriting, power, and ethical practice: Reflections from an adult educator. *Studies in the Education of Adults, 35*(1), 35–53.

Cho, S., Crenshaw, K., & McCall, L. (2013). Toward a field of intersectionality studies: Theory, applications, and praxis. *Signs, 38*, 785–810.

Christensen, P., & Prout, A. (2012). Anthropological and sociological perspectives on the study of children. In S. Greene & D. Hogan (Eds.), *Researching children's experience* (pp. 42–60). Thousand Oaks, CA: Sage.

Chung, Y. B., & Singh, A. A. (2009). Lesbian, gay, bisexual, and transgender Asian Americans. In A. Alvarez & N. Tewari (Eds.), *Asian American psychology: Current perspectives* (pp. 233–246). New York, NY: Taylor & Francis.

Collins, P. H. (1990). *Black feminist thought: Knowledge, consciousness, and the politics of empowerment*. Boston, MA: Unwin Hyman.

Collins, P. H. (2007). Pushing the boundaries or business as usual? Race, class, and gender studies in sociological inquiry. In C. Calhoun (Ed.), *Sociology in America: A history* (pp. 572–604). Chicago, IL: University of Chicago Press.

Corsaro, W. A. (1997). *The sociology of childhood*. Thousand Oaks, CA: Pine Forge Press.

Costello, G. C. (2014). Are trans communities losing intersex allies in the TERF wars? *TransAdvocate*. Retrieved from https://www.transadvocate.com/an-intersex-perspective-on-the-trans-intersex-and-terf-communities_n_14539.htm.

Crenshaw, K. (1989). Demarginalizing the intersection of race and sex: A Black feminist critique of antidiscrimination doctrine, feminist theory, and antiracist politics. *University of Chicago Legal Forum, 14*, 538–554.

Crenshaw, K. W. (1991). Mapping the margins: Intersectionality, identity politics, and violence against women of color. *Stanford Law Review, 43*, 1241–1299.

Dahlberg, G., & Moss, P. (2005). *Ethics and politics in early childhood education*. London: Routledge.

Dahlberg, G., Moss, P., & Pence, P. (2013). *Beyond quality in early childhood education and care: Postmodern perspectives* (3rd ed.). London: Falmer Press.

Davies, B. (2014). *Listening to children: Being and becoming*. New York, NY: Routledge.

Deleuze, G., & Guattari, F. (1987). *A thousand plateaus: Capitalism and Schizophrenia*. London: Athlone Press.

DePalma, R., & Atkinson, E. (Eds.). (2009). *Interrogating heteronormativity in primary schools: The no outsiders project*. Stoke on Trent, UK: Trentham Books.

Derman-Sparks, L., & The A.B.C. Task Force. (1989). *Anti-bias curriculum*. Washington, DC: National Association for the Education of Young Children.

Derman-Sparks, L., & Olsen Edwards, J. (2010). *Anti-Bias education for young children and ourselves* (2nd ed.). Washington, DC: National Association for the Education of Young Children.

de Vries, A. L., & Cohen-Kettenis, P. T. (2012). Clinical management of gender dysphoria in children and adolescents: The Dutch approach. *Journal of Homosexuality, 59*(3), 301–320.

Dill, B. T., & Zambrana, R. E. (2009). Critical thinking about inequality: An emerging lens. In B. T. Dill & R. E. Zambrana (Eds.), *Emerging intersections: Race, class, and gender in theory, policy, and practice* (pp. 1–21). New Brunswick, NJ: Rutgers University Press.

Dray, B. J., & Wisneski, D. B. (2011). Mindful reflection as a process for developing culturally responsive practices. *Teaching Exceptional Children, 44*(1), 28–36.

Drescher, J. (2014). Gender identity diagnoses: History and controversies. In B. Kreukels, T. Steensma, & A. de Vries (Eds.), *Gender dysphoria and disorders of sex development: Progress in care and knowledge* (pp. 137–150). New York, NY: Springer.

Edwards, C., Gandini, L., & Forman, G. (Eds.). (2011). *The hundred languages of children: The Reggio Emilia experience in transformation* (3rd ed.). Santa Barbara, CA: Praeger Publishers.

Ehrensaft, D. (2011). *Gender born, gender made: Raising healthy gender-nonconforming children.* New York, NY: Experiment Books.

Ehrensaft, D. (2016a). *Contemporary understandings of gender development.* Lecture at Mills College, Oakland, CA.

Ehrensaft, D. (2016b). *The gender creative child: Pathways for nurturing and supporting children who live outside of gender boxes.* New York, NY: Experiment Books.

English, L. M. (2005). Foucault, feminists and funders: A study of power and policy in feminist organizations. *Studies in the Education of Adults, 37*(2), 137–150.

Erikson, E. (1968). *Identity: Youth and crisis.* New York, NY: W. W. Norton and Company.

Ewick, P., & Silbey, S. (1995). Subversive stories and hegemonic tales: Toward a sociology of narrative. *Law and Society Review, 29*(2), 197–226.

Fast, A. A., & Olson, K. R. (2017). Gender development in transgender preschool children. *Child Development, 89*(2), 620–637.

Fausto-Sterling, A. (2000). *Sexing the body: Gender politics and the construction of sexuality.* New York, NY: Basic Books.

File, N., Basler Wisneski, D., & Mueller, J. (2012). Strengthening curriculum in early childhood. In N. File, J. Mueler, & D. Basler Wisneski (Eds.), *Curriculum in early childhood education: Re-examined, rediscovered, renewed* (pp. 200–205). New York: Routledge.

Fletcher, J. (1999). *Disappearing acts: Gender, power and relational practice at work.* Cambridge, MA: MIT Press.

Foucault, M. (1980). Truth and power. In C. Gordon (Ed.), *Power/knowledge: Selected inter-views and other writings, 1972–1977* (pp. 109–133). New York: Pantheon.

Foucault, M. (1981). *A history of sexuality, Volume 1: An introduction.* Trans. R. Hurley. Harmondsworth, UK: Penguin.

Freire, P. (2018). *Pedagogy of the oppressed* (50th Anniversary Ed.). New York, NY: Bloomsbury Publishing USA.

Fricker, M. (2007). *Epistemic injustice: Power and the ethics of knowing.* Oxford University Press.

Funk, C., & Lugo, L. (2012). *Asian Americans: A mosaic of faiths.* Retrieved from http://www.pewforum.org/files/2012.07/Asian-Americans-religion-full-report.pdf.

Gendler, T. S. (2000). The puzzle of imaginative resistance. *The Journal of Philosophy, 97*(2), 55–81.

Graham, A., & Fitzgerald, R. (2010). Children's participation in research: Some possibilities and constraints from the current Australian research environment. *Journal of Sociology, 46*(2), 133–147.

Greene, S., & Hill, M. (2012). Researching children's experience: Methods and methodological issues. In S. Greene & D. Hogan (Eds.), *Researching children's experience* (pp. 2–21). Thousand Oaks, CA: Sage.

Greene, S., & Hogan, D. (Eds.). (2012). *Researching children's experience.* Thousand Oaks, CA: Sage.

Greenberg, J. A. (1999). Defining male and female: Intersexuality and the collision between law and biology. *Arizona Law Review, 41*, 265.

Grieshaber, S., & McArdle, F. (2010). *The trouble with play.* New York, NY: Open University Press.

Hackett, C., Connor, P., Stonawski, M., & Skirbekk, V. (2015). *The future of world religions: Population growth projections, 2010–2050: Why Muslims are rising fastest and the unaffiliated are shrinking as a share of the world's population.* Retrieved from http://pewforum.org/files/2015/03/PF_15.04.02_ProjectionsFullReport.pdf.

Haddock, V. (2004). *The gay panic defense in the Araujo case.* SF Gate (May 16, 2004). Retrieved from https://www.sfgate.com/opinion/article/Gay-panic-defense-in-Araujo-case-2758581.php.

Haig, D. (2004). The inexorable rise of gender and the decline of sex: Social change in academic titles, 1945–2001. *Archives of Sexual Behavior, 33*(2), 87–96.

Halim, M. L. D., Bryant, D., & Zucker, K. J. (2016). Early gender development in children and links with mental and physical health. In *Health promotion for children and adolescents* (pp. 191–213). Boston, MA: Springer.

Halim, M. L., & Ruble, D. (2010). Gender identity and stereotyping in early and middle childhood. In *Handbook of gender research in psychology* (pp. 495–525). New York, NY: Springer.

Harry, B., & Klingner, J. (2006). *Why are so many minority students in special education? Understanding race and disability in schools.* New York, NY: Teachers College Press.

Haynes, J. (2009). Listening to the voice of child in education. In S. Gibson & J. Haynes (Eds.), *Perspectives on participation and inclusion: Engaging education* (pp. 27–43). London: Continuum.

Hill Collins, P. (2015). Intersectionality's definitional dilemmas. *Annual Reviews of Sociology, 41*, 1–20. doi: 10.1146/annurev-soc-073014-112142.

Hogan, D. (2012). Researching "the child" in developmental psychology. In S. Greene & D. Hogan (Eds.), *Researching children's experience* (pp. 22–41). Thousand Oaks, CA: Sage.

Human Rights Campaign (2018). *A national epidemic: Fatal anti-transgender violence in America in 2018*. Retrieved from https://www.hrc.org/resources/a-national-epidemic-fatal-anti-transgender-violence-in-america-in-2018.

International Code of Ethics for Educators (2008). Washington, DC: Childhood Education International. Retrieved from https://ceintl.wpengine.com/wp-content/uploads/2019/04/ICOEE2019.pdf.

Intersex Society of North America. Retrieved from http://www.isna.org/.

InterAct Advocates for Intersex Youth. Retrieved from https://interactadvocates.org/.

James, S. E., Herman, J. L., Rankin, S., Keisling, M., Mottet, L., & Anafi, M. (2016). *The report of the 2015 U.S. transgender survey*. Washington, DC: National Center for Transgender Equality.

John, M. (2003). *Children's rights and power: Charging up for a new century*. London: Jessica Kingsley.

Kalma, X. (2016). Mind your words. In Z. Sharman (Ed.). *The remedy: Queer and trans voices on health and health care* (pp. 203–206). Vancouver, British Columbia, Canada: Arsenal Pulp Press.

Keo-Meier, C., & Ehrensaft, D. (2018). *The gender affirmative model: An interdisciplinary approach to supporting transgender and gender expansive children*. Washington: American Psychological Association.

Kohlberg, L. (1966). A cognitive-developmental analysis of children's sex-role concepts and attitudes. In E. Maccoby (Ed.), *The development of sex differences*. London, Tavistock.

Kroeger, J. (2006). Ism moments and children's becoming. *Journal of Equity and Innovation in Early Childhood Education, 4*(1), 32–47.

Kroeger, J., & Regula, L. (2017). Queer decisions in early childhood teacher education: Teachers as advocates for gender non-conforming and sexual minority young children and families. *International Critical Childhood Policy Studies, 6*(1), 106–121.

Lee, C. (2008). The gay panic defense, No. 42. *U.C. Davis Law Review, 471*. Retrieved from https://scholarship.law.gwu.edu/faculty_publications/788/.

Liebel, M. (2012). *Children's rights from below: Cross-cultural perspectives*. New York: Palgrave MacMillan.

Loveridge, J. (Ed.). (2010). Involving children and young people in research in educational settings. *Report to the Ministry of Education: Victoria University of Wellington, Jessie Hetherington Center for Educational Research* (pp. i–161). Retrieved from http://www.educationcounts.govt.nz/__data/assets/pdf_file/0005/80708/957_Involving-CYP-020 92010.pdf.

MacNaughton, G. (2005). *Doing Foucault in early childhood studies*. London: Routledge.

Malaguzzi, L. (1994). *Your image of the child: Where teaching begins*. Comments translated and adapted from a seminar presented Reggio Emilia, Italy, June 1993. Retrieved from https://www.reggioalliance.org/downloads/malaguzzi:ccie:1994.pdf.

Mallon, G. P., & DeCrescenzo, T. (2006). Transgender children and youth: A child welfare practice perspective. *Child Welfare, 85*(2), 215–241.

Martalock, P. (2012). What is a wheel? The image of the child: Traditional, project approach, and Reggio Emilia perspectives. *Dimensions of Early Childhood 40*(3), 3–12.

Medina, José (2013). *The epistemology of resistance: Gender and racial oppression, epistemic injustice, and resistant imaginations.* New York, NY: Oxford University Press.

Mezirow, J. (1991). *Transformative dimensions of adult learning.* San Francisco: Jossey-Bass.

Miller, S. J. (2016). *Teaching, affirming, and recognizing trans and gender creative youth: A queer literacy framework.* New York, NY: Palgrave Macmillan.

Mirandé, A. (2014). Transgender identity and acceptance in a global era: The Muxes of Juchitán. In J. Gelfer (Ed.). *Masculinities in a global era: International and cultural psychology* (pp. 247–263). New York, NY: Springer. http://dx doi.org/10.10007/978-1-4614-6931-5_14.

Money, J. (1955). Hermaphroditism, gender and precocity in hyperadrenocorticism: Psychologic findings. *Bulletin of the Johns Hopkins Hospital, 96*(6), 253.

Money, J., & Ehrhardt, A. A. (1972). Man and woman, boy and girl: Differentiation and dimorphism of gender identity from conception to maturity (from Faustc-Sterling).

Morrar, S. (2019). Rocklin school board OKs textbooks with LGBT figures after heated late-night debate. Retrieved from https://www.sacbee.com/news/local/education/article229905214.html.

Murris, K. (2013). The epistemic challenge of hearing child's voice. *Study in the Philosophy of Education.* doi 10.1007/s11217-012-9349-9.

Murris, K. (2016). *The posthuman child: Educational transformation through philosophy with picturebooks.* London: Routledge.

Murris, K. (2017). Reading two rhizomatic pedagogies diffractively through one another: A Reggio inspired philosophy with children for the postdevelopmental child. *Pedagogy, Culture & Society.* http://dx.doi.org/10.1080/14681366.2017.1286681.

Murris, K. (2018). Posthuman child and the diffractive teacher: Decolonizing the nature/culture binary. In A. Cutter-Mackenzie et al. (Eds.), *Research hardbook on childhood nature* (pp. 1–25). New York, NY: Springer International Publishing. https://doi.org/10.1007/978-3-319-51949-4_7-2.

Murris, K. (2019). Children's development, capability approaches and postdevelopmental child: The birth to four curriculum in South Africa. *Global Studies of Childhood, 9*(1) 56–71.

Muska, S. (1999). *The Brandon Teena story.* Marketed and distributed by New Video.

National Association for the Education of Young Children (2005, 2011) *Code of ethical conduct and statement of commitment (A position statement).* https://www.naeyc.org/sites/default/files/globally-shared/downloads/PDFs/resources/position-statements/Ethics%20Position%20Statement2011_09202013update.pdf.

Nicholson, J. (2017). *Emphasizing social justice and equity in leadership for early childhood: Taking a postmodern turn to make complexity visible.* Lexington Press.

Nicholson, J., Kurtz, J., & Perez, L. (2018). *Trauma-informed practices for early childhood educators: Relationship-based approaches that support healing and build resilience in young children.* New York, NY: Routledge.

Núñez, A. M. (2014). Employing multilevel intersectionality in educational research: Latino identities, contexts, and college access. *Educational Researcher, 43*(2), 85–92.

Olson-Kennedy, A., & Tando, D. (2018). *How much distress is enough distress?* Gender Odyssey Conference (June 22, 2018). Seattle, Washington.

Oyêwùmí, O. (2011). *Gender epistemologies in Africa: Gendering traditions, spaces, social institutions, and identities.* New York, NY: Palgrave Macmillan.

Pastel, E. (2018). *Qualities to look for in gender expansive children's literature.* Retrieved from https://www.genderjusticeinearlychildhood.com/resources.

Pastel, E., Steele, S., Nicholson, J., Maurer, C., Hennock, J., Julian, J., Unger, T., & Flynn, N. (2019). *Supporting gender diversity in early childhood classrooms: A practical guide.* London, UK: Kingsley Press.

Patel, L. (2016). *Decolonizing educational research: From ownership to answerability.* New York, NY: Routledge.

Payne, E., & Smith, M. (2014). The big freakout: Educator fear in response to the presence of transgender elementary school students. *Journal of Homosexuality, 61,* 399–418.

Perry, B., Pollard, R. A., Blakely, T. L., Baker, W. L., & Vigilante, D. (1995). Childhood trauma, the neurobiology of adaptation, and "use-dependent" development of the brain: How "states" become traits. *Infant Mental Health Journal, 16,* 271–291.

Petty, K. (2010). *Developmental milestones of young children.* St. Paul, MN: Red Leaf Press.

Piaget, J. (1958). The growth of logical thinking from childhood to adolescence. *AMC, 10,* 12.

Pollock, M. (Ed.). (2008). *Every day anti-racism: Getting real about race in school.* New York, NY: The New Press.

Pyne, J. (2014). Gender independent kids: A paradigm shift in approaches to gender non-conforming children. *Canadian Journal of Human Sexuality, 23*(1), 1–8.

Quinn, P. C., Yahr, J., Kuhn, A., Slater, A. M., & Pascalis, O. (2002). Representation of the gender of human faces by infants: A preference for female. *Perception, 31*(9), 1109–1121.

Revathi, A. (2010). *The truth about me: A Hijra life story.* Penguin Books India.

Rich, A. (1994/1986). *Blood, bread, and poetry: Selected prose 1979–1985.* New York, NY: W. W. Norton & Company, Inc.

Rinaldi, C. (2001). Documentation and assessment: What is the relationship? In Project Zero and Reggio Children's. In *Making learning visible: Children as individual and group learners* (pp. 78–93). Reggio Emilia, Italy: Reggio Children.

Rogers, S. (Ed.). (2011). *Rethinking play and pedagogy in early childhood education: Concepts, contexts and cultures.* New York, NY: Routledge.

Rogoff, B. (2003). *The cultural nature of human development.* Oxford, United Kingdom: Oxford University Press.

Roscoe, W., & Murray, S. O. (2001). *Boy-wives and female husbands: Studies of African homosexualities.* New York, NY: St. Martin.

Ruffolo, D. (2009). Queering child/hood policies: Canadian examples and perspectives. *Contemporary Issues in Early Childhood, 10*(3), 291–308. http://dx.doi.org/10.2304/ciec.2009.10.3.291.

Russell, S., Pollitt, A., Li, G., & Grossman, A. (2018). Chosen name use is linked to reduced depressive symptoms, suicidal ideation, and suicidal behavior among transgender youth. *Journal of Adolescent Health, 63*(4), 503–505. doi: https://doi.org/10.1016/j.jadohealth.2018.02.003.

Scheman, N. (1997). Queering the center by centering the queer: Reflections on transsexuals and secular Jews. In D. T. Meyers (Ed.), *Feminists rethink the self* (pp. 124–162). New York, NY: Westview.

Schore, A. N. (2003). Early relational trauma, disorganized attachment, and the development of a predisposition to violence. In M. F. Solomon & D. J. Siegel (Eds.), *Healing trauma: Attachment, mind, body, and brain* (pp. 107–167). New York, NY: Norton.

Sensoy, O., & DiAngelo, R. (2017). *Is everyone really equal? An introduction to key concepts in social justice education* (2nd ed.). New York, NY: Teachers College Press.

Serano, J. (2016). *Whipping girl: A Transsexual Woman on Sexism and the Scapegoating of Femininity*. Berkeley, CA: Seal Press.

Sharman, Z. (Ed.). (2016). *The remedy: Queer and trans voices on health and health care*. Vancouver, BC: Arsenal Pulp Press.

Solnit, R. (2015). *Men explain things to me*. Chicago, IL: Haymarket Press

Solórzano, D. G., & Yosso, T. J. (2001). Critical race and LatCrit theory and method: Counterstorytelling Chicana and Chicano graduate school experiences. *International Journal of Qualitative Studies in Education, 4*, 471–495.

Solórzano, D. G., & Yosso, T. J. (2002). Critical race methodology: Counter-storytelling as an analytical framework for education research, *Qualitative Inquiry, 8*(23), 23–44.

Sorrels, B. (2015). *Reaching and teaching children exposed to trauma*. Beltsville, MD: Gryphon House.

Steele, K. (2016). *Looking back and looking forward: An inquiry into the lived experiences of Trans adults as young children*. Unpublished manuscript. Mills College, Oakland, CA.

Steensma, T. D., Biemond, R., de Boer, F., & Cohen-Kettenis, P. T. (2011). Desisting and persisting gender dysphoria after childhood: a qualitative follow-up study. *Clinical Child Psychology and Psychiatry, 16*(4), 499–516.

Steensma, T. D., McGuire, J. K., Kreukels, B. P., Beekman, A. J., & Cohen-Kettenis, P. T. (2013). Factors associated with desistence and persistence of childhood gender dysphoria: A quantitative follow-up study. *Journal of the American Academy of Child & Adolescent Psychiatry,52*(6), 582–590.

Stryker, S. (2008). *Transgender history: The roots of today's revolution*. New York, NY: Seal Press.

Surtees, N. (2005). Teacher talk about and around sexuality in early childhood education: Deciphering an unwritten code. *Contemporary Issues in Early Childhood, 6*(1), 19–29.

Taylor-Shaughnessy, K. (2016). Name game: Being seen in my entirety. In Z. Sharman (Ed.). *The remedy: Queer and trans voices on health and health care* (pp. 25–29). Vancouver, British Columbia, Canada: Arsenal Pulp Press.

Tuck, E. (2009). Suspending damage: A letter to communities. *Harvard Educational Review, 79*(3), 409–428.

Vade, D. (2005). Expanding gender and expanding the law: Toward a social and legal conceptualization of gender that is more inclusive of transgender people. *Michigan Journal of Gender and Law, 11*(2), 253–316. Retrieved from https://repository.1aw.umich.edu/mjgl/vol11/iss2/4.

Young-Bruehl, E. (2012). *Childism: Confronting prejudice against children.* New Haven, CT: Yale University Press.

Williams, B. (2004). *Truth and truthfulness.* New Jersey: Princeton University Press. Kindle Edition.

Woods, J. B. Sears, B., & Mallory. C. (2016). *Model legislation for eliminating the gay and trans panic defenses.* Los Angeles, CA: The Williams Institute, UCLA School of Law.

Zimmermann, J. (2015). *Hermeneutics: A very short introduction.* Oxford: OUP.

Zosuls, K. M., Ruble, D. N., Tamis-Lemonda, C. S., Shrout, P. E., Bornstein, M. H., Greulich, F. K. (2009). The acquisition of gender labels in infancy: Implications for gender-typed play. *Developmental Psychology, 45*(3), 688–701. doi: 10.1037/a0014053.

Zucker, K. J., Bradley, S. J., Owen-Anderson, A., Kibblewhite, S. J., & Cantor, J. M. (2008). Is gender identity disorder in adolescents coming out of the closet? *Journal of Sex & Marital Therapy, 34*(4), 287–290.

Index

Alcorn, Leelah, 49–51, 126, 128–29, 137, 139, 141–42, 150, 162
anatomy, 25, 26, 27–29, 31–36, 41, 45, 59, 64, 90–91, 123
Anthias, Floya, 78–81, 84–85
anti-bias education (ABE), 12–13, 16, 59, 66–67, 83, 119, 156
Anzaldúa, Gloria, 10–11
authentic gender self, 12, 17, 36, 40, 48, 92, 99, 118, 140–49

beneficial epistemic frictions, 52–54
Blaise, Mindy, 66, 101–4, 106
Bonilla-Silva, Eduardo, 78
Bornstein, Kate, 25, 32, 36, 41

cisgender, 37
cisnormative/cisnormativity, 20, 23–24, 37, 47, 57, 68, 102, 112, 114, 115, 123, 127–28, 132–36, 138, 140, 143, 145, 161
cissexism, 94–98, 158
commitment to the nonideal, 12, 99, 122, 144, 159
counterstories (counterstorytelling, counter narratives), 8, 10–11, 119–20, 128, 134–35, 139–40, 146, 148–50, 153

credibility judgments, 12, 104, 105–7, 109, 115, 121–22, 124
critical reflection, 11, 52–53, 54, 57, 85, 87, 122, 131, 151–53, 162

Davies, Bronwyn, 101, 122–24, 147, 152
Derman-Sparks, Louise, 4, 13, 16, 48, 66, 119–20, 156, 159
dominant discourse, 131, 133, 135, 139
dominant group, 7, 23–24
dominant knowledge projects, 52, 162
Dray, Barbara, 54–58

Ehrensaft, Diane, 4, 17, 33, 36, 40, 64, 68, 72, 74, 76, 90–92, 111–12, 140, 143
emergent listening, 84, 122, 123–24, 143–44, 151, 153, 158
empiricism, 99–100, 122, 144
epistemic injustice, 4, 48, 161
epistemic resistance, 119–20, 146, 159
Erikson, Erik, 65

fallibilism, 99–100, 122, 144
false gender self, 40

Fausto-Sterling, Anne, 25–30, 33–34, 40, 47
Foucault, Michal, 23–24, 127
Freire, Paulo, 136, 151
Fricker, Miranda, 3–5, 7, 12, 48, 104–6, 114–15, 117, 127–33, 135, 141–43

gender, 45
gender attribution, 41, 42–45, 54–55, 57–58, 61, 67, 76, 85, 88, 158
gender awareness/milestones, 11, 17–18
gender-based oppression, 12, 18, 27, 30, 34, 37, 46–47, 65, 76, 78, 87–88, 92–98, 100, 154, 156–59
gender binary, 4, 9, 17–18, 22–24, 25, 26–31, 33–35, 37–38, 43, 45–47, 57, 61, 64–67, 69–70, 83, 90–95, 97–100, 108–9, 113, 119, 122, 124, 130–31, 133, 135, 139–40, 148–54, 158–59
gender boxes, 11, 63, 65–66, 67, 68–70
gender dysphoria, 34, 83, 111–12
gender expansive(ness), 3, 8, 10, 11, 44, 45–46, 47–48, 60, 67, 69, 74, 76, 84, 103, 106, 108–9, 112, 119–20, 125, 127–28, 130–31, 135, 137, 139–42, 145, 149, 152, 155–56
gender expression, 19, 39–41, 42–43, 45, 47, 54–56, 59, 62, 64–66, 68–71, 74, 76, 88, 90–91, 95, 97–98, 103, 106, 112, 118–20, 123, 132, 136, 139, 149, 158
gender health, 18, 55, 57, 59, 74, 83–84, 92, 99, 118, 124, 142
gender identity, 4–5, 7, 9, 13, 17–19, 24, 31–32, 35, 36–39, 41, 43, 45–48, 54–56, 59, 64–70, 73–75, 82–83, 90–91, 93–95, 102–3, 106, 108–12, 114, 117, 119, 129–31, 132–24, 134, 137, 139, 143, 152, 155–56, 158, 161
gender justice, 99–100
gender pronouns, 13, 42–46, 125, 145, 154–55
gender roles, 27–28, 30–32, 40, 78, 101, 154

gender theories & models, 67–98; gender boxes, 11, 63, 65–66, 67, 68–70; GenderBread Person, 67, 70–72; gender galaxy, 67, 74–76, 88, 90–92, 95, 103, 134, 159; gender spectrum(s), 67, 69–72, 74–76, 88, 90, 95; Gender Unicorn, 67, 71–72; gender web, 67, 72–74, 75–76, 88, 90–92; intersectional gender constellation, 11, 45, 63, 67, 76, 77–78, 84, 87–92, 95, 98–99, 101, 103, 123, 134, 153, 158, 163

hermeneutical injustice, 4–5, 12, 126, 128; harms of, 141–42
hermeneutical tools, 5, 7–8, 126–28, 130–34, 137–40, 141–46, 158
heteronormative/heteronormativity, 9, 20, 47, 68, 102, 106, 127–28, 133, 161

identity power, 12, 80, 85, 88, 96–97, 129
identity prejudice, 12, 20, 104–5, 115, 123, 128, 133, 141, 161
image of the child, 19–22, 49, 52, 65, 83, 102, 107–16, 119, 121–22, 124, 138, 143, 145–46, 149, 151–2
intersectional identities, 76–82, 84–87, 100, 119
intersex, 28–33, 35, 38, 43, 47, 61, 69–70, 75, 91, 119, 134, 145
ipso gender, 38, 45, 75, 139

Keo-Meier, Colt, 17, 64, 74
Kohlberg, Lawrence, 64–65

legal designation, 17, 33–36, 40, 45, 56, 59, 64, 68, 74, 82, 88, 94, 109

MacNaughton, Glenda, 23–24, 127
Medina, Jose, 12, 52–53, 57, 87, 99–100, 120, 122, 127–34, 140–41, 144, 147–48, 150, 159, 162–63
meliorism, 99–100, 122, 145

Mezirow, Jack, 52
mindful reflection, 54–61, 121–22, 130, 136, 144, 151
misgender, 46, 92, 96, 118
Murris, Karin, 19–20, 22, 48–49, 107, 109–10, 113

negative cultural images, 12, 19–20, 102, 105–14, 124, 152; of children, 107–8; of TGE children & youth, 111–13; of TGE individuals and young children as less than fully human, 113–14; of transgender people, 108–10; of transgender people in medical and psychological fields, 110–11
nonbinary, 5, 16, 38, 41–42, 47, 62, 74, 78, 83, 92–93, 95–96, 128, 156
Núñez, Anne-Marie, 79–81, 84–85

Olsen Edwards, Julie, 4, 13, 16, 48, 65–66, 119–20, 156, 159
oppositional sexism, 93–98, 157–58

particularism, 99–100, 122, 144
Pastel, Encian, 54, 58, 116, 119–20, 154–57
Payne, Elisabethe, 5, 8, 66, 138–39, 145–46
pedagogy of listening, 50–52, 57
persona dolls, 60, 119–20, 145
physiology, 25–36, 41, 45, 59, 64, 68, 71, 88, 90, 131
Piaget, Jean, 65
postdevelopmental, 22, 66
poststructuralists/poststructuralism, 23, 106
Pyne, Jake, 5, 17

queer theory, 22, 106

Rinaldi, Carlina, 36, 50–52, 103

Serano, Julia, 5, 92–95, 108–9, 124, 133
sex, 27–33, 33–36, 38, 46–47, 61–62, 66, 69–70, 74, 76, 93, 95, 100, 117, 124, 133, 138–39
sex-gender distinction, 27–33, 34–36, 46–47, 69–70, 74, 76, 95, 117, 124
sexual orientation, 39, 46–47, 68, 70, 80, 137
signification, 23–25, 37, 53, 66, 81, 86, 127, 129–30, 132, 135, 139, 159–60
Smith, Melissa, 5, 8, 66, 138–39, 145–46
social categories, 4, 10, 22, 25–38, 65, 77–88, 96, 98, 104, 106, 113, 117, 119, 141, 147, 150
social imagination, 3, 12, 98, 140, 147–63; resistant, 12, 140, 147–63

testimonial injustice, 4–5, 7, 12, 104, 125, 130–32, 141, 143; harms of, 114–18
theory of gender constancy, 64–65
traditional sexism, 92–98, 110, 158
transformative learning, 11, 52–57, 85
transformative social actions, 53–54, 87, 156, 162
transgender/trans, 38
trustworthiness, 105–6

Vade, Dylan, 28, 31, 36, 74–76, 88, 108

Wisneski, Debora, 54–58

About the Authors

Katie Steele, MBA, is a queer and nonbinary transgender educator, learner, and activist. As a member of the Gender Justice in Early Childhood team, he has presented in conferences and classrooms around the San Francisco Bay Area and in Washington, D.C., on shifting mindsets and creating space for young children of all genders. With that same team, he is also a coauthor of the book *Supporting Gender Diversity in Early Childhood Classrooms: A Practical Guide*. Katie's passions have always been education and social justice. He is currently the director of operations at AnnieCannons, Inc.—a nonprofit organization in Oakland, California, that provides software engineering education and career-launching employment opportunities to survivors of human trafficking and gender-based violence.

Julie Nicholson, PhD, is professor of practice in the School of Education at Mills College and a senior fellow for Childhood Education International in Washington, D.C. Dr. Nicholson conducts community-engaged scholarship and her teaching, research, publications, and advocacy emphasize issues of equity and social justice in early childhood. Her recent books address leading for social justice, responsive practices for children experiencing homelessness, play-based learning, disrupting suspensions and expulsions for young boys of color, trauma-informed practice, and culturally responsive self-care for early childhood educators. She is a proud member of the Gender Justice in Early Childhood team. She regularly gives keynotes and presentations at conferences and events nationally and internationally.

www.ingramcontent.com/pod-product-compliance
Lightning Source LLC
Chambersburg PA
CBHW061715300426
44115CB00014B/2705